SCHOOLHOUSE ACTIVISTS

SCHOOLHOUSE ACTIVISTS

African American Educators and the Long Birmingham Civil Rights Movement

TONDRA L. LODER-JACKSON

SUNY PRESS

Cover photograph of the Lincoln School faculty in Birmingham circa 1939 reprinted with permission from the Birmingham, Ala. Public Library Archives.

Published by State University of New York Press, Albany

Printed in the United States of America

For information, contact State University of New York Press, Albany, NY
www.sunypress.edu

Production, Jenn Bennett
Marketing, Fran Keneston

Library of Congress Cataloging-in-Publication Data

Loder-Jackson, Tondra L., 1967–
Schoolhouse activists : African American educators and the long Birmingham civil rights movement / Tondra L. Loder-Jackson.
pages cm
Includes bibliographical references and index.
ISBN 978-1-4384-5861-8 (hc : alk. paper)—978-1-4384-5860-1 (pb : alk. paper)
ISBN 978-1-4384-5862-5 (e-book)
1. African American educators. 2. African Americans—Education. 3. Civil rights movement—Alabama—Birmingham. I. Title.

LA2311.L63 2015
370.92—dc23
[B] 2014048843

10 9 8 7 6 5 4 3 2 1

In memory of my grandparents, Mack and Martha Loder,
and with desperate hope for my nieces, Kimya and Kamaya Loder

Tell your children about it in the years to come, and let your children tell their children. Pass the story down from generation to generation.

—Joel 1:3 (New Living Translation)

CONTENTS

ILLUSTRATIONS

FIGURES

TABLES

PREFACE

In 2005, I was asked to interview for the Southern Oral History Project's (SOHP) chronicling of the "The Long Civil Rights Movement" in the U.S. South.[1] The interviewer was interested in learning about my perspectives as a post–civil rights generation student who attended integrated Birmingham City Schools (BCS).[2] He knew I was engaged in my own research on Birmingham's educational history, so we were able to converse both as academic researchers and interviewer and interviewee.

Participating in the SOHP helped crystallize my previous thinking and assumptions about the salience of multigenerational participation in the mid-twentieth century, or what has been called the "classical phase" of the civil rights movement.[3] Similar to the SOHP, this book acknowledges that this movement is more aptly titled "the long civil rights movement," one that has been described as "a living, breathing animal that grows and morphs in different directions" over time, and by some accounts, spans from as early as the nineteenth century through the integration eras of the 1970s and 1980s.[4]

As a third-generation citizen of Birmingham and a BCS alumna, I have an affinity for the city, which is undergirded by my intellectual understanding and appreciation of its pivotal role as a battleground for the civil rights movement. I am dismayed yet motivated by scholarly and anecdotal contentions that younger generations of African American educators, being too far removed from the activist traditions and experiences of older generations of African Americans, are ill-equipped to address modern-day problems in schools and communities.[5]

After devoting fourteen years to public education in the Midwest and Northeast, I was beckoned by a "call to home" in 2003 to fulfill a lifelong yearning to give back to Birmingham and the BCS.[6] One of the initial teacher education courses I taught at UAB was "The Birmingham Civil Rights Movement," which was spearheaded by my School of Education colleague, Lois Christensen, along with two local educators.[7] Other courses on this subject had been taught on campus, but none at that time or since then has focused squarely on the struggle for educational equity in Birmingham. Our guest speakers not only included icons of the Birmingham civil rights movement, such as Reverend Fred Shuttlesworth, the founder of the Alabama Christian Movement for Human Rights (ACMHR) and widely acknowledged leader of the Birmingham movement, and Reverend James Bevel, a leading strategist of children's and youths' activism, but also relatively unknown educators, who were instrumental in desegregating schools and instituting Black History programs and curriculum in Birmingham when it was still risky and dangerous to do so. As the course's youngest collaborator, it was not lost on me that, over time, I would become increasingly responsible for teaching about the Birmingham civil rights movement. The unexpected death in 2009 of one of our collaborators, Lillie Fincher, was a somber reminder of my obligation.[8]

My role as a local professor, who was only seven months old when Martin Luther King Jr. was assassinated on April 4, 1968, and has longstanding family ties to Birmingham, undoubtedly afforded me the privilege to pursue a relatively large life story project featuring a multigenerational sample of educators, most of whom consented to having their transcripts eventually housed in local public archives. In addition to collaborating with local public school educators through my employment as a university educator of teachers and school administrators, I also work closely with parents, community members, and civic organizations to mobilize grassroots support for urban education reform. My social, professional, generational, and geographic locations uniquely shape my perspectives, insights, and biases concerning this book's content.

In the wake of Birmingham's commemoration of fifty years of civil rights history in 2013, and the sixtieth anniversary of the landmark *Brown versus the Board of Education of Topeka, Kansas* Supreme Court case in 2014, I believe now is the time to examine more closely the role and involvement of African American educators during the long civil rights movement. I am struck by how little we know about how African American educators figured into the local, regional, and national civil rights movements. In Birmingham, very few connections have been made to link the struggles between educators and students in the 1950s and 1960s and those still living today, and then to situate these generations within the historical quest for quality public schooling, which began shortly after the first African Americans arrived in post–Civil War Birmingham. Another neglected and related matter concerns a longstanding and controversial historical debate about whether African American educators in the U.S. South helped or hindered the civil rights movement. To state the matter plainly (and, admittedly, too simplistically), were they activists or accommodationists? The ambitious aim of this book is to interrogate these issues utilizing alternative methods, some unearthed data, and new historical interpretations.

This is the first book of its kind devoted primarily to the multigenerational perspectives of African American educators in the U.S. South and their perceived roles and contributions to the civil rights movement.[9] Several notable works by historians of education examine African American educators in the U.S. South between the periods of enslavement and the classical phase of the civil rights movement.[10] However, disciplinary boundaries and scope preclude these works from addressing, in elaborate depth, contemporary African American education. *Schoolhouse Activists* is a continuation of this historical dialogue but with a primary emphasis on the perspectives of a multigenerational sample of African American educators working in twenty-first-century schools in Birmingham, Alabama.

This book is divided into two parts. Part I chronicles the history of Birmingham education in relation to African American educators between the late nineteenth century and the mid-twentieth-century classical phase of the civil rights movement drawing on extensive primary and secondary sources. Part II amplifies the voices of African American educators who came of age before, during, and after the classical phase of the movement through interviews I conducted with more than forty-five educators. Although these interviews bracket a multigenerational cadre of educators born between the 1920s and the early 1980s, and emphasize their memories of and experiences during the most commemorated phase of the Birmingham civil rights movement, the chapters in Part I situate their life stories within a perpetual movement for educational equity, which encompasses the establishment of Birmingham's first Black school in the late nineteenth century, segregated schooling and school integration in the twentieth century, and emergent educational problems in the twenty-first-century era of resegregation, No Child Left Behind, and the "neoliberal" school reform movement.[11]

Schoolhouse Activists might interest anyone following the current crisis in public education confronting African American and other socially disenfranchised children. I believe it would be of particular interest to education scholars, historians of education, civil rights historians, scholars focused on generations and social change, social studies teachers, teachers unions, school reformers, community activists, and social justice organizations. Faculty and students in the fields of educational foundations, African American Studies, and sociology of education would also find this book instructive, namely those who teach course titles such as the Civil Rights Movement, Social Movements in Education, African American Education, and Urban Education.

ACKNOWLEDGMENTS

If you want to go fast, go alone. If you want to go far, go together.

—African Proverb

My journey to publishing this book began long before I penned its initial pages. It originated in the 1940s with my paternal grandparents' migration from rural Selma to industrial Birmingham, Alabama, in search of a better life. I owe to them my earliest social consciousness of Birmingham's significance as a bastion of the civil rights movement. My grandmother, who earned a living performing domestic service "over the Mountain" (local color for affluent White independent suburbs in southeastern Birmingham), took great pride in treating my younger brother and me to lunch at Woolworth's and an Easter shopping spree at Newberry's in downtown Birmingham. Unbeknownst to us at that time, our Saturday excursions through the full range of downtown retail stores would have been off-limits only a few years prior to our arrival in Birmingham in 1974.

I am honored and humbled that more than forty-five educators entrusted me to probe into their personal and professional lives in order to write this book. Unfortunately, some of them have already passed away, but thankfully all of them received a copy of their interview transcripts well before this book's publication. I also thank the numerous informants who helped me locate this special cadre of educators.

The critical, insightful, and supportive feedback I received from the editorial staff and anonymous peer reviewers of SUNY Press helped take this book to another level. In addition, several colleagues granted me invaluable opportunities to present and hone earlier versions of this book in scholarly forums: Kofi Lomotey, George Noblit, Linda Tillman, Diana (formerly Slaughter-Defoe) Kotzin, Jerome Morris, Sheryl Conrad Cozart, Paula Groves Price, Hilton Kelly, Camille Wilson, Karen Johnson,

Horace Huntley, Daniella Cook, and Richard Lofton. I am also grateful for the coveted time Tonya Perry and her UAB Red Mountain Writing Project afforded me, first, to craft my book prospectus during a faculty writing retreat, and then to highlight its findings at a preconference seminar for the 2013 National Writing Project's Urban Sites Conference held in Birmingham. I also presented preliminary findings and ideas at annual meetings and conferences convened by the American Educational Research Association (AERA), American Educational Studies Association, Association for the Study of African American Life and History, National Association for Multicultural Education, Oxford (England) University Roundtable on Social Justice, and the Research on Women and Education Special Interest Group of AERA.

Portions of this book appeared in different forms in "Hope and Despair: Southern Black Women Educators across Pre– and Post–Civil Rights Cohorts Theorize about their Activism," *Educational Studies: The Journal of the American Educational Studies Association* 48, no. 3 (2012): 266–95, and "Bridging the Legacy of Activism across Generations: Life Stories of African American Educators in Post–Civil Rights Birmingham," *The Urban Review* 43, no. 2 (2011): 151–74.These sections are reprinted with kind permissions of Taylor and Francis and Springer Science + Business Media respectively.

I gratefully acknowledge the generous support of the Lyle M. Spencer Foundation's Small Grants Program (#200500140) and the UAB Vice President's Office of Equity and Diversity's Minority Faculty Development Fund.

Birmingham houses a treasure trove of archives managed by unbelievably knowledgeable archivists, most notably, Laura Anderson and formerly, Horace Huntley, at the Birmingham Civil Rights Institute (BCRI), as well as Jim Baggett, Don Veasey, and staff members managing the Southern History, Government Documents, and Rare Books collections at the Birmingham Public Library (BPL). Special thanks to Jim Baggett and Laura Anderson, along with other current and former staff leaders at the BCRI—Ahmad Ward, Priscilla Hancock Cooper, Sylvea Hollis, Wayne Coleman, and Lawrence Pijeaux—for inviting me to disseminate preliminary findings and ideas at community forums sponsored by their respective organizations. I also appreciate the assistance of other archival, library, and school staff: Howard Robinson, Tyra White, and Jason Trawick, Alabama State University Archives and Special Collections Department; Imelda Vetter, Heather Martin, and Godfrey Watkins, UAB Mervyn H. Sterne Library; Joe Mosnier, formerly the SOHP at the University of

North Carolina at Chapel Hill; Geraldine Bell and Candace Murdock, Miles College Learning Resource Center; and Nez Calhoun and Martha Bouyer, Jefferson County Public Schools. The aforementioned archival organizations, along with Duke University's Behind the Veil Project, the Alabama Department of Archives and History, and Anne Rutledge, granted me privileges to reprint all photographs and archival document quotations that required permissions.

The UAB School of Education afforded me a semester sabbatical, and I appreciate my Educational Foundations Program colleagues, Samantha Elliott Briggs and Andrew McKnight, for standing in for me during that time. Michael Chambers II, Sylvia Hollins, Debrie Woods, Natalie Woods, Inas Mahdi, and Elizabeth Varghese provided critical research or administrative support during the grant phase.

I am grateful for the fervent prayers, support, and encouragement of my family, friends, pastor, church, and colleagues, especially current and former UAB sister-colleagues. My husband, Herb Jackson, has been my sounding board, confidant, and tireless supporter from start to finish. I also thank my parents, Lee and Juanita Loder, and my brother and his wife, Lee Wendell and Adrianne Loder, for their exemplary servant leadership to Birmingham. My mother-in-law, Ola Jackson, took a special interest in attending community forums where my work was featured. I am especially appreciative of the genuine support for this book's success that I received from my sister-friends, Dwinelva Zackery, Charlotte Hicks, Nesi Porter, Judy Stewart, Ruby Mendenhall, and Cynthia Reavis.

In tune with the reverent benediction of James Weldon Johnson's "Lift Every Voice and Sing," I am wholly indebted to the "God of our weary years, God of our silent tears, Thou who has brought [me and this book] this far on the way."

ABBREVIATIONS

ACMHR	Alabama Christian Movement for Human Rights
ADAH	Alabama Department of Archives and History
AERA	American Educational Research Association
A. G. Gaston	Arthur George Gaston
A. H. Parker	Arthur Harold Parker
ALSDE	Alabama State Department of Education
ASNLH/ASALH	Association for the Study of Negro Life and History/Association for the Study of African American Life and History
ASTA	Alabama State Teachers Association
ASU	Alabama State University
ATA	American Teachers Association
BCRI	Birmingham Civil Rights Institute
BCS	Birmingham City Schools
BPL	Birmingham Public Library
BPS	Birmingham Public Schools
Birmingham BOE	Birmingham Board of Education
CME	Colored Methodist Episcopal Church
HBCU	Historically Black Colleges and Universities
ICC	Interstate Commerce Commission
JCNTA	Jefferson County (AL) Negro Teachers Association
JeffCo Schools	Jefferson County (AL) Schools

KKK	Ku Klux Klan
NAACP	National Association for the Advancement of Colored People
NABSE	National Alliance of Black School Educators
NATCS	National Association of Teachers in Colored Schools
NCLB	No Child Left Behind
NCTA	National Colored Teachers Association
NEA	National Education Association
SACS	Southern Association of Colleges and Schools
SCLC	Southern Christian Leadership Conference
SNYC	Student Negro Youth Congress
SNCC	Student Non Violent Coordinating Committee
SOHP	Southern Oral History Program
UA	University of Alabama
UAB	University of Alabama at Birmingham
UPWA-CIO	United Public Workers of America-Congress of Industrial Organizations

INTRODUCTION

ACTIVISTS OR ACCOMMODATIONISTS?

Recasting the Role of African American Educators in the Civil Rights Movement

A familiar story in Birmingham's civil rights history and folklore showcases the bravery of schoolchildren, who on May 2, 1963, marched through the streets of downtown Birmingham in droves during what would later be called "The Children's Crusade."[1] They are portrayed as youthful stand-ins for parents, educators, and neighbors deemed too fearful and risk averse to defy Jim Crow laws.[2] While students jumped out of classroom windows and barged through schoolhouse doors to stake their claim for civil rights, their teachers reportedly dissuaded them with threats of suspension and expulsion. Principals, in particular, are vilified in this narrative as accommodationists who literally stood in the doorway of progress.[3]

The narrative of the Children's Crusade reflects a common refrain among local historians, archivists, and activists who are asked to reflect on the role of African American educators in the Birmingham civil rights movement. Their customary response is that "educators weren't really involved in the Birmingham civil rights movement."[4] Some even charge that African American educators were more of a hindrance than a help to the movement. Much of the published record on Birmingham's civil rights history reinforces this sentiment, as this history has focused primarily on the contributions of renowned preachers, civil rights leaders, attorneys, and even children.[5] When African American educators are mentioned in the scholarship, they are typically portrayed as fearful bystanders attempting to circumvent reprisals from the White community by shunning activism. For example, civil rights historian Glen Eskew portrayed African American principals and teachers in Birmingham who stood their ground against student protestors by locking school gates and suspending pupils who participated during the school day. Yet in a singular sentence in his extensive account of Birmingham's civil rights history, he acknowledged that "[s]ome teachers joined their pupils in the protest."[6] If indeed African American educators were more involved in the movement than has been portrayed, then why are their experiences largely overshadowed in Birmingham's civil rights history?

AN INCONCLUSIVE HISTORICAL RECORD

The story of Birmingham's civil rights struggle has rarely been told from the perspective of educators. Extant historical accounts of educators' involvement in the classical phase of the civil rights movement rely largely on historians' interpretations of limited archival data. The U.S. Southern regional coverage of African American educators' participation in the civil rights movement, albeit sparse, is strikingly similar to Birmingham's documented history. By far the most attention African American educators have received in the civil rights scholarship is associated with the NAACP's campaigns for equalization of teachers' salaries and the landmark *Brown v. Board of Education* Supreme Court case.[7] But even this documentation is incomplete, as it typically glosses over the painstaking pre-*Brown* era of educational infrastructure building, and is eclipsed by the crucial albeit far from singlehanded activism of the NAACP Legal Defense Fund.[8]

Those civil rights historians who have devoted some attention to African American educators tend to cast them as ancillary or inconsequential to the movement. For example, Adam Fairclough, who has written extensively about the contributions of African American educators to the long civil rights movement, surmised that they were largely averse to protesting *publicly* because "the disruption of school routine and discipline violated the professional instincts of many black educators."[9] Although Fairclough credited African American educators for organizing themselves behind the scenes to support the long civil rights movement, other scholars have paid less attention to these subtle activities and focus more on their presence, or lack thereof, in high-profile protests. John Dittmer, for example, in his examination of Mississippi's civil rights struggle, concluded that "as a group black teachers in the 1950s refused to take a stand and the movement of the early 1960s passed them by."[10] Similarly, Idus Newby deduced that the civil rights movement in South Carolina occurred not so much because of, but rather despite the contributions of African American schools and colleges.[11] Historian David Garrow implicated African American educators by inference in his critique of Birmingham's middle class, which he portrays as self-preservationist and only tepidly involved in the civil rights movement. Garrow concluded, "The black elite [in Birmingham] failed to push strongly for significant racial reforms."[12]

A notable group of historians whose research is focused on African American education offer a more affirmative account. In spite of their contributions, some scholars counter that such accounts are overly nostalgic about the status and condition of African American education in the pre-*Brown* era.[13] However, the Herculean efforts of formerly enslaved African Americans' struggle to promote literacy, advocate for the inclusion of their children in common schools, bolster teacher training, and establish high schools in the face of violent resistance and oppression should not be diminished.[14] Neither should "glass half-empty" perspectives on pre-*Brown* African American education be embraced unquestioningly as normative. James D. Anderson contended that the educational system established by African Americans during the post–Civil War years "was not necessarily deleterious, nor was all of black education repressive in reality."[15] In a similar vein, Vanessa Siddle Walker cautioned that "to remember segregated schools largely by recalling only their poor resources presents a historically incomplete picture."[16] The conditions and status of African American education pre-*Brown* were quite dire but not bereft of excellence, bravery, and perseverance.

One historian observed that "[h]istory is full of people who seemed unimportant to their contemporaries but, through some process that produced a surviving structure, have become important to us."[17] Unearthing this "surviving structure" is perhaps one of the most daunting challenges in documenting a more robust account of African American educators' involvement in the long civil rights movement. Good faith efforts to document this history adeptly are complicated by the fact that there is very limited archival evidence of direct classroom observation data, and the evidence that does exist derives from the 1930s Depression and 1940s pre–World War II eras, which depicts an overly dire history of African American schools.[18] Therefore, historians have relied heavily on memoirs, oral histories, school memorabilia, and a few surveys to recount African American educational history.[19] An overreliance on this data is problematic when considering the "politics of commemoration," whereby memory elites (e.g., museum curators, scholars, prominent activists, and the media) often determine who gets remembered and who does not.[20] Consequently, not enough is known and analyzed about "what ordinary people do with their collective pasts."[21] The sparse publicly archived information that does exist, especially related to the role of African American educators in the Birmingham civil rights movement, tends to instigate a "Rashomon effect" whereby scholars and laypeople alike draw their own myopic, and at times, polemical "truths" concerning these educators' involvement.[22]

The limited archival data of African American educators' civil rights participation are further complicated by a historical debate regarding whether these educators were characteristically activist or accommodationist. This dichotomy is admittedly much too simplistic for characterizing the complexity of African American educators' contributions to the movement.[23] Yet the civil rights movement sometimes prompted harsh criticisms about the perceived accommodationist tactics of African American teachers, principals, and higher educators.[24] Some historically Black colleges and universities (HBCUs) have been depicted as irrelevant or even detrimental to integration efforts. Civil rights leaders sometimes accused African American higher educators of failing to support the struggle against segregation.[25] The NAACP chastised HBCUs for implementing Jim Crow graduate programs as an alternative to banned White graduate programs.[26] At times, HBCU presidents were charged with being "Uncle Toms" for bowing to segregationist politicians' demands to expel student activists, and some were accused of acting as informants to expose members of civil rights organizations.[27] As noted previously, in Birmingham, some prominent African American principals were criticized for not allowing students to participate in protest marches and demonstrations, suspending them for their participation, and thereby kowtowing to the threats of reprimand from White school district leaders.[28]

The aforementioned problems of limited archival data and debates about whether African American educators were friends or foes of the civil rights movement are exacerbated by a disciplinary disjuncture between historical and contemporary research on African American education.[29] The legacy of excellence, endurance, and rich cultural heritage of all-Black, primarily rural Southern schools during the pre- and immediate post-*Brown* eras has been fairly well documented.[30] This documentation is critical to establishing a historical record of what existed and what was lost during this time period. However, an augmentation of this scholarship is desperately warranted.

Any undertaking that aims to link historical and contemporary perspectives about African American education in the U.S. South must take into account the decidedly altered social context of African American schools, communities, and families in the decades after the classical phase of the civil rights movement.[31] Many African American middle-class, working-class, and poor residents are no longer relegated to living together in segregated neighborhoods.[32] The Jim Crow era's close-knit, racially segregated yet economically heterogeneous communities, where teachers, principals, students, and parents lived, worked, and attended church and community events together, are no longer a reality for many African American residents in Birmingham.[33] This means many contemporary African American schools and communities have not experienced the same cohesiveness and collective capacity to mobilize social change as those of yesteryear. Furthermore, the students and parents whom veteran African American educators encounter today may be generationally distinctive from their previous students and parents.[34] For example, students born in the latter twentieth and early twenty-first centuries are influenced by the prominence of hip-hop culture.[35] In essence, the still not fully documented loss of professional and community cohesion among African Americans from diverse social classes and racially segregated schools and professional teacher and administrator associations places younger generations of African American educators, along with their students, and in many instances their students' relatively young parents, at an unprecedented disadvantage for mobilizing themselves collectively to address pressing contemporary problems in their schools and communities.[36]

In his analysis of the activist tradition of African American educational leadership from the late eighteenth century to the 1954 *Brown* case, V. P. Franklin concluded that contemporary African American educators have failed to perpetuate this activist tradition, as evidenced by the perils confronting contemporary urban schools and the lack of urgency to address these problems as a collective.[37] Even with respect to delivering critical pedagogy, some scholars believe African American educators have wavered in their activism since the classical phase of the civil rights movement. They contend that African American activist educators in the 1960s and 1970s distanced themselves from progressive pedagogical approaches to the study of social and political life.[38] Furthermore, they argue that in the wake of what was then a waning (classical phase) civil rights movement and Black Panther activism, these once cutting-edge "Black Power" schools, which were designed to help students challenge and usurp the status quo, eventually morphed into more traditional and less ideologically threatening educational programs focused on reading, mathematics, writing, self-concept, and global awareness.[39] Yet some recent scholarship suggests a perpetuation of this activist tradition through a commitment among contemporary African American educators to nurture and love African American children and engage in social justice advocacy.[40]

If historians focus their attention on the past, and education scholars generally examine contemporary educational issues, then how do we ensure that questions about historical continuities and discontinuities in African American education are addressed within a compartmentalized academy? This question points to a need for alternative frameworks that link past and present investigations of African American education.

ALTERNATIVE FRAMEWORKS

Patricia Hill Collins's seminal work on Black feminist thought, namely her reconceptualization of *activism*, is focal to this book's analysis.[41] With careful acknowledgment that Black feminist thought is situated in and intended to speak expressly to the lived experiences of Black women, its conceptual re-visioning of "activism" is useful in crafting an alternative framework for examining the multigenerational life stories of African American women *and* men, particularly those born in the post–civil rights era.

Given that women have comprised the majority of the African American teaching force prior to *Brown* through the present day, Black feminist thought is essential for reexamining educator activism.[42] Prevailing conceptions of social and political activism and resistance misunderstand the meaning of activism in Black women's lives, as they focus on formalized and visible political activity and miss "unofficial, private, and seemingly invisible spheres of social life and organization."[43] African American women in the U.S. South have been traditionally excluded from or relegated to subordinate roles within formally organized civil rights, women's rights, and labor rights groups.[44] In turn, with the exception of a few notable works primarily authored by women scholars, their contributions also have been marginalized in the published history of civil, educational, and freedom rights struggles in the United States.[45] Barnett referred to African American women civil rights leaders as a "category of invisible, unsung heroes and leaders" due to the constraining interlocking oppressions of racism, sexism, and classism.[46] She credited women such as Septima Clark, Diane Nash, and Joann Robinson, along with many others, as being the unsung heroines who initiated protests, strategized tactics, and contributed significant dollars to the civil rights movement.[47] Historian Glenda Gilmore characterized the activism of African American women in the U.S. South in the late nineteenth and early twentieth century as a unique brand of "racial diplomacy" that required them to walk a fine line between advocating for racial justice and quelling the fears and ire of White Southerners.[48] In light of this context, Patricia Hill Collins proposed assessing Black women's activism not so much by their ideology (i.e., whether they possess conservative progressive, or radical views) or association with formal political organizations but rather by their strategic responses to their daily encounters with domination in their communities, schools, and workplaces.[49]

The terms *activism* and *activist*, as articulated by the participants in the life stories featured in Part II of this book, reflect Patricia Hill Collins's conceptual denotations, which are defined as two distinct yet interrelated dimensions of activism: *struggles for group survival* and *struggles for institutional transformation*.[50] The former dimension points to Black women's creative strategies to resist and subvert oppressive structures, either as individuals or in groups, typically through means other than direct confrontation, which might not be the most preferred, opportune, or safest approach. Collins cites the historical struggles of Black women teachers as exemplary of this dimension. In contrast, struggles for institutional transformation are described as any efforts to challenge or dismantle discrimination in the public spheres of the workplace, media, and other social institutions, quite often in solidarity with larger-scale, formal organizations.[51] From the standpoint of Black feminist thought any collaborative actions Black women take to directly challenge institutionalized racism, sexism, and other forms of subordination would fall within the realm of struggles for institutional transformation.[52]

In light of the aforementioned perspectives, there are three assumptions which guide this book's analysis. First, activism may be expressed in both conventional and unconventional ways. Second, the activism of African American educators in the U.S. South, especially women, is deeply intertwined with their teaching and leading practice. Third, activism changes over time in response to new and emergent generational challenges.

Conventional and Unconventional Activism

The activism of African American educators during the long civil rights movement is both similar to and distinctive from the activism enacted by Birmingham's civil rights "foot soldiers."[53] Conventional forms of civil rights activism include those widely embraced in the civil rights scholarship and media as well as by residents of historic civil rights cities in the U.S. South. These forms tend to be visible, collective, and valorized in both academic and public discourse. They are also widely associated with the classical phase of the civil rights movement. Some notable examples include visible and active participation in protest marches, boycotts, sit-ins, jail-ins, and high-profile civil rights organizations. Unconventional forms of activism presented in this book are more closely associated with the professional milieu of teachers and administrators. They sometimes involve educators as a collective but very often feature an individual educator carrying out an act behind the scenes or clandestinely. Some examples include, but are not limited to: engaging in subversive acts to avoid jeopardizing the livelihoods and futures of student-protestors; contributing materially, temporally, and financially to civil rights causes through professional teachers associations; and promoting voters' education and rights among fellow educators and students.[54] While there is limited primary and secondary source documentation of African American educators' participation in conventional forms of civil rights protest,[55] a closer examination of extant scholarship and public archives indicates that these educators were often involved behind the scenes in both conventional and unconventional ways that helped to propel the movement.[56]

Educational Praxis as Activism

A second assumption is that teaching and leading in schools are activist practices in their own right.[57] I acknowledge a philosophical tension in the Black feminist scholarship related to this assumption.[58] Activist pedagogy may be liberating or constraining depending on the context. The teaching profession typically reinforces the status quo, which in turn undermines activist aims of educators (and their students). Yet many educators have used the classroom to teach powerful lessons about freedom, justice, and democracy, which have stirred younger generations of students to action. Paulo Freire referred to this kind of teaching as *praxis,* which challenges the notion of a demarcation between theory and practice.[59]

The subtle contributions of many African American educators during the long civil rights movement may be characterized as "intellectual activism" or acts of "intellectual resistance" and subversion in the classroom and school.[60] Successful revolutions are undergirded by the contributions of intellectual elites.[61] African American educators have produced a robust tradition of Black intellectual thought, which has bolstered their arduous fight for justice and equality.[62] Education historian Derrick Alridge has chronicled the contributions of nineteenth- and early–twentieth-century African American scholars and educators—Alexander Crummell, Anna

Julia Cooper, Booker T. Washington, W. E. B. Du Bois, Carter G. Woodson, Mary McLeod Bethune, and Charles S. Johnson—and their impact on education, politics, and society.[63] Crummell, described as a "civilizationist," believed that a classical education, as opposed to an industrial education, undergirded by deeply rooted Christian principles, was the ticket to freedom for African Americans.[64] His protégés, Anna Julia Cooper and W. E. B. Du Bois, also promoted classical education for African Americans.[65] Alridge described Anna Julia Cooper as "the Victorian feminist educator," who argued in one of her earliest writings, *A Voice from the South*, that African American women were "an integral part of the race uplift movement of the late 19th century and must, therefore, obtain higher education to prepare themselves for the mission of race uplift."[66] Carter G. Woodson, in particular, has been heralded for his ambitious and exhaustive project to integrate Black history curriculum across the multiple sites of higher education, public schools, and community institutions during the pre-*Brown* era.[67] Woodson's contributions laid the foundation for African American teachers' critical pedagogy throughout the long civil rights movement. Even nineteenth-century educational figures that have been typically portrayed as accommodationist—namely, Booker T. Washington, Nannie Helen Burroughs, and Mary McLeod Bethune—were known to espouse dialectical views about the pedagogy and politics they deemed most appropriate and expedient for advancing Black progress.[68]

The praxis of African American educators in the U.S. South during the pre-*Brown* era, especially female teachers, entailed promoting positive images in a White supremacist culture through teaching Black heritage and history; instilling a strong sense of racial pride in their students; teaching about democracy, civil, and human rights; spearheading efforts to liberate African Americans through literacy; and producing and utilizing research and scholarship to advance educational and professional equity.[69] The voter literacy schools of South Carolina teacher-activist Septima Clark, who lost her job and economic livelihood after she refused to defect from the NAACP when membership had been outlawed by her state, is illustrative of this kind of activism, although she also linked her praxis to conventional civil rights activism.[70] Likewise, Charles Hamilton Houston, John Hope Franklin, Kenneth and Mamie Clark, and Marion Wright Thompson used their research and scholarship to tip the *Brown* decision on the side of desegregation.[71] Furthermore, African American teachers in the early twentieth century prepared students for a democracy not yet fully realized in a Jim Crow society by teaching and modeling civic action, self-respect, and decision-making and survival skills for protection.[72] In spite of working in woefully underfunded and underresourced schools, they enabled their students to acquire "educational capital" by generating materials and supplies, situating curriculum and instruction within a more affirming framework, and mobilizing human resources.[73]

Activism and Generational Change

A third assumption, informed by life course perspectives that consider the interplay among human agency, history, and social change, is that activism may change over time as successive generations confront emergent social concerns and political realities.[74] A case in point is the generational tension that existed between the Southern Christian Leadership Conference (SCLC) and the Student Nonviolent Coordinating Committee (SNCC) during the 1960s.[75] Mentored by Ella Baker and others, SNCC members insisted on being recognized as a student-led grassroots activist organization with protest strategies that should be recognized in their own right. Conversely, the more established SCLC was generally comprised of ministers, teachers, attorneys, and other Black professionals. Martin Luther King Jr. initially supported the efforts of SNCC but grew increasingly anxious with their bold strategies, most notably, the 1961 Freedom Rides and proposed protest involvement in Albany, Georgia, in 1961 and 1962.[76]

Generational tension persists today among African Americans born across the spectrum of the long civil rights movement. African Americans born on opposite sides of the classical civil rights movement confronted vastly divergent opportunities and constraints for "what [they] could be and do."[77] For example, African American educators born a few decades prior to and immediately following *Brown* ranged from childhood to young or middle adulthood during the height of Birmingham's civil rights movement. This means many of them came of age as youth and adult professionals during the passage of the Civil Rights Act of 1964, the Voting Rights Act of 1965, and Malcolm X's and Martin Luther King Jr.'s assassinations in 1965 and 1968, respectively. Demographic research on African American "baby boomers" indicates that this generation, born between 1946 and 1964, grew up in a world of segregation and racism yet had more opportunities for formal schooling than did its parents' generation, the silent generation born between 1925 and 1945.[78]

African Americans born between 1965 and 1984 and beyond this bracket are influenced by the prominence of hip-hop culture,[79] which makes them arguably more generationally distinctive than previous generations of African Americans.[80] The generation X and hip-hop generation came of age in an era of ambivalent opportunities.[81] This generation is the first among African Americans that is more fully "enjoying the fruits of the civil rights and black power movements," yet it is also experiencing the "reversal of civil rights gains."[82] On the one hand, several decades after *Brown*, the African American middle class grew and rates of college attendance and graduation increased; on the other hand, there is an increasingly impoverished urban and rural African American population in the United States, with poverty rising in the suburbs, rising crime rates in urban neighborhoods, and increasingly punitive and inequitable political and judicial responses to crime, which have resulted in a strikingly disproportionate African American prison population.[83] Moreover, the hip-hop generation has been described as possessing a worldview that is more materialistic and less morally rigid with respect to values about marriage, divorce, sexual relations, and lifestyle, compared to previous generations of African Americans.[84] The traditional influences of family, church, and school have been supplanted partly by the powerful culture and pervasive influence of technology, popular entertainment, particularly rap music, and globalization, which has exacerbated unemployment and poverty rates among African American youth.[85]

Many African Americans in the generation X/hip-hop generation and beyond have little to no direct experiential knowledge of the historical tradition of activism that has more closely aligned the United States with its espoused democratic principles. This limited knowledge has left an increasing number of younger African Americans wholly unprepared to effectively confront modern-day iterations of racism, sexism, and other forms of oppression.[86] In the field of education, this reality has disconcerting implications for the transmission of knowledge and culture. Patricia Hill Collins cautioned that in the post–civil rights era "large numbers of Black children remain warehoused in inner-city schools, sadly, many of them taught by Black teachers who have little institutional memory of . . . activism."[87] Consequently, a number of newly minted teachers experience frustration, despair, and inefficacy to mobilize transformative changes in contemporary public schools.

Notably, in spite of their limited or nonexistent direct experiences with the classical phase of the civil rights movement, young people in the United States who were not yet born during this era remember this phase at unexpectedly high rates, which speaks to the powerful influence of memory elites, schools, families, and communities to mediate compelling information about this era.[88] Younger generations of African Americans make sense of what they know vicariously about the most commemorated phase of the long civil rights movement through "liberatory education and pedagogy."[89] As Alridge observed,

> While hip hop is far from perfect in addressing the problem of education in black communities, it has carried on the tradition of calling for African Americans to take control of their education and to obtain the educational tools that will enable them to improve their lives.[90]

Similar to Black feminist thought, hip-hop scholars purport that the political views of this generation are not as clearly distinguishable as more classical conceptualizations of Black political thought, activism, and "re-actionism" such as revolutionary, radical, reformist, accommodationist, and nationalist schools of thought.[91] In response to this political nebulousness, some observers have categorized the hip-hop generation as spurring more of a cultural than a political movement.[92] However, hip-hop commentators contend that hip hop is indeed an emergent political movement with an "off-the-radar segment" that is busy creating a national infrastructure and mobilizing a national youth culture at local and regional levels in the United States through political rallies, voting blocs, and cultural-political bridge building.[93]

In response to this new context, some African Americans are calling for new "tools" to address persistent racism in the twenty-first century. To explicate this analogy, the (classical) civil rights generation used a hammer to solve its problems whereas the hip-hop generation might need a screwdriver to fix unprecedented problems.[94] As one scholar-commentator cautioned: "We can't keep yelling at them to use a hammer for a new problem."[95] Echoing this sentiment, Reverend Joseph Lowery, considered the "dean" of the classical phase of the civil rights movement, noted that the problems younger generations of African Americans confront "aren't as obvious, as brutal" as they were for previous generations.[96] He went on to say that these problems "are so systematic, camouflaged that the task is much more difficult in many ways."[97]

In light of this hip-hop generational context, young self-proclaimed activists contend that new strategies for resistance are needed to fight the complex issues of their day such as poverty, inequitable education, police brutality, homicide, and environmental racism. In the field of education, there are calls for new pedagogical strategies to prepare today's students to confront a modern-day post–civil rights racial context.[98] As one young activist put it, "Everyone tends to think that activism is marching in the streets. But not everybody can or wants to do that. For them, writing might be a form of resistance and activism."[99]

LOOKING BACKWARD TO MOVE FORWARD

As noted previously, historian V. P. Franklin concluded that contemporary African American educators have failed to work collectively to carry the torch of traditional activist leadership, as evidenced by the perils confronting inner city schools.[100] His conclusion raises the question of whether or not younger generations of African American educators are even cognizant of a longstanding tradition of activist educational leadership and their place within it. Indeed, Franklin's admonition calls for a reexamination of the African American tradition of educational activism from a multigenerational perspective. This particular perspective lends itself, first, to extrapolating an "activist trajectory" inclusive of past and present generations of African American educators, and second, to deducing whether this trajectory has declined over time. In the spirit of the Akan word *sankofa,* in order to move forward one must first look backward for a beginning point of sorts, which in Birmingham, originates around the time of the city's post–Civil War establishment.[101]

PART I

BREAKING GROUND AND LAYING THE FOUNDATION

1

PIONEERING BLACK SCHOOLS SECOND TO NONE

EMANCIPATED TO EDUCATE

Former Birmingham resident Esther King Casey was one of the first Black[1] public school teachers in the U.S. South to rise up from slavery and emancipate her community by way of the schoolroom.[2] She was described as cultured and refined with speech "surprisingly devoid of the usual Negro dialect."[3] Her most vivid childhood memory was walking with her father past President Abraham Lincoln "hanging" (as an effigy) in the courthouse square, riddled with the bullets of Confederate soldiers embittered by their Civil War defeat. After the Emancipation Proclamation, most freed Blacks were "leased out" to plantation owners and continued to work under an oppressive and exploitive sharecropping system not too far removed from slavery.[4] Casey fared better than most Blacks, however. After her family's emancipation, similar to many freed Blacks, Casey remained with her mother and the wife of her former slave owner, Susan King, to whom she referred as "the White lady." King was one of many Civil War widows left to manage the plantation after her husband, Captain Henry King, went off to, and later died in, war. She taught Casey to read and write as a child during slavery, and then insisted that Casey's mother enroll her in the newly opened school for freed Blacks. Whether King was anxious to abide by new laws requiring former slave owners to care for and educate freed Black children until age fifteen is not clear,[5] but she willingly assumed responsibility for paying the required monthly school fees of fifty cents as long as Casey remained under her care. When Casey turned eighteen, she had acquired enough education to qualify her to become a teacher. She taught for three years before marrying Jim Casey, and eventually moved to Birmingham under her grandson's care.

For Esther King Casey's generation, the long civil rights struggle for educational equity began shortly after the Civil War ended. The end of the

Civil War brought an influx of freed Blacks to Birmingham, which was founded in 1871, and other cities in the U.S. South in search of a better way of life.[6] During slavery, Blacks in Alabama were generally forbidden from being taught to read and write, and poor Whites were not much more literate.[7] Therefore, the establishment of schools was the first order of business for White and Black Alabamians alike but it proved to be an uphill battle in a post–Civil War state whose economic livelihood was practically decimated by the legal dismantling of slavery. An anti–public education sentiment, deeply rooted in the American South's colonial period and continuing into the modern era, also undermined early efforts to establish public schools in Birmingham and its surrounding Jefferson County seat.[8]

While White Alabamians appealed to prominent local business and civic leaders for new schools, Black Alabamians had to rely more heavily on their own communal efforts and support from Northern White philanthropists and missionaries.[9] As a result, the first school for freed Blacks in Alabama was established in Huntsville in 1863 in partnership between a U.S. Army base and a Northern missionary board.[10] A Freedmen's Bureau followed in 1865, serving as the federal government's primary vehicle for relief and rehabilitation in Alabama's first freedmen's schools established in 1866.[11] The American Missionary Association (AMA) was the predominant mission group in Alabama advocating education for Black people in the post–Civil War era.[12] While the Freedmen's Bureau primarily provided the physical building infrastructure, the AMA mostly recruited and paid an integrated teaching staff to work in Black schools.[13]

Black education during the Reconstruction era was regarded as the responsibility of the federal government and private philanthropy rather than as a local government function.[14] Despite this view, Black Reconstructionist legislators, community members, and educators fought painstakingly to establish schools for Black children in Alabama.[15] Yet in the midst of their self-determination, it was the intent of many White Southerners to relegate Black education to a substandard system dictated by White benevolence rather than by state-mandated support.[16] As Bullock concluded, the late nineteenth century marked the beginning of a very long period of Black education that placed the interest of Black children "out of the mainstream of American culture and into the bayous."[17]

There was a glimmer of hope for Blacks in 1867 when delegates to the Alabama Constitutional Convention, which included eighteen Black Alabama legislators out of nearly one hundred, laid the foundation for a state-supported school system for Black and White children.[18] However, the constitution did not materialize without racial political strife. Black legislators fought vociferously against an amendment to establish racially segregated schools.[19] Although the amendment failed to pass, it foreshadowed a system of educational apartheid that would become commonplace in Alabama.[20] The contingent of White legislators who aimed to thwart Black education, even if it meant dismantling the state's fledgling public education system altogether, finally had its day in 1875 when it replaced the 1867 constitution with one that called for abolishing the state board of education, reducing administrative expenses, forbidding payments to any denominational or private school, and mandating racially separate schools.[21] Throughout the Reconstruction era White legislators in Alabama and across the South were unrelenting in their schemes to allocate money inequitably for Black versus White public schools.[22] Between 1875 and 1891 these legislators passed several constitutional amendments intended to thwart and eventually dismantle Alabama's fledgling public education system writ large in order to circumvent racial integration and Black progress.

In the midst of Reconstruction-era political battles, Birmingham's Black community continued to press forward to establish schools for their children. The public school was paramount of any government service for Birmingham's recently freed Black community. Unlike Black-owned and -operated organizations such as churches and fraternal associations, which were sustained by small leadership staffs, the Black community was hard put to sustain an adequate teaching force solely on its own resources.[23] Public schools depended in large part on tax revenue collected and allocated by the White-dominated state and local governments, which meant that the advancement of Black education often involved wrangling and compromising with White public officials.[24]

Birmingham's first school for White children was opened for occupancy in March 1874.[25] The land deed drafted by Elyton Land Company stipulated that the school be built "for the white children now residing in, and who may reside hereafter in said city for no other purpose and use whatever. The school is to be taught by white teachers."[26] It was not until the Black community petitioned the board of aldermen in 1876 for "a free colored school" that they made headway in establishing its first publicly supported school for Black children.[27] In response, the only contribution the board made was an agreement to hire and compensate a teacher.[28] The building itself was to be provided by the Black community. In 1882 the mayor appointed a committee to select a lot for the erection of the first Black school.[29] It was in 1883, nine years after the establishment of the first school for White children, that Black children in Birmingham finally were able to attend their own quasi-public school on the north side of the city, followed by a second school on the south side in 1884.[30] Although Birmingham's emergent Black public schools were supported by White Northern philanthropic societies and some White Birmingham school and civic leaders, by and large the Black community had to rely upon its own toil and resources to educate Black children.[31] Throughout the late nineteenth and early twentieth centuries, Black educators in Birmingham joined ranks with local businessmen and community leaders to establish schools, upgrade facilities, advocate for higher teacher salaries, garner resources for faculty and students, and promote racial pride through Black History programs and curricula.[32] In the absence of this persistent agitation for resources, Birmingham's Black citizens would not have progressed as far as they did during the Jim Crow era, which is comparable to the experience of Blacks throughout the U.S. South.[33]

BIRMINGHAM EDUCATORS AND BOOKER T. WASHINGTON: PARALLELS AND INTERSECTIONS

Booker T. Washington's Campaign to Build Black Schools

While Black citizens worked tirelessly to establish Birmingham's first public schools, Booker T. Washington was initiating an ambitious plan to educate Blacks throughout the rural South, West, and Mid-Atlantic regions with the help of the Black community and several prominent and interconnected White Northern philanthropists and civic leaders, namely, George Foster Peabody, John F. Slater, Julius Rosenwald, and Anna T. Jeanes.[34] Peabody, a native of Massachusetts, a Baltimore, Maryland, merchant, and a London banker, established the Peabody Educational Fund in 1867 to promote common school education and assist in establishing a permanent system of public schools in impoverished areas of the South and Southwest.[35] Notably, Washington also received philanthropic support from a prominent White Alabamian and former state-legislative opponent of Black education, Jabez L. M. Curry, who became the chief agent of the Peabody Fund.[36] Washington's vision for Tuskegee Institute benefited from the Peabody Fund's shift in direction to support normal schools focused on teacher training in 1880.[37] In addition, Slater, a native of Norwich, Connecticut, was inspired by Peabody's philanthropic success and started a fund in 1882 to support Black schools, namely teacher training programs.[38]

The most well-known of Washington's philanthropic relationships was with Illinois businessman and philanthropist Julius Rosenwald, who served as president and later chairman of Sears, Roebuck & Company.[39] Rosenwald launched into large-scale philanthropy during his fiftieth birthday when he gave away $700,000, a portion of which went to Tuskegee Institute. He also set aside a notable sum of this investment to partner with Washington to establish Black schools in primarily poor rural areas throughout the U.S. South. In the long run, the ambitious Rosenwald Fund project invested an estimated four million dollars to build nearly five thousand schools across a swath of states between Texas and Maryland. But the Washington-Rosenwald vision could not have been realized without the strong monetary and nonmonetary support of Black community members, which included a number of educators.[40] Black teachers, principals, and curriculum supervisors, referred to as "Jeanes Supervisors" after their namesake the Anna T. Jeanes Fund, which based its program on the ideas of Black teacher and school founder Virginia Randolph, led community campaigns to raise thousands of dollars for schools.[41] As one author noted, "Local people did not wait for someone to offer them a Rosenwald school."[42] Notably, of the total dollars expended on Rosenwald Schools over the years, 64 percent came from publicly collected taxes, 17 percent was invested by the Black community, 15 percent was donated by Rosenwald and the Rosenwald Fund, and only 4 percent came from other private white donors.[43] In Alabama, the Black community's donations exceeded contributions made by Whites, tax funds, and Rosenwald.[44] Yet only one school in the Birmingham area, Miles Memorial College, which would later be named Miles College, is recorded as receiving a Rosenwald Fund grant in 1929 to upgrade its library resources.[45]

Booker T. Washington is widely acknowledged to be the foremost leader in Black education during the late nineteenth and early twentieth century, and the fact that he hailed from Alabama made his influence even more formidable among Birmingham's Black turn-of-the-twentieth-century education pioneers.[46] His endorsement of industrial education afforded many formerly enslaved Black Americans like himself with a practical education and a modest trade. This educational philosophy resonated with his worldview and humble beginnings. However, his approach to Black progress was not embraced universally by some of his Black contemporaries who advocated a classical or Black heritage curriculum and more direct confrontations to Jim Crow.[47] Yet, his approach appeased many White Northern and Southern philanthropists and business leaders, with Rosenwald being one of his most ardent supporters.[48] As one scholar noted, "Washington was extremely skilled at wearing masks and operating behind the scenes."[49] His critics, however, contended that his accommodationist tactics in soliciting White philanthropic support for Black schools undermined the aims of equality and reinforced second-class citizenship for Blacks in the U.S. South. This criticism was validated to some degree in Birmingham where in 1907 Blacks were used as common laborers in the steel industry.[50] Local White media and school leaders rationalized Black workers' relegation to unskilled and semiskilled labor by demeaning their intelligence.[51] Notably, Birmingham Public School (BPS) superintendent John Herbert Phillips, often characterized as a loyal supporter of Black education, once claimed, "Whatever anthropologists may report, the black race is to all intents and purposes a young race; therefore it is imitative."[52] Yet in spite of Washington's often derided approach, his influence on Birmingham's Black education pioneers was far-reaching.

Arthur Harold Parker and Birmingham's First Black High School

While Booker T. Washington embarked on his mission to build Black schools throughout the South, one of his admirers, Arthur Harold Parker, was a leading figure in establishing Birmingham's first Black high school.[53] Parker was a fair-skinned man with Caucasian features, born in Springfield, Ohio, in 1870 on the homestead his mother inherited from her former White slave owner and biological father. Both of his parents were products of a mixed ancestry of White, African, and Native American. His father was also born into slavery in Decatur, Alabama, although he escaped through the Underground Railroad, making his way all the way up to Canada.[54] His mother was raised and worked on a Virginia plantation where she was taught to write and read alongside the White children who lived in the main interior of the slave owner's house, commonly referred to as "the big house."[55]

Parker attended an all-Black elementary school, but later enrolled in an integrated high school, which made him highly cognizant of his racial status in America. He recalled: "I remember well that I did not care for the high school as I did for the elementary school. Gradually, I came to understand."[56] When his plans to attend Oberlin College were diverted by his parents' physical incapacitation, he migrated to Birmingham in 1887 where his two uncles lived. One of his uncles encouraged him to pursue

Figure 1.1. Arthur Harold Parker, principal of Birmingham's first Black high school. Photo: Birmingham, Ala., Public Library Archives.

the teacher's examination. It was not difficult to convince Parker to pursue teaching because he held the profession in high esteem, recognizing it as one of the few routes Blacks could embark upon to become white-collar professionals. In 1888, Parker became only the thirteenth Black teacher in Birmingham when he accepted a position at Slater School. After grieving the losses of his mother and first wife, Parker pursued the principalship. Upon losing his second wife during childbirth, a despondent Parker left the education field briefly to work for the Internal Revenue Service. It was his third wife, Anna Gilbert, who encouraged him to return to teaching and administration in 1899.

When several prominent Black businessmen and community members petitioned the board of education for a high school in 1899, BPS superintendent Phillips asked Parker to serve as the school's first principal. In his reflections on Phillips's invitational meeting with him, Parker recalled: "I gave him my word that I would roll up my sleeves and go to work with all my might. I never faltered in my faith and belief that we would succeed and Dr. Phillips never faltered in his help of me."[57] Parker assumed the helm of Industrial High School in September 1900 with eighteen students in one room on the second floor of the all-Black Cameron School building. Initially, he served as the school's first principal and teacher, eventually hiring two more teachers in the second and third year of his tenure. Over time, Parker would employ many well-credentialed Black educators who had been denied jobs in other sectors.[58] Many of Parker's newly hired teachers had master's degrees and doctorates from Northern universities and were eager to return to Birmingham to work.[59]

Following in the footsteps of his role model, Booker T. Washington, Parker instituted a primarily industrial education curriculum. Although the curriculum emphasized industrial education, it also included a number of academic classes such as English, Algebra, Plane Geometry, Civics and History, including "Negro History," Science, and even Spanish.[60] In fact, the second teacher Parker hired during the school's early years, J. R. Coffey, made it clear that he was not interested in teaching industrial classes but rather academic classes such as science, philosophy, and foreign languages. Parker gave no indication that he failed to oblige Coffey's curricular preferences, but he found a kindred spirit in his third hire, Miss O. D. Kennedy, who assumed responsibility for teaching female students sewing, cooking, and singing skills.

Although Parker's endorsement of an industrial education curriculum has been characterized as an appeasement strategy akin to Washington's tactics, his penchant for industry was deeply rooted in his upbringing.[61] As the second oldest of five children, Parker was responsible for a great deal of housecleaning. During his four years of high school he did all of the family's washing and ironing. As he reminisced: "Each Monday morning I would get my tubs, water and soap ready—put the clothes to soak and have them out by seven or eight o'clock."[62] On Saturdays and alternating weekday afternoons, Parker would report to his father's barbershop to shine shoes and learn the barber's trade. By the time he graduated, as he put it: "I was holding down a barber's chair—with quite a number of regular customers."[63] One of Parker's former teachers, Carol W. Hayes, who would later become the longtime "Director of Negro Education" for the BPS, wrote in a foreword to Parker's autobiography that "[Parker], like the late Booker T. Washington, believed that the foundation of every race must be laid in the common every-day occupations that are right about our doors."[64]

Since it was the only Black public high school in Birmingham at the time, Industrial High School drew its students from a cross-section of socioeconomic classes. Students traveled from diverse areas such as Woodlawn, South Birmingham, and the more middle-class communities of Smithfield and Enon Ridge. But some of Birmingham's middle-class Black families opted to send their children to private schools because they did not approve of the industrial curriculum.[65] Ellen Tarry, who attended Industrial High School for her final year of school, recalled in her memoirs that some Black parents sent their children to boarding schools because of their aversion to the Birmingham Board of Education's emphasis on industrial education for Blacks at that time. She recalled that "[m]any parents felt that our [Industrial] high school did not measure up and that their children would be handicapped by attendance there."[66] Some parents became even more disenchanted upon receiving correspondence from their former neighbors who migrated to the North only to find that their children were retained in lower grades because "they had no Latin or French and found it impossible to keep up with their classes in mathematics."[67]

Oral histories of former Birmingham educators who attended Industrial High School as students in the 1930s reveal the indelible print of the city's social class schisms. Gertrude Crum Sanders recalled that wearing school uniforms "was one of the best things that could have happened to the black folks" because they helped to mask social class differences.[68] She explained that she and her sister only had four dresses between them: "one on and one off, and when that one's off it better be in the wash, getting ready for the next day."[69] Similar to Black Pentecostal church culture, Sanders noted that girls could not wear lipstick or jewelry at Industrial High School.[70] She described the curriculum as including "cooking, sewing, washing and the laundry, [and] beauty culture."[71] Sanders recalled Parker summoning her to his office to her initial chagrin, only to learn that he had decided to skip her one grade level due to her high scholastic performance. But her memories of skin color discrimination were not as flattering, as she recounted her teachers' preference for "half white girls" and conversely, their prejudice against darker-skinned students.[72] However, the fact that Parker acknowledged her aptitude by promoting her a grade ahead demonstrates his egalitarianism in interacting with some of his darker-skinned students.

Undeniably, Parker was a member of Birmingham's Black bourgeoisie, based on several factors.[73] First, he could readily trace his White heritage on both sides of his family. Second, he was visibly fair-skinned, and no doubt often mistaken for White by many during his day. Third, he could boast of a family heritage of land and property inheritance as well as pre–Civil War emancipation and literacy. Finally, by virtue of his profession as a teacher and school administrator, he was a part of an educated and credentialed class. Yet in spite of his pedigree, Parker showed signs of leveling the playing field at Industrial High School. Once when a White news reporter mistook a female student who was sweeping the floors during his visit for a "janitress," Parker laughed in jest at his misjudgment, noting that the girl's father was one of the "most wealthy Negroes in the city."[74] He proudly proclaimed to the reporter: "No difference who they are. When they enter high school they know that [they're] going to have to work with brooms as well as with books."[75]

Parker was not only revered in his school but also in his professional associations and throughout the Birmingham community. In 1900, he was elected president of the Alabama State Teachers Association.[76] As a long-tenured principal, he went on to make major building and program improvements, which included moving the school to a new location that his students helped to renovate, and establishing a night school and a summer school for teachers. During an influenza epidemic in 1918, the school closed temporarily and was converted into a hospital where the students served the community as nurses. Parker received many distinctions from the Black community, including a Negro Citizens' Loving Cup for "that citizen that had done the most for his race in 1924," and an honorary Doctor of Letters from Miles College in 1933.[77] A former Industrial High School student, Juanita Waiters Clarke, recalled that Parker and her teachers were "revered by everybody and everybody in Birmingham knew them by name."[78] In spite of the industrial curriculum critiques leveled by some Black middle-class parents, Ellen Tarry attested that she and her fellow Industrial High School classmates never wavered in their pride for their beloved school and principal: "I. H. S. was our school and we loved it. We loved our principal Professor A. H. Parker, too."[79]

However, Parker also had his fair share of critics in his day who winced at his perceived accommodationism in courting White patrons to support Industrial High School. A member of the Birmingham NAACP once complained that his silence on political equality for Blacks did more harm than good and made him a sellout.[80] Parker was known to acquiesce to Phillips's requests for his high school choir to sing Negro spirituals in order to remain in his good stead.[81] One common explanation for Parker's tactics is that, similar to Booker T. Washington, he viewed accommodationism as a necessary evil to withstand in order to realize his vision for Black education in Birmingham.[82] But it is also likely that Parker genuinely liked Negro spirituals, and therefore, did not view showcasing this genre as self-abasement. Furthermore, the school's choir was well renowned throughout the Black community, and Parker scoffed at the notion that Negro spirituals were degrading. A chapter in his autobiography, "The High School as a Musical Factor" is devoted to highlighting Industrial High School students' musical acumen, especially in singing spirituals.[83] Parker also expounded on a May 1914 *Birmingham News* article, titled "Folk Songs of Negroes Praised by Dr. Phillips," where during a commencement program, Phillips was reportedly so moved by the Negro spirituals that he threatened not to grant Parker with an orchestra director, "lest they stop singing the spirituals."[84] The news reporter noted several "amens" and even weeping from the primarily Black audience when Phillips "declared [the spirituals] were born when the Negro race was in its tragic period."[85] It is quite probable that Parker's sentiments about industrial education and spirituals coincided with Phillips's paternalism, and that Parker exploited their commonality on these two matters for the good of his school and community.[86]

Parker was also genuinely fond of Phillips and considered him to be a friend and ally. Phillips was arguably one of the most ardent White supporters of Black education in Birmingham at that time.[87] Even though his views on Black intelligence reflected the White supremacist thinking of his day, Phillips advocated fairly strongly for the establishment of Birmingham's Black public schools. His advocacy for Black schools aside, Parker spent time getting to know him personally during their trips between Tuskegee Institute, where Parker taught for five summers and Phillips was an annual keynote speaker, and Birmingham. During one trip, they encountered a violent thunderstorm that struck and killed several people in a "colored church."[88] Phillips got out of the car and assisted people until medical staff arrived. He was detained for over an hour, apparently ignoring Parker's warning that he would miss his train to Birmingham, which he did. On another excursion, Parker walked alongside a public highway to pick blackberries while waiting for a flat tire to be repaired, only to be accosted by a White man who forbade him from doing so. Phillips immediately got out of the car and intervened by asking the man when it became a crime to pick fruit on a public highway where private owners had no claim to its property rights.[89] Upon learning of Phillips's death, Parker attended his funeral and remained "until the last sad, touching rite was finished at his tomb."[90] A mournful Parker reflected: "As I turned away and almost groped my way back home, the feeling surged over me that I had lost one of the best friends that had yet touched my life."[91]

After serving as principal of the Industrial High School for thirty-nine years, Parker went into "semi-retirement" due to illness, serving briefly as principal emeritus and Director of Guidance for Negroes for the school board.[92] Industrial High School was soon named after him. He died shortly after his retirement and was funeralized in the renamed A. H. Parker High School auditorium. By newspaper accounts, his reputation among Black and White Birmingham residents alike was admirable. The White-owned *Birmingham News* published elegiacally: "And now that the death which knows no color line has come to claim Dr. Parker, the mourning and the sense of loss transcend all racial lines."[93] The newspaper went on to describe Parker's important role in promoting positive race relations in the city, noting that "the always delicate and sensitive problems of race relationship found help in the sane and informed viewpoints of Dr. Parker."[94] Many Birmingham residents during that time and since then believed that his dream "to see built in Birmingham a high school for Negro boys and girls that would be second to none in the South" was realized under his nearly forty-year tenure as Industrial High School's inaugural principal.[95]

Carrie Tuggle, Tuggle Institute, and Colored Women's Clubs

Although prominent Black men helped found and establish Birmingham's first Black schools, Black women were also important contributors. During the height of Colored Women's Clubs at the turn of the twentieth century,[96] Black women educators in Birmingham fought for educational equality and voter enfranchisement.[97] Among these women, Carrie Tuggle is an exemplar.[98]

Born into slavery, Tuggle overcame the poverty of her early life to become one of Birmingham's prominent Black community leaders. In 1903 she founded Tuggle Institute, a combined school and home for poor Black children and youth, with only $2.50. Tuggle was affiliated with a number of Colored Women's Clubs such as the Courts of Calanthe, Knights and Ladies of Honor of the World, and Rising Sons and Daughters of Protection. She created the Rising Sons and Daughters solely for the purpose of supporting Tuggle Institute. Club members and Black community residents supported Tuggle Institute during a time when public monies generally supported White institutions. Many of Tuggle's fellow club members served as teachers and administrators at the school. Tuggle also doggedly solicited support from Birmingham's White philanthropic community. In fact, prominent White Birmingham businessmen and their

Figure 1.2. Carrie Tuggle, founder of Tuggle Institute. Photo: Birmingham, Ala., Public Library Archives.

wives, such as "Mr. and Mrs. Louis Pizitz" and "Mrs. A. B. Loveman," lent their financial support to Tuggle Institute. Over time, Tuggle expanded her school's wooden makeshift building to include an integrated academic and industrial curriculum, nursing training, music instruction, and character education. Tuggle also emphasized lessons on racial pride and self-esteem development using books written by Booker T. Washington and other Black leaders of her day.

Tragically, in 1919, when Tuggle was just shy of paying off the school building's mortgage, the school burned down in a suspicious fire that killed two orphans. In response, Birmingham's Black and White citizens banded together to raise funds to rebuild the school. Tuggle Institute's teachers moved operations to a nearby church and did not miss a beat with respect to teaching and caring for the children. Despite these struggles, Tuggle Institute was rebuilt and touted as "one of the most effective and beneficial institutions of the South."[99]

There are notable commonalities between Tuggle and her Black school-founding contemporaries. Tuggle and Washington shared a common heritage of being born into and later progressing "up from slavery."[100] Akin to Washington and Parker, Tuggle was successful in soliciting funding from prominent Whites in the U.S. South who were a far cry from being diehard advocates for the Black community's advancement. For example, Hugo Black, a controversial Alabama figure who had ties to the Ku Klux Klan, yet later became a "liberal" Supreme Court Justice who ruled in favor of *Brown* and other desegregation cases, served on Tuggle Institute's advisory board.[101] The Institute actually originated from Tuggle's plea during her early career as a social worker to a court judge not to send two young juvenile delinquents to prison but rather to her home for her loving brand of reform. Some of Birmingham's prominent Black residents at that time, for example, A. G. Gaston, credited Tuggle for rescuing them when their lives were spiraling out of control.[102]

Although the Institute initially emphasized an academic curriculum, Tuggle eventually adopted Washington's model of industrial education. Similar to Washington, she encountered criticism for adopting the industrial education curriculum. Her advocacy of industrial education may have even put her at odds with her son-in-law, Oscar W. Adams Sr., a successful leader and publisher of the Black-owned newspaper *The Birmingham Reporter,* who might have had "Du Boisian" philosophical leanings.[103] Yet in spite of her characterization by some as an accommodationist, Tuggle was the first Black woman to register to vote in Jefferson County, and often was called upon to vouch for many other Black women to be permitted to register, including a number of teachers.

Unfortunately, Tuggle suffered more tragedies after the deadly fire. One of her two daughters, Mamie Adams, who was a prominent civic leader in her own right, preceded Tuggle in death. Furthermore, the never-ending need for fundraising also took a tremendous toll on her. Consequently, she was in confinement for six months prior to her death due to exhaustion and an emotional breakdown. Upon her death in 1924, the *Birmingham News* remembered her as the "female Booker T. Washington."[104]

Indiana Little: Colored Women's Club Activist and Educator

Notably, a lesser-known contemporary of Tuggle's, Birmingham women's club member, and teacher Indiana Little paid an even higher price for her voting rights activism.[105] As a part of a larger campaign for Black Alabamians to recoup voting rights lost after the adoption of the infamous

1901 Alabama Constitutional Convention, in 1926 Little led a thousand Black women and men to the Jefferson County Board of Registrars to demand their right to vote. Little charged the board of registrars with giving intelligence tests to Blacks but not to Whites. She was arrested and charged with vagrancy and disorderly conduct. Regrettably, the board of registrars did not budge in its position and none of the group members were registered on that day. But Little's protest eventually mobilized Black community protest ten years later. It would not be until thirty-one years later that Little would become a registered voter, at age fifty-five.

FOUNDING HBCUS AND NORMAL SCHOOLS IN BIRMINGHAM AND ALABAMA

The early efforts of Birmingham's Black citizens to establish schools for their children resulted in twenty-four elementary schools and two high schools by 1939.[106] Establishing elementary and secondary public schools proved to be an uphill battle. An equally ambitious project was to build higher education institutions to train Black professionals. Given that teaching was one among a few professional careers that educated Blacks could pursue at that time, the establishment of teacher training programs, or normal schools as they were called during that time, was especially important. The demand for Black teachers was especially pressing given that many Blacks were confined to teaching in private versus public schools. A 1918 report of the U.S. Commission on the Southern States underscored Black underrepresentation in the teaching field, documenting that Black educators comprised only 36,920 or 17.4 percent of the region's 211,900 teachers while Blacks made up 30 percent of the U.S. South's population.[107] The advancement of Black education in the U.S. South during the early twentieth century depended desperately on the bolstering of teacher training programs.[108]

The founding of HBCUs was critical for advancing Blacks' struggle for educational equity after slavery. Once again, Booker T. Washington was at the forefront of this ambitious project in Alabama. Washington and others founded Tuskegee Institute in 1881, where he employed a primarily industrial education curriculum.[109] His efforts benefited from the Peabody Fund's shift in 1880 from focusing on elementary schools to normal schools.[110] Through this new emphasis, Washington was able to secure Peabody funding for Tuskegee Institute, Talladega College, and the state normal schools in Huntsville and Montgomery.[111] The Jeanes Fund also gave generously to Alabama's Black higher education institutions, especially Tuskegee Institute.[112] A particularly large endowment of

$1 million, stewarded by Washington, Andrew Carnegie, and other trustees, was set aside to supervise and train Black teachers.[113]

The primary training site for Black teachers in Alabama during the latter part of the nineteenth century and throughout the twentieth century was Alabama State University (ASU), which descended from the Lincoln Normal School established in 1867. ASU went through several subsequent iterations and name changes, a few of which included State Teachers College and Alabama State College for Negroes.[114] It would become the first state-sponsored liberal arts institution for the higher education of Blacks.[115] The school's main campus was located in Montgomery, but one of its two satellite campuses was situated in Birmingham, which helped to fortify its influence on Black education in this city.[116]

Another HBCU that greatly influenced Birmingham's Black educators was Miles College.[117] Miles College was established in a community east of Birmingham in 1905 by leaders and members of the Colored Methodist Episcopal Church.[118] Similar to ASU, Miles College was also a key

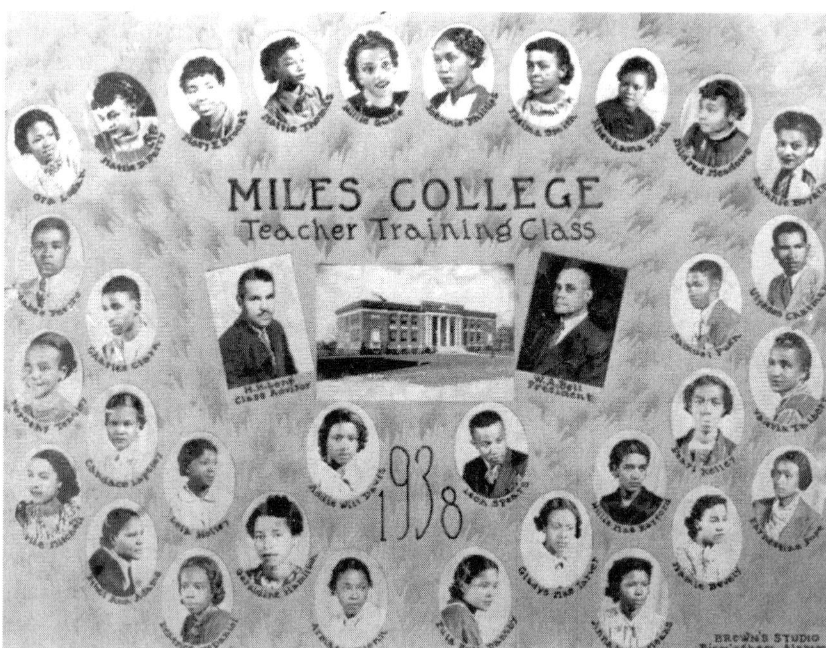

Figure 1.3. Miles College teacher training class featuring President William A. Bell, 1938. Photo: Birmingham, Ala., Public Library Archives.

training site for Black teachers in Birmingham in the late nineteenth century throughout the twentieth century. The college originally had grammar school and "normal preparatory" sections, with an overwhelming majority of Black women in the student body. In the 1909–10 academic year, Miles College educated 139 female students out of a total of 158 students in the grammar, sub-normal, normal preparatory, and college preparatory classes. Willie Selden McDaniel became the first woman to receive a bachelor's degree from Miles in 1918 and entered the teaching profession, as did most of Miles College's female graduates. Unlike many other HBCUs in the U.S. South, Miles offered a number of classical education courses, including Greek, Latin, literature, and rhetoric. But the curriculum also included traditional industrial education classes. Both Miles College and ASU would later become hotbeds of civil rights activity during the height of the civil rights movement in Birmingham and Montgomery respectively.[119]

FROM AN EPIC TO A COLLECTIVE NARRATIVE

Birmingham educators began setting the stage for their involvement in the mid-twentieth-century phase of the civil rights movement as early as the city's establishment in 1871. The fight for public schooling began with Reconstruction-era Black state legislators advocating for the legal foundation to educate Black children. This fight continued when Black educators such as Booker T. Washington, A. H. Parker, and Carrie Tuggle joined ranks with community leaders and educators to establish schools of their own. The historical record bears out that it took a strategic, multipronged plan of action to petition White-dominated local and state governments for the establishment of public schools for Black children, raise money, garner land and pool together nonmonetary resources from the Black community, and solicit support from White Northern and a few Southern philanthropists while alternately trying to temper violence and threats to Black livelihood and progress by appeasing (at least on the surface) White Southerners.

Notably, the figures featured in this chapter have more name recognition than other unsung educators in Birmingham's and Alabama's history and folklore. Those educators who pursued what some historians and observers have described as an accommodationist approach to advancing Black education have been memorialized in the names of contemporary Birmingham City Schools—Booker T. Washington Elementary School, A.

H. Parker High School, and Carrie A. Tuggle Elementary School. In the case of Carrie Tuggle, White civic leaders of her day led the campaign to memorialize her legacy.[120] Yet there are no visible historical markers honoring firebrand educators such as Indiana Little, who chose a more conventional activist approach to challenge Jim Crow. Furthermore, it is difficult to determine exactly how many other Black educators during Little's day chose conventionally activist strategies because their reputations were typically sullied by their bold actions, a reality that disqualified them from being heralded as "credits to their race" and thereby overshadowed their legacy in the history of education and civil rights canons.[121] But it is important to note that Birmingham educators with a more prominent history were not immune from retribution. The suspected arson of Tuggle Institute is a case in point. Reportedly there were two foiled arson attempts prior to the one that was sinisterly successful.[122] Even A. H. Parker alluded to the suspiciousness of another fire that burned down the all-Black Thomas School in 1894, recalling: "How it caught [on fire] was never known."[123]

Not only have familiar narratives about Birmingham's and Alabama's early education pioneers focused primarily on educators often characterized as accommodationist, these narratives also tend to emphasize the feats of heroic figures striving almost singlehandedly (with the exception of their reliance on support from prominent Whites) to establish elementary and secondary schools and HBCUs. But these educators were actually part of an elaborate, interconnected network of local, state, and national Black educators whose existence is virtually absent in civil rights history and underplayed in many histories of education.[124] Of utmost concern to these educators was the establishment of a physical and academic educational infrastructure for Black children. Their second and concurrent order of business was to organize themselves to promote educational equity for students *and* educators.

2

ORGANIZING FOR EDUCATIONAL EQUITY

> There are in our ranks to-day, many good, strong teachers, who know and feel what they are doing,—men and women whose lives are consecrated to their calling and whose quiet but persistent and effective work is seldom understood and more seldom appreciated. We need more of this kind of teachers. He who would be a real teacher must first get a fulness of that spirit that loves service and loves to live for service. This spirit makes bricks without straw and converts mountains into molehills. It is this spirit that makes and creates, that lives and conquers, and triumphs!!
>
> —A. H. Parker, Speech to Alabama State Teachers Association (ASTA)

At the dawn of the twentieth century, A. H. Parker gave an uplifting presidential address at the ASTA conference to encourage his fellow educators to press on during a "Negro Nadir" period when their second-class citizenship in America seemed inevitable.[1] Parker harkened his audience to a familiar Biblical Old Testament parallel between the oppression of Hebrews enslaved in Egypt and the plight of Black Americans in the Jim Crow South. The Exodus reference tells of how Pharaoh withheld the straw necessary for the Hebrews to make bricks, and then charged them to "go and gather straw for themselves."[2] Parker knew this metaphor would resonate with fellow educators who attended church and built schools with paltry support from White public school and government officials. In light of their kindred burden, he impressed upon his audience members the importance of their solidarity as Black educators, not only to survive Jim Crow oppression but also to thrive in their schools and communities.

THE LABYRINTH OF BLACK TEACHERS ASSOCIATIONS

Understanding the aims, structure, leadership, and inner workings of Black teachers associations is crucial to deciphering the nature and extent of Black educators' involvement in the long civil rights movement.[3] These associations were the linchpin for educational and political activism in a racist society that made it virtually impossible for Black educators to fight alone without retribution.[4] Rather than cower in the face of mounting oppression and violent backlash to Black progress, educators across the U.S. South and other regions in the country, "elected to organize, to teach, to study, and to work diligently together rather than individually to secure the constitutional rights they were denied."[5] By banding together within an intricate network of local, state, and national organizations, Black educators found that they had more influence and a stronger collective voice to effect change.

State and National Black Teachers Associations

Black teachers associations typically originated at the state level in the post–Reconstruction Era South in response to the erosion of hard-fought political gains and increasingly violent resistance to Black political and educational advancement.[6] The first Black state teachers association of note was the Kentucky State Association of Colored Teachers, founded in 1877.[7] After Kentucky's association was established, Black educators followed suit in Georgia (1880), North Carolina (1881), Alabama (1882), Texas (1884), and fifteen other states, located primarily in the U.S. South but also spanning the Northeast.[8] By the time of the 1954 *Brown* decision, there were twenty Black state teachers associations across the country.[9]

As Black educators organized themselves at the state level, a college educator in Alabama set his sights on founding a national Black teachers association. During his tenure as president of ASTA, J. R. E. Lee spearheaded the founding of the National Colored Teachers Association (NCTA) in 1903.[10] Lee, who was the director of the academic department at Tuskegee Institute and a protégé of Booker T. Washington, was elected as the organization's first president at its inaugural meeting in Nashville, Tennessee. He held the presidency until 1909, and then continued to serve in other offices until 1917. The organization strengthened its base by periodically convening national meetings jointly with well-established organizations of Black preachers, parents, and youth, and then merging with the National Association of Land Grant College Presidents in 1907. In fact, a number of college presidents served as presidents of the association, including Mary McLeod Bethune, who became the first female president in 1923. At its 1907 meeting, the organization changed its name to the National Association of Teachers in Colored Schools (NATCS) because its original name seemed exclusive to Black educators when in fact a number of White teachers taught in Black schools. Among the signers of the organization's certificate of incorporation were prominent men and women including Harlem Renaissance writer and college professor Alain Locke and women suffragists and educators Nannie H. Burroughs and Lucy Diggs Slowe. Under the leadership of Alabama State College president H. Councill Trenholm, in the 1920s NATCS strengthened its ties to the leading White national teachers association through its interface with the National Education Association (NEA) Committee on Problems in Negro Education and Life, which eventually became the Committee to Cooperate with the National Association of Teachers in Colored Schools. The committee's objectives were to strengthen relationships with NATCS, support studies on the problems of Black education and life, and promote positive interracial relationships. In 1937 NATCS' name was changed once more, to the American Teachers Association (ATA), before the organization merged with the NEA in 1966.

Alabama State Teachers Association

ASTA originated in 1882 at a meeting held in Selma, Alabama, where more than one hundred Black and White mostly male educators (only thirteen were women) attended.[11] The two-day meeting proved to be productive, resulting in a draft of ASTA's first constitution, which set forth the duties and election of officers, annual membership dues, and process for amendments.[12] The momentum for this inaugural meeting began with the practice of educators in Alabama attending state-mandated, racially segregated teacher institutes, or one-week seminars on teaching methods, convened between local public schools and normal schools.[13] The teacher institutes afforded Black educators a forum to meet and discuss problems and concerns.[14] As these institutes waned in 1895, Black educators in Alabama found it even more important to connect with their state teachers association.[15] Furthermore, Jim Crow's legal barriers to travel and accommodations meant that ASTA's meetings offered Black teachers in Alabama a rare opportunity for face-to-face interactions with educators outside of their school districts.[16]

The inaugural ASTA meeting was convened by William Paterson, a Scotsman, who immigrated to New York as a youth and eventually made his way to Alabama to work in the shipyards.[17] Paterson, who became ASTA's first president, served for thirty-seven years at precursor institutions that would later became known as Alabama State University (ASU). Also among the founding members was Booker T. Washington, who had arrived to Alabama in the previous year to serve as the founding principal of Tuskegee Institute. During this inaugural meeting Washington gave a speech on the virtues of industrial education where he exhorted teachers to promote "mental and manual training" for Black students.[18] Washington's message likely resonated with many educators in Alabama, but not all educators within the ranks of state and national Black teachers associations, particularly those from the Northeast, agreed with his brand of industrial education and accommodationism for advancing Black education.[19] In spite of these "cleavages," Washington's influence on NATCS was notable, particularly in the number of his Tuskegee protégés who became national officers in the organization.[20]

Although there were no racial restrictions at the outset, ASTA transitioned from being integrated to predominantly Black after the 1896 *Plessy v. Ferguson* Supreme Court decision sanctioned "separate but equal" as the law of the land. There are notable gradations in two historical accounts of why this racial transition transpired. One explanation is that in the wake of *Plessy*, White members no longer felt comfortable associating with an integrated professional organization.[21] Another more detailed and politicized explanation suggests the surfacing of underlying racial tensions between Black and White ASTA leaders and members in 1892.[22] As noted previously, ASTA originated as an integrated organization, and its first two presidents were White men. But when William Hooper Councill, the Black leader of Alabama Agricultural and Mechanical (A&M) normal school in Huntsville, Alabama, made William Paterson's racial identity an issue in their competition for a Morrill Land Grant, Paterson and several of his supporters refused to attend the 1892 ASTA convention in Huntsville.[23] Councill had already demonstrated his willingness to pursue activist stances against Alabama's Jim Crow laws when he lodged a complaint against the Interstate Commerce Commission (ICC) in 1887 for being forcibly removed from a first class section of a train even though he possessed a first class ticket.[24] Councill lost this battle when the ICC endorsed the railroad's separate-but-equal policy. Consequently, the Alabama legislature pressured Councill to resign from his college presidency.[25] Although he was reinstated the following year, the legislature sent a clear message to Black educators that they had no recourse if they challenged Jim Crow laws singlehandedly.[26] In response to the flap between Paterson and Councill, Booker T. Washington attempted to placate Paterson through letters urging him not to defect from the organization.[27] Adding fuel to the fire were the actions of some ASTA delegates, who wrote letters declaring that the organization had passed resolutions calling for the state of Alabama to "have [only] colored teachers in all the State colored public and Normal Schools."[28] By implication, this meant that ASTA, too, should become an all-Black organization. Irrespective of the real impetuses for ASTA's racial transition, the organization became the largest predominantly Black professional association for educators in Alabama until its merger in 1969 with the state arm of NEA, known as the Alabama Education Association (AEA).[29]

Prior to merging with AEA in 1969, ASTA counted among its numerous professional activities several that were focused expressly on gaining civil, political, and educational rights and reshaping curricular content to reflect Black cultural heritage and pride. These activities included: documenting racial disparities in education; promoting advancing levels of education for Black children; voting rights advocacy; Black History program development; participation in the Montgomery Bus Boycott; the establishment of a welfare and legal fund to support educator-activists in jeopardy of losing their jobs; and legal support to the 1967 *Lee v. Macon* case, which ordered full desegregation of Alabama's public schools.[30] ASTA also advocated for an equitable sick leave plan given that Black teachers were not paid for any absences due to illness in the 1940s. In the late 1950s, ASTA fought to protect and reinstate state tenure laws, which were being dismantled county by county as a means to fire politically active teachers.

Notably, ASTA's activities mirrored many of the activities of national Black teachers associations, and even had connections to prominent national figures.[31] For example, H. Councill Trenholm, president of ASTA between 1931 and 1933, was a close friend of Carter G. Woodson, founder of the Association for the Study of Negro Life and History, an organization where Trenholm jointly held office as vice president.[32] As a member of the NEA Committee to Cooperate with the NATCS, Trenholm and his colleagues encouraged scholars to study problems affecting Black Americans with a special emphasis on their portrayal in school textbooks. Under Trenholm's leadership, ASTA's Negro History Project, which had the expressed aim of "developing racial self-respect through a study of Negro life and history," promoted Black Americans' contributions to American life and culture through a number of activities.[33] One of the Project's key initiatives was developing and disseminating Negro History Project kits to Black teachers throughout Alabama. This effort led to a number of annual Negro History Week programs and the acquisition of classroom and library books authored by and written about Black people. The Negro History Project also documented racial disparities in education, which laid the groundwork for legal challenges to Alabama's inequitable system of education.

Arguably, one of ASTA's most important contributions to the early struggle for civil rights was its financial, legal, and moral support to teachers who fought for equal salaries, voting rights, and other civil rights. In 1938, ASTA established a Vote Commission, under the leadership of its president, W. McKinley Menchan, "to encourage teachers to push for their political and citizenship rights and to develop strategies for black teachers in Alabama to become registered voters."[34] Menchan, who migrated to Alabama from Pennsylvania, was a staunch advocate for Black educators' voting rights. He used the summer school program at Alabama State Teachers College as a forum to encourage and train teachers to make connections between obtaining their voting rights and addressing educational inequities. Moreover, Menchan drove the message home to his constituency that "[t]he share we get . . . will depend on the number of votes we have."[35] The Vote Commission included educators and community leaders, two of whom were from Birmingham (Emory O. Jackson, who is discussed later in this chapter, and Felix Paul).[36] One of the commission's first orders of business was to determine key reasons why so many Black educators were not qualified to vote. Some of the contributing factors included the financial burden of the poll tax, resistance from White boards of registrars, lukewarm support for Black voting rights among White school officials, and Black teachers' failure to recognize the importance of voting. In order to protect ASTA from unwanted scrutiny and professional retribution against its membership, the Association's leaders often camouflaged overtly political agenda items in their public recordings of meetings by listing voting rights clinics as "Presentation of a Special Project" or "Special Project Reports."[37]

Black teachers' enfranchisement became even more salient in the years leading up to *Brown*. At ASTA's 1940 annual convention, convened in Birmingham at A. H. Parker High School, Zelia S. Evans, one of the organization's only three female presidents, chose a theme focused on education's role in advancing democracy to complement the work of the Vote Commission and the Education Commission. Evans encouraged her constituency to prepare students to participate as first-class citizens in an American democracy not yet fully realized. Discerning the urgency of the times, J. D. Thompson, the thirty-sixth president of ASTA between 1952 and 1954, appropriated money for a Black teachers' voter registration drive because he believed that "obtaining the ballot was the prelude for better schools and salaries for blacks."[38] ASTA leaders also spent considerable time documenting and reporting racial disparities in educational resources and publishing their findings in periodic reports, which helped raise awareness among its constituency about "the extent to which they were being shortchanged."[39]

Birmingham's Connection to Black Teachers Associations

Notably, Birmingham educators were not represented at ASTA's founding meeting in 1882. Yet, over time, they quickly became more visible both in the leadership structure and rank and file membership. In the same year that A. H. Parker was appointed principal of Industrial High School, he became the ninth president of ASTA, serving in this capacity from 1900 to 1902.[40] His membership in ASTA connected him and Industrial High School to a complex multiorganizational network of local, state, and national Black educators. Several ASTA conventions, including its fiftieth jubilee anniversary meeting, were held in Birmingham at A. H. Parker High School. Moreover, Birmingham produced eight presidents and five vice presidents as well as several other officers. As only the ninth president of the emergent organization, Parker's legacy was to restructure ASTA into departments by dividing members according to their affiliations with elementary schools, high schools, normal schools, and colleges and universities. These departments, which were institutionalized in 1905, would convene separate meetings, each presided over by a leader drawn from their respective professional ranks who could understand the department's unique needs and interests. Parker's proposal would help a diverse class of Black educational professionals throughout the state—teachers, principals, college presidents—to connect with likeminded colleagues with whom they could relate professionally. But this departmentalization also reinforced the sex segregation inherent in the teaching (mostly female) and K–12 school and college leadership (virtually all male) ranks.[41]

While participating in state and national teachers association activities somewhat buffered Black educators from intense scrutiny at their school sites, some educators were active in local Black teachers associations, which placed them in direct confrontation with their immediate supervisors and school district officials. In the Birmingham-area Jefferson County (JeffCo) Public School district, Black teachers formed the Jefferson County Negro Teachers Association (JCNTA).[42] According to its constitution, JCNTA had several objectives, which included: promoting professionalism by providing a medium for professional affiliation; creating a unified purpose based on majority rule; cultivating appreciation for literary culture; and serving as a liaison between teachers and the school board. These objectives were developed ultimately for the express purpose of ensuring that "all the children of the people may receive the very best training possible for useful citizens."[43] In some instances, the JeffCo school board provided matching funds to JCNTA for purchasing materials and establishing libraries.[44] Perhaps the most activist of JCNTA's agendas was spearheading teacher salary equalization cases, in collaboration with the NAACP and an elaborate network of local, state, and national Black teacher associations.

BLACK EDUCATORS' ALLIANCE WITH NAACP AND TEACHERS ASSOCIATIONS

In the decades preceding *Brown*, many Black educators joined ranks with the NAACP in the fight for educational equity. An exemplary alliance between Black educators and the NAACP is the campaign for the equalization of teachers' salaries, which spanned between 1936 and 1948 as part of a larger, ambitious NAACP strategy to dismantle *Plessy*, case by painstaking case. Although this campaign is viewed by some scholars as foundational to the NAACP's early legal strategy for arriving at *Brown*, it has been woefully neglected in civil rights history.[45] This overshadowed history not only marginalizes the role that Black educators played in the NAACP's early civil rights struggles, it also reinforces the invisibility of Black women educators' contributions to the civil rights movement.[46]

Compared to conventional civil rights protests, the teacher salary equalization cases may not be viewed by some scholars and observers as particularly activist, but, as one historian noted, "in the context of the 1930s and 1940s [they were] a bold strike against white supremacy."[47] The most important outcomes of the teacher salary equalization campaigns were "its impact on local African American activism and the growth of the NAACP in the South."[48] The lawsuits brought forward by local educators often represented their foray into formal protest.[49] Furthermore, the presumed correlation between racial discrimination in educational resources (e.g., teacher salaries, school funding, buildings, curriculum, material resources, etc.) and the decline in Black voting power in the early twentieth century, particularly in Birmingham,[50] lends credence to the activist characterization of the teacher salary equalization cases. In other words, if Black teachers could not wield the fight for professional equity through the ballot, then they would have to do so boldly through the courts.

Thurgood Marshall became the general counsel of the NAACP after his mentor and legal civil rights pioneer, Charles Hamilton Houston, stepped down. Using the NAACP-commissioned Margold Report as a guide, Houston was a forerunner of the campaign for teacher salary equalization, brilliantly forecasting the appeal and potential economic impact these cases would have on a Black middle-class constituency (i.e., teachers) that could bolster the NAACP's membership rolls.[51] The campaign to dismantle Jim Crow would require the national office of the NAACP to work closely with local and state educators and attorneys, who had a better pulse on what was happening on the ground.

In the years leading up to the teacher salary equalization campaign, Black educators and NAACP attorneys alike were deeply concerned about educational disparities between White and Black schools in the 1940s, particularly inequities in average per pupil spending, access to schooling, teacher training, and salaries.[52] The differential statistics during this decade were particularly revealing for the state of Alabama.[53] For example, the per pupil expenditure for White children in Alabama in 1940 was $50.14, compared to $21.54 for Black children.[54] By 1952 these expenditures rose to $164.83 and $115.08 per White and per Black pupil respectively.[55] White and Black children attended school for an average of 157 and 147 days respectively in 1940, but reached parity by 1954 (i.e., 176 for both groups).[56] There were also striking differences in teacher training. For example, in 1940, White teachers had a reported average of 3.2 years of college training compared to Black teachers, who had an average of 2.1 years.[57] These numbers increased to 4.1 and 3.4 years for White and Black teachers respectively in 1952.[58] No doubt the narrowing of these gaps was due in large part to Black educators' persistent and strategic efforts to advocate for educational equity.

With respect to teacher salaries, the NAACP published a pamphlet in 1941 entitled "Teacher Salaries in Black and White," which further documented gross racial disparities.[59] The report found that Black teachers on average earned 40 to 50 percent of what their White counterparts earned.[60] Other data during this period reinforced the NAACP's salary findings. Based on one report, White teachers earned more than double of Black teachers in 1940 at an average of $848 compared to $402.[61] By 1952, this gap had decreased, yet not closed altogether, with White teachers earning $2,541 and Black teachers earning $2,359.[62] According to one estimate, the overall salary differential between Black and White teachers amounted to the loss of approximately $10 million each year to Black teachers.[63] Yet Black teachers taught with fewer resources, larger classroom sizes, and higher demands for remediating illiteracy in the aftermath of historical legal prohibitions on Black education.[64]

Birmingham Teacher Salary Equalization Campaign

To address educational inequities, the NAACP did not typically institute litigation directly, but rather through local educators or their professional organizations.[65] Birmingham educators involved as plaintiffs were linked to an intricate internal and external multiorganizational strategy executed across local, state, and national levels.[66] This strategy involved NAACP, ASTA, NATCS, and Birmingham-area Black teachers associations.

Brief History of the NAACP Birmingham Chapter

In order to understand how the NAACP joined ranks with local attorneys and educators, a brief history of the fits and starts of the NAACP's Birmingham chapter is warranted. The establishment of state and local NAACP chapters in Alabama and Birmingham in 1918 and 1919 respectively were critical to creating a political infrastructure for dismantling Jim Crow and gradually gaining civil rights.[67] During this period, the Birmingham chapter of the NAACP would become the state's largest unit, skyrocketing from fifty to one thousand members within five months. The most pressing issue for the Birmingham chapter was suffrage. Although Black citizens were granted voting rights at the state's Reconstruction Constitution convention of 1868, they were denied the right to vote in city democratic primaries in 1888, and were virtually disenfranchised by the 1901 Alabama Constitution.[68] Consequently, by 1920 the number of Black voters on the county rolls diminished to only a few hundred in the Birmingham-Jefferson County area.[69] Yet, Black residents in Birmingham continued to fight for suffrage. The passage of the Nineteenth Amendment of the U.S. Constitution in 1920 granting women the right to vote spurred mass voter registration campaigns among the Colored Women's Clubs, which boasted a number of Black women teachers in their ranks.

On the heels of the Nineteenth Amendment's passage, a large contingent of Black women attempted to register but were refused by the Jefferson County Board of Registrars.[70] This blatant disenfranchisement angered many Blacks and prompted several mass meetings and NAACP branch discussions.[71] In the aftermath of World War II, which elevated hope for a new American racial order, the Black community's commitment to the NAACP nationwide was revived in the 1940s as evidenced by a spike in national membership from 50,000 in 1940 to 450,000 in 1946; in addition, the number of local branches increased from eighty in 1939 to fourteen thousand in 1948.[72]

Arthur D. Shores: NAACP Attorney and Educator

During the NAACP's period of revival, a young rising attorney in Alabama, Arthur D. Shores, was making headway to become the organization's lead counsel in the U.S. Southern region during the 1940s and 1950s.[73] Shores passed the Alabama Bar examination in 1937, and two years later he became the only Black practicing attorney in Alabama for the next ten to fifteen years, litigating numerous high-profile civil rights cases as an associate and regional representative for the NAACP.[74] Most histories either minimize or fail to acknowledge Shores's pre-attorney days as an educator. Prior to pursuing law, Shores was a teacher in the JeffCo public schools, a principal in the Bessemer, Alabama, public schools, and a vice president of NATCS.[75] In order to move up the ranks to the vice presidency of NATCS, Shores had to be quite visible and well respected within his state teachers association. Illustratively, Shores gave one of the keynote addresses at ASTA's 1936 annual convention convened in Birmingham at the Industrial High School.[76] Without question Shores's close connections to both state and national Black teachers associations facilitated his adeptness in targeting educators for a NAACP teacher salary equalization campaign that would boldly challenge Jim Crow's chokehold on Black education in Alabama.[77] As 1941 came to a close, the NAACP could proclaim victory in half of the Southern states in which it wielded the teacher salary equalization campaign.[78] But the campaign in Birmingham proved to be an uphill battle.

Black Teachers Associations' Support for Birmingham Teacher Salary Equalization Cases

As noted previously, ASTA began raising awareness among its constituency regarding teacher salary inequities as early as 1930 through its Negro

Figure 2.1. Arthur D. Shores, former educator and civil rights attorney. Photo: Birmingham Civil Rights Institute.

History Project's systematic study of racial disparities in education.[79] In addition, the organization established the Committee for the Equalization of Teacher Salaries and School Facilities, which was comprised of teachers association members and community leaders.[80] ASTA President Menchan called a special meeting with his executive committee in August 1938 to report on his attendance at a recent NATCS conference along with a meeting he had with Thurgood Marshall.[81] At the NATCS conference, Menchan learned that several Black state teachers associations had been successful in their campaign to equalize teacher salaries. He also reported that Marshall, no doubt inspired by his mother, who was a teacher, believed conditions were favorable to challenge teacher salary inequities in Alabama but that "great courage would be needed to undertake such a fight and that ASTA must be prepared to support the teachers who made the sacrifice."[82] ASTA's Education Commission, which was appointed by Menchan, was also closely involved, meeting in May

1938 to endorse a proposal for a salary equalization contest in Alabama.[83] This action signaled ASTA's initiation into formally supporting the litigation of its members on this issue. In July of that same year, ASTA's Education Commission, in collaboration with its Citizenship Commission, comprised of prominent Black citizens from across the state, met jointly with Thurgood Marshall to discuss plans for equalizing teacher salaries in the state.[84] Although local and state community members played an important role in the teacher salary equalization campaign, ASTA's correspondence to its membership on December 6, 1938, made clear this campaign was ultimately a "teacher's fight."[85] In the same correspondence, ASTA informed its constituency about the campaign and sought financial support of $1.00 per member for "studying and providing ways and means for conducting a campaign for the equalization of teacher's salaries and educational opportunities in Alabama."[86] A little over two years later, on February 11, 1941, Black teachers in Birmingham, Bessemer, Fairfield, and Tarrant, Alabama, joined ranks to pass a resolution in support of educational equity "for all citizens."[87]

JeffCo Principal William Bolden's Case

William Bolden formally initiated the legal fight for teacher salary equalization in the JeffCo Public Schools on March 27, 1942.[88] Black teachers rallied to Bolden's defense by projecting to raise the initial $3,000 required to fight his case.[89] Prior to 1942, the JeffCo board, under J. E. Bryan's superintendence, operated a racially disparate salary schedule modeled after one Bryan learned about during his matriculation at the University of Chicago.[90] Under Bryan's model, teacher salaries were determined by training and experience rather than by the previous criterion of state certification status.[91] White teachers and Black teachers were ranked at three levels respectively: Masters, Bachelors, and Below College Graduate; and College Graduate, Two Years College or Junior College, and Below Two Years College.[92] Teachers with ten or more years of service were ranked at the "Super Maximum" level, but Black teachers could not exceed $100 under this category.[93] The minimum salary for White teachers under this schedule ranged from $65–$120 whereas the minimum salary for Black teachers ranged from $40–$70.[94] Moreover, the supplement for principals and coaches was grossly inequitable, with the supplements to White teachers totaling $6,000 and the supplements to Black teachers totaling a mere $262.40.[95] Some school board members justified these inequities with the rationale that White teachers were better trained than Black teachers.[96] Furthermore, the Alabama state superintendent presented his rationales for the racial disparities, explaining that any attempt to close the gap would reduce White teachers' salaries and require the school term to be shortened.[97] However, two progressive White JeffCo school board members, Raymond Thomason and Harry Denman, voiced their grievances about the disparities and urged the board to mitigate the gap.[98] In response, Bryan instituted a single salary schedule for the 1941–42 school year, which stipulated a common minimum salary and degree attainment system that applied to all teachers irrespective of race.[99] But since the new schedule overlay old salary schedules rife with gross inequities, the new schedule failed to level the playing field.[100] Furthermore, the new schedule did not set a maximum salary cap, and any salary above the minimum could be passed upon the discretion of the superintendent and the school board, which typically privileged White educators.[101]

JeffCo Teacher Ruby Jackson Gainer's Cases

When the school district refused to comply with the court's ruling on Bolden's court case, Ruby Jackson Gainer confronted the board, first by letter and later by a contempt of court lawsuit through her local teachers union.[102] To bolster her case, Gainer followed suit with Bolden, and enlisted the legal support of attorneys Shores and Marshall.[103] In her letter to the board, Gainer noted that "a recent investigation conducted by the JeffCo Teachers Union, Local 683, UPWA-CIO, revealed that the Decree has not been complied with and that the Negro teachers and principals in Jefferson County, Alabama, are still being discriminated against in the payment of salaries on account of race and color."[104] In addition to the salary dispute, Gainer also challenged the disparities in credit for experience between Black and White teachers.[105] Gainer and Bolden originally added an amendment naming 379 plaintiffs, but this amendment was reduced by 175 teachers, due to the defecting teachers' allegations that they had not consented to having their names listed in the lawsuits.[106]

The plaintiffs eventually won their lawsuit. However, this legal victory was hollow because the JeffCo board was not quick to comply with the court's ruling in the teacher salary equalization case. After testifying in court, Gainer and another teacher, Maenetta Steele, who was president of her school's UPWA-CIO, were both fired.[107] Gainer's employment contract was terminated after fourteen years of service for alleged "insubordination, neglect of duty and other good and just causes," which JeffCo superintendent Bryan claimed were "substantiated by records in [JeffCo Board of Education] office furnished by principals, supervisors and directors over a period of years."[108] Once again, Gainer sought legal counsel from Shores and Marshall to file a wrongful termination lawsuit with the Birmingham Circuit Court.

Although Gainer made enormous personal and professional sacrifices on behalf of Black educators in Jefferson County and Birmingham, she did not stand alone in her quest for justice. She received support from ASTA both in her teacher salary equalization and employment termination lawsuits.[109] Throughout Gainer's litigation, ASTA's Education Commission served as a liaison between the association and educator-plaintiffs. Correspondence between ASTA's president and its Education Commission illustrates how the organization worked both internally and externally, in concert with other Black teachers associations and the NAACP, on behalf of activist educators. It also sheds light on how these organizations negotiated their own sustainability while simultaneously advocating for Black educators in very costly and time-consuming litigation, which school districts typically dragged out in hopes of eroding the plaintiffs' resolve and resources. In a series of letters exchanged between ASTA's Education Commission chairman and its president, the two men cordially but emphatically attempt to keep the lines of fiscal authority straight concerning Gainer's case.[110]

After a lengthy legal battle, Gainer eventually won her job back when the Alabama Supreme Court decided on January 15, 1948, to reverse a lower court's decision to uphold her dismissal.[111] Yet even after this decision more legal wrangling with the lower court ensued until Gainer finally was reinstated to her teaching position and received a monetary court settlement for back pay on the salary she did not receive during her termination period.[112] Gainer subsequently resigned from JeffCo and moved to Pensacola, Florida, where she and her husband already had a home. Even after moving to Pensacola, Gainer persisted in her lawsuit for teacher pay equity all the way up to the U.S. District Court and won a partial victory after a long drawn-out court battle.[113] During her tenure as a Pensacola educator, Gainer continued her activist pursuits through the Florida State Teachers Association and became only the third Black elected vice president of the Association of Classroom Teachers of the NEA in 1969.[114] Gainer taught in the Pensacola public school system until she retired.[115]

Figure 2.2. Ruby Jackson Gainer and Emory O. Jackson at Gainer's celebration, sibling teacher-activists. Photo: Birmingham, Ala., Public Library Archives.

Emory O. Jackson: From Teacher's Desk to Editor's Chair

Gainer was not the only activist sibling in a family of thirteen children deeply devoted to Christianity and democracy.[116] Her older brother, Emory O. Jackson, is customarily noted for his longtime editorship of the Black-owned *Birmingham World* newspaper. However, quite similar to the treatment of Shores's life story, an aspect of Jackson's biography that is often overlooked is his earlier role as a teacher and its influence on his activism. Jackson had only a brief tenure as a teacher in the JeffCo and Dothan, Alabama, public school systems due to his outspokenness and activism.[117] During his stint as a teacher, he was known to encourage his students to declare activist stands about race relations through written assignments. Jackson once publicly criticized discriminatory policies at North Highland School in Dothan, Alabama, which resulted in his teaching contract not being renewed. In another incident, he was fired for protesting the differential treatment of Black and White educators at a public school banquet, where the Black attendees received the measly portions of chicken whereas the White attendees received the choicest portions.[118] Jackson's ardent support for teacher litigation, especially his sister's teacher salary equalization cases, also likely caused him some problems with school district officials.[119]

Following his abbreviated teaching career, Jackson eventually became the publisher of the *Birmingham World* newspaper between 1941 and 1975.[120] He was also the founder and first president of the Alabama State Conference of the NAACP. Using the Black press as his mouthpiece, Jackson came to his sister's as well as other Birmingham teachers' defense during their arduous fight for teacher salary equalization.[121] In fact, Jackson viewed his role at the press as simply an extension of his previous role as a teacher. He once said, "To me an editor's chair is little more than a teacher's desk moved into the public square."[122] By working closely with civil rights organizations and Black teachers associations (as noted previously, he served on ASTA's Vote Commission, which promoted voting rights, and contributed to its Negro History Project), Jackson rallied local activists, educators, and citizens to finance and defend the rights of Birmingham teachers.[123]

At times Jackson's relationship with Black educators was adversarial. He was known for publicly chastising Black teachers in his newspaper, many of whom he deemed too fearful to stand up for their rights and financially support local Black teachers' organizations. He publicly criticized JeffCo teachers for not paying dues to ASTA's Education Committee to support the legal causes of their fellow educators. Furthermore, in response to several teacher-plaintiffs' decisions to drop their names from Gainer's teacher salary equalization lawsuit due to fear of reprisals from JeffCo school officials, Jackson retorted: "Teachers who don't give a hoot about equal salaries for themselves cannot be expected to give a yip about the education of the children they are supposed to teach. I am not anti-teacher but I am anti–Jim Crow."[124] The husband of a principal who formerly supervised Gainer once confronted Jackson and Gainer at the *Birmingham World* downtown office because of Jackson's negative news story about the man's wife. His wife had apparently written a negative performance evaluation on Gainer, which most likely produced the circumstantial evidence the JeffCo Board used to justify Gainer's dismissal from her teaching job.[125] According to the testimony of a former *Birmingham World* reporter, when the man physically assaulted Gainer, Jackson grabbed a chair and broke it over the man's head, exclaiming: "Don't hurt my sister now!"[126] The reporter recalled that the broken chair remained in the newspaper's Fourth Avenue office until the business relocated long after Jackson's death.[127]

As editor, Jackson used the *Birmingham World* to keep the public abreast of every detail of Gainer's and other educators' court battles to gain teacher salary equity. In fact, his editorials were responsible for drawing a crowd to Gainer's court hearings to regain her job. Jackson drew national support from teachers unions, the NAACP, the Sociology Department at Columbia University, the Congress of American Women, the Negro Chamber of Commerce, and other Black newspapers such as the *Pittsburgh Courier*.[128] Although he worked closely with ASTA for years in their mutual fight for political and educational justice, Jackson was angered by what he viewed as the organization's conciliatory response to resolving its involvement in the JeffCo teacher salary case.[129] Yet he continued to work in solidarity with Black institutions to advance the cause of civil rights both inside and outside of the education arena.

CHANGES ON THE HORIZON

As teachers throughout the city of Birmingham, the state of Alabama, and the United States organized and mobilized themselves for educational equity during the first half of the twentieth century, no doubt they foresaw unprecedented changes on the horizon. Black teachers associations on the local, state, and national levels were growing in their ranks, establishing new and modernized headquarters, raising their profile in the struggle for civil rights, and even winning some notable legal victories.[130] Post–World War II Black activism was on the rise as NAACP membership rolls skyrocketed.[131] Even the sports arena showed promising signs of transforming American race relations with Jackie Robinson's integration of major league baseball in 1947.[132] At the federal level, President Harry Truman was calling for more racial equity and demonstrated that his sentiments were more than hollow political promises when he ended racial segregation in the armed forces and civil service jobs in 1948.[133] The NAACP's mounting legal successes in higher education equity cases, and its strategic transition to litigating public elementary and secondary cases in 1952, which led the way to victory in the formidable 1954 *Brown* case, signaled that school integration was imminent.[134]

Yet in the midst of these prophetic signs, Black educators were cautiously optimistic about the prospects of school integration. On the one hand, they saw the promise of integration as a culmination of their arduous struggle to be recognized as first-class citizens in America. On the other hand, they were uneasy about the fate of Black schools, teachers associations, and other institutions, for which they labored painstakingly to edify nearly a century after their legal emancipation from slavery. A question posed in a letter penned by ASTA president J. D. Thompson immediately following the *Brown* decision articulated the collective uncertainty of the moment: "What position is one to take when the decisions of the highest Court do not suit him [or her]?"[135] Although the full context of Thompson's letter suggests that his question was more of a commentary on the mounting White resistance and threats of violence in response to the *Brown* decision, it also alludes to the wariness many Black educators felt about integration at that time. Black educators in Birmingham would soon find out where they stood on school integration as *Brown*'s nine-year deferral in the city spurred unprecedented civil rights activism that reverberated locally, nationally, and internationally.

3

SUPPORTING THE MOVEMENT INSIDE AND OUTSIDE OF THE SCHOOLHOUSE

BROWN AND EARLY STRUGGLES TO INTEGRATE BIRMINGHAM SCHOOLS

The role of Black educators in desegregating public schools in Birmingham is best understood within the context of community. These educators lived, worked, and socialized with neighbors from different socioeconomic status yet they were linked together by a common racial stratum and destiny. Depending on where they attended church, their pastors and visiting preachers were likely at the forefront of the Birmingham civil rights movement, using their churches for mass meetings and taking up monetary collections to support the cause.[1] The pioneering families who risked their lives to put *Brown* to the test early on included children enrolled as students in all-Black schools where their educators taught, led, and counseled them. Black educators frequented barbershops, beauty salons, and other neighborhood businesses where the merits and shortcomings of school desegregation were being deliberated. They also interacted with fellow educators in Black professional teachers associations, social clubs, and civic organizations. In light of this context, chronicling the early struggles of local civil rights activists, attorneys, and preachers along with ordinary citizens—parents, students, church members, and neighbors—helps set the stage for examining how Black educators both contributed to and were impacted by the long drawn-out struggle to integrate schools in Birmingham.

BROWN'S NINE-YEAR DEFERRAL

Public school officials in Alabama did not get serious about desegregating public schools until nine years after the 1954 *Brown* decision.[2] In the year preceding *Brown*, the Alabama legislature drafted legislation to preserve segregation. Albert Boutwell, a state senator from Birmingham, who was a leading proponent of segregation, chaired the Interim Committee of Segregation, which had the express charge of undermining the anticipated *Brown* ruling. Shortly after the *Brown* decision, the Alabama State Superintendent of Education sent a letter and resolution to the Birmingham Public School (BPS) board stating that Alabama schools would remain segregated in the 1954–55 academic year pursuant to state law mandating racially segregated schools.[3] At stake was Section 256 of the Alabama Constitution of 1901, which sanctioned racially segregated schools.[4] In anticipation of *Brown*, the state legislature amended Section 256 so that it eliminated "the express prohibition against the operation of mixed schools, attended by both races" but made clear that the state would not coerce anyone to attend integrated schools, and furthermore, would not assume fiscal obligation to "operate any such mixed schools at all."[5] Moreover, Alabama legislators convened a special session in January 1956 to denounce school desegregation, the NAACP, and the U.S. Supreme Court.

The Alabama legislature's Jim Crow legal precedents and its unrelenting attempts to create new roadblocks did not deter Autherine Lucy from attempting to integrate the University of Alabama (UA) in the early 1950s. Lucy and another Black student, Polly Myers, applied for admissions at UA as early as September 4, 1952, forgoing opportunities to study at Yale and Columbia respectively.[6] Both of them were accepted to the university, and were even assigned dorm rooms with the UA president's assurance that they would be successfully enrolled. However, they were both prohibited from enrolling when UA informed them that the courses they sought were offered at the all-Black Alabama State College.[7] Civil rights attorneys Arthur Shores and Thurgood Marshall languished with their cases for several years until they foresaw an unprecedented legal breakthrough with *Brown*. On December 30, 1955, Lucy's admission was upheld by the federal court, and she finally enrolled at UA in February 1956. But after weeks of encountering mob violence, she was first "excluded" from campus by the UA Board of Trustees, and subsequently expelled for legally challenging the board's exclusion.[8]

Fred Shuttlesworth and Birmingham Families' School Desegregation Battles

Fred Shuttlesworth's Family's Fight

With the sanction of Alabama law, by all accounts, Birmingham's White public officials had no intention of heeding *Brown*, that is, until their legal showdown with Fred Shuttlesworth and other families in 1957.[9] Similar to desegregation struggles in other Southern states, court cases initiated by Shuttlesworth and his own young children, along with other families, were critical to dismantling Jim Crow schooling.[10] Shuttlesworth's organization, the Alabama Christian Movement for Human Rights (ACMHR), a group comprised largely of pastors and local church members, was organized to fill the gap left by the NAACP, which had been banned altogether in Alabama after suffering incremental bans such as barring schoolteachers' membership in the organization.[11] ACMHR petitioned the Birmingham Board of Education (BOE) on August 21, 1957, to admit Black students.[12] In response, the Alabama State Superintendent of Education wrote a letter "urgently recommend[ing]" Shuttlesworth and the adult petitioners to "fully support" the BOE in its decision to place students according to the provision of the Pupil Placement Law, and reminding them that "the people of Alabama voted to change the Constitution of this State, and thereby abolished the right of education or training of any individual at public expense."[13] The superintendent went on to warn them: "I think you will destroy what you already have if you refuse to cooperate with the decision of the local school board of education to place your child in the school they think will be best for your child."[14]

On September 17, 1957, Birmingham's school and municipal officials contended with *Brown* head-on when Shuttlesworth and his family joined ranks with other Black families in an attempt to integrate Phillips High School.[15] Shuttlesworth and his family paid dearly for their activism. They were attacked by an angry White mob, which left Shuttlesworth badly beaten, his wife stabbed, and his daughter suffering a broken ankle. Yet this setback did not stop Shuttlesworth from issuing another petition dated October 26, 1959, and signed by fifty-eight individuals and married couples.[16] The petition again called for "the public schools of Birmingham, Alabama to be desegregated, and opened to all children without regard to race, creed, or color, according to the Supreme Court Decisions of May, 1954 and June, 1955."[17] In response, the Birmingham BOE built new all-Black schools to thwart *Brown*.[18] Similar actions to upgrade and build new facilities for Black students occurred throughout Alabama.[19] In an oral history account, former BPS teacher Lillie Fincher recalled that the Birmingham BOE erected the all-Black Carver High School "right in Shuttlesworth's back door" so that he would be forced to send his children there instead of Phillips High School.[20] Fincher noted that local residents referred to Carver High School as the "Shuttlesworth School" because his children were required to attend.[21] Former BPS teacher Willie Mae Crews also asserted that Black BPS high schools such as Carver and Hayes "were built to keep [Black] children from attending . . . Phillips High School and Woodlawn High School, which were all-white."[22] Subsequently, Shuttlesworth filed a lawsuit with his daughter Ruby and James Armstrong's daughter Denise as the two leading plaintiffs in *Ruby Fredericka Shuttlesworth et al. versus Birmingham Board of Education*.[23] In this suit, the plaintiffs urged the court to declare several sections of the state Pupil Placement Law unconstitutional, including stipulations for psychological testing as a requisite for desegregation transfers.[24] Shuttlesworth and his plaintiffs lost their case, and it would not be until six years later that BPS would finally desegregate.

James Armstrong's Family's Fight

In addition to the Shuttlesworth case, the *Dwight Armstrong et al. v. The Board of Education of the City of Birmingham et al.* case was pivotal in mobilizing student and faculty desegregation efforts throughout Birmingham.[25] Civil rights attorney W. L. Williams referred to *Armstrong v. Board of Education* as "the case that broke the back of discrimination in the Birmingham school system."[26] The case was filed in 1957, yet took six years before it was eventually adjudicated in federal court. James Armstrong and his children (which included plaintiff Dwight Armstrong) had previously joined ranks with Shuttlesworth in the initial battle to integrate Phillips High School.[27] It was his family's unwavering determination not to retreat in the face of violent threats from Birmingham's White community, coupled with mounting fear from its Black community—including many of his barbershop customers—that eventually convinced BPS Superintendent of Negro Schools Carol Hayes to stop dissuading Armstrong's family's integration efforts and to "[get] on his side."[28]

The *Armstrong* case resulted in a plan to integrate West End and Ramsay high schools and Graymont Elementary School. But this plan was almost thwarted by school board–mandated school closings on September 5, 1963.[29] The registration of the Armstrong children at Graymont Elementary on September 4 set off a firestorm in the state's capitol as Governor George Wallace sent state troopers to block the students' enrollment.[30] On September 9, 1963, Dwight and Floyd Armstrong were joined by their father, Shuttlesworth, and attorneys Oscar Adams and Ernest Jackson, to integrate Graymont.[31] During that same week, Robert Walker attempted to integrate Ramsay, and Patricia Marcus and Josephine Powell tried to integrate West End.[32] All five students were blocked by state troopers and officials sent under Governor George Wallace's orders, but they eventually succeeded in attending these formerly all-White schools. The following day President John F. Kennedy federalized the Alabama National Guard and gave U.S. Secretary of Defense Robert McNamara leeway in employing any of the armed forces he deemed necessary to enforce school desegregation.[33] Whereas integration at Graymont did not result in arrests, this was not the case at West End, where nine students were arrested and one thousand refused to attend classes.[34] White students also walked out of Ramsay High School in protest of integration. According to one eyewitness account, anti-integration protestors drove across the city from school to school waving Confederate flags and urging White students to walk out of their schools in protest.[35]

BIRMINGHAM EDUCATORS' CIVIL RIGHTS ACTIVISM

While Black families, civil rights activists, and attorneys were at the forefront of fighting for school desegregation in Birmingham, educators were also involved both on the frontlines and behind the scenes. A closer examination of the historical record of Black educators in Birmingham challenges the dominant fear-and-evasion narrative that pervades civil rights histories and many histories of Black education. As discussed in chapter 2, there were Birmingham educators who were actively involved in local, state, and national civil rights organizations and professional teachers associations. Some marched in public protests even at the risk of their jobs and economic security. Many others engaged in subtle acts of resistance concealed inside of the schoolhouse.

Activism Outside of the Schoolhouse

Lucinda Robey was one among a notable number of Black educators who was openly and unabashedly active in the Birmingham civil rights movement.[36] Robey was a life member of the Birmingham chapter of the NAACP, serving as its youth director before assuming this same role at the state level.[37] As a school principal, she led youth to participate in local civil rights activities, often transporting them to mass meetings.[38] Robey was also the sole woman listed on the charter of the ACMHR, and one among a few women who served in a leadership role in the organization.[39] In addition, Robey served as chairperson of her local delegation to the ASTA as well as on the board of the Birmingham Negro Teachers Association.[40] In ASTA, she was actively involved in representing the interest of the Department of Classroom Teachers, which was established latently in 1963 to be more sensitive to and inclusive of the interests of the organization's primarily Black female teaching constituency.[41] Robey's professional risk as an educator was not lost on Shuttlesworth, who warned her about potential retribution for her public activism: "I used to tell her, 'Lucinda, you can't teach school from jail.' " To this she replied, "I'll do what I can do."[42]

Former BPS teacher, Lillie Fincher remembered Lucinda Robey as a role model. She recalled that Robey's car "always had her toothbrush and a change of underwear in it just in case she had to go to jail."[43] It was Robey who strengthened Fincher's resolve when she fretted about losing her job because of her NAACP membership. According to Fincher, Robey attended "every one of those [mass] meetings at night."[44] When the school district refused to supply Robey a secretary to support her in

Figure 3.1. Lucinda Robey, former Birmingham activist educator pictured (top row third from the left) with Reverend Fred Shuttlesworth and members of the Alabama Christian Movement for Human Rights. Photo: Birmingham Civil Rights Institute.

her role as principal, Fincher recalled that she paid for her own secretary and purchased school supplies from both her and her husband's (who was also an educator) salaries.

Robey's civil rights comrade, Lola Hendricks, remembered that "Robey was under constant threat of the loss of her job but was bold."[45] Hendricks also noted that Robey threatened to sue the school superintendent if he fired her from her job.[46] But Robey was not the first socially conscious teacher whom Hendricks encountered. As an A. H. Parker High School alumna, Hendricks recalled how her teachers prepared her for activism. Her former history teacher, Henry Williams, spoke to students candidly about suffrage as a part of his lessons and encouraged them to become registered voters.[47] Hendricks credited Williams with inspiring her to register to vote as soon as she turned eighteen.

Former BPS teacher Jesse Champion Sr. illustrated soberly the professional risk encountered by teachers who participated publicly in the movement. Champion lost his teaching job in 1963 for preventing the citizen's arrest of one of his students, an action that he believed would turn violent upon the arrival of the Birmingham Police Department at the scene.[48] Upon orders from notorious Police Commissioner Eugene "Bull" Connor, Champion was arrested to "teach him a lesson."[49] Champion knew full well what this lesson meant: "Teachers were not supposed to be a part of the Civil Rights Movement."[50] He felt that his arrest was retribution for his previous involvement in mass meetings, marches, and demonstrations, including the Selma to Montgomery march. Consequently, Champion was charged with inciting a riot, and was instructed by the school superintendent to resign or be fired. According to Birmingham BOE minutes, the superintendent stated that he was informed by the Birmingham Police Department that Champion was convicted in Police Court on May 7, 1963, of assault and battery and disorderly conduct charges associated with his attempt to protect his student.[51] In his oral history, Champion acknowledged that he conceded to submitting a resignation letter to avoid having a termination on his employment record.[52] In response, Black principals and teachers in Birmingham rallied to his cause by taking up money to keep him and his family from being homeless. A few months after the incident, he accepted a teaching and coaching job in Flint, Michigan. He later returned to Birmingham in 1970 to become the first Black news reporter at a local radio station. Champion concluded that the fate of his BPS teaching career deterred his fellow teachers from becoming more actively involved in the civil rights movement.[53]

Figure 3.2. Jesse Champion Sr., former Birmingham teacher fired for activism. Photo: Birmingham Civil Rights Institute.

Activism inside the Schoolhouse

In light of the retribution that Lucinda Robey and Jesse Champion Sr. suffered, some Birmingham educators deemed it necessary to conceal their civil rights involvement behind schoolroom doors. Fincher acknowledged that although she felt she could not march with her students without risking her family's economic livelihood, "she could work with and teach them in the classroom so that history would become real for them."[54] Fincher was also inspired by her mother's personal battle to become a registered voter. She recalled that her mother, Gertrude Crum Sanders, felt compelled to wear her own mother's maid uniform and speak "the language of an uneducated person" to temper any White antagonism she might encounter as an educated Black teacher attempting to register to vote.[55] No doubt the high price for registering to vote, or even encouraging and registering others to do so, was fresh on her mind as the tragic Mississippi "Freedom Summer" of 1964 resulted in one of the most heinous and high-profile civil rights murders, which made martyrs of three young voting rights activists, James Earl Chaney, Andrew Goodman, and Michael Schwerner.[56] Sanders's shrewd self-abasement proved successful in securing her voter's registration. When the 26th Constitutional Amendment granting eighteen-year-old citizens the right to vote was passed in 1971, as the Social Studies department head, and following in her mother's footsteps, Fincher set out to "register every eighteen year old in our student body" using both her and another teacher's signature as application references.[57] She organized bus transportation by soliciting the assistance of a local NAACP president to transport more than three hundred students to the JeffCo Courthouse.[58]

Other Birmingham teachers such as Carolyn Cunningham noted the "unwritten type of proclamation" that Black teachers and administrators were not supposed to participate in the civil rights movement.[59] She acknowledged that she felt as if she had to "sneak" to mass meetings along with other teachers from Ullman High School, which was one of only three all-Black high schools during Birmingham's Jim Crow era that was subsequently closed during integration.[60] Former educator Ruth Barefield-Pendleton also reinforced the subtle resistance narrative shared by other BPS teachers.[61] She mentioned that civil rights leaders such as Andrew Young and James Bevel occasionally asked teachers to transport students from distant marching sites back to their homes and communities. She also admitted smuggling a copy of the voter registration questions she was required to take to become a registered voter, and using it as a teaching tool for her American History course. Barefield-Pendleton recalled: "I gave it to my students and they took it home to their parents and the parents studied them so they could pass the test to qualify [to vote]."[62]

Lydia Alexander, a former JeffCo public high school teacher, expressed some regret for not being involved in the movement more publicly as a teacher. But similar to other teacher narratives, she acknowledged the supportive role of Black educators.

> I wish I could tell you that I led the demonstrations. I wish I could tell you that I was one of those foot soldiers that just marched. But I was scared. To tell you the truth, we were threatened beyond belief about what we could and could not do. So

> behind our classroom doors, we urged our students to get out and march; and they did. They went in droves, and that's the biggest part that we could play in encouraging them to go. But we were threatened to lose our jobs if we dared join them.[63]

Alexander's perspective points to a need to revisit the May 1963 Children's Crusade from the perspective of Black educators' involvement.

The Children's Crusade and Black Educators

While Black educators grappled with what their role should be in the civil rights movement, children, youth, and college students were stepping up their involvement. One of the most pivotal acts of heroism in the Birmingham civil rights movement involved the bravery of children and youth. In 1963, after efforts to keep the civil rights movement on the national radar screen had stalled, Martin Luther King and other leaders were in search of a game changer. Some SCLC strategists, namely James Bevel, a twenty-four-year-old preacher and SNCC member, along with Isaac "Ike" Reynolds, Dorothy Cotton, Bernard Lee, and Andrew Young, had been actively engaged in inspiring and organizing young people to participate in the movement.[64] As youth participation in picketing and sit-ins continued to increase, Bevel and Reynolds urged King and other leaders to recruit schoolchildren to advance their involvement to the next level.[65] Initially, King and A. G. Gaston vehemently opposed the idea of using children in marches that would pit them against the notorious Birmingham police force led by Bull Connor.[66] But Bevel and Reynolds persisted until King and other civil rights leaders acquiesced.[67]

On May 2, 1963, a day that Bevel dubbed "D-Day," nearly one thousand students from across the city skipped school to converge on downtown Birmingham.[68] Many students walked miles from schools as far west as Wenonah and as far north as Carver high schools. On that day nearly one thousand protestors were arrested, which changed the tenor and dynamics of the Birmingham campaign.[69] The Children's March continued on through May 7, with only a one-day reprieve for a Sunday "kneel-in" at White churches.[70] On May 6, Birmingham's Black public schools could only account for fewer than nine hundred students out of 7,500 enrolled due to their activist-inspired truancy.[71] Yet after experiencing elation about their brave efforts, Birmingham students had to come to terms with the very high price they paid for freedom. They served jail time, incurred juvenile arrest records, and were suspended from school.[72]

The Birmingham BOE issued an order to expel or suspend 1,081 protesters on May 20, 1963.[73]

According to minutes of the central committee of the joint ACMHR and the SCLC, some members asked, "What about the children?," in response to the glaring omission of their mass expulsions and suspensions in Shuttlesworth's and King's briefings on the prepared statements they were to present at a news conference later that afternoon.[74] In response, the central committee, which included prominent civil rights leaders and attorneys such as King, Shuttlesworth, Andrew Young, Ralph Abernathy, and Arthur Shores, along with local educators such as Miles College president Lucius Pitts, deliberated several courses of action. King called a special meeting on May 20 to continue mulling over strategies for overturning the students' expulsions and suspensions. At the meeting, King stated that he knew nothing about the handbills calling for a mass student walkout until one was placed in his hand. He and other leaders chastised Bevel and other adult youth leaders for their unapproved actions. The committee designated Pitts to serve as a liaison between it and the Birmingham BOE to petition on behalf of the expelled and suspended students. Shores worked with other civil rights lawyers, including one of *Brown*'s NAACP Legal Defense Fund strategists, Constance Baker Motley, to enjoin the Birmingham BOE from expelling or suspending the students. Consequently, the United States Fifth Circuit Court of Appeals ruled in favor of plaintiff Linda Cal Woods, the daughter of civil rights activist Reverend Calvin Woods, who asked for a reversal of the BOE's suspension of his daughter for participating in the Children's March on a Saturday while school was not in session.[75] This case resulted in the dropping of charges against several students.

Based on the oral histories of student activists and their teachers, Birmingham educators played a mostly supportive role in The Children's Crusade although some were viewed as hindrances to the youthful protest. Several student activists recalled that teachers supported their activism clandestinely by pretending not to see them leave the classroom, facilitating classroom discussions about their involvement, and refusing to suspend or expel them, a perspective that is validated by the relatively low numbers of students who were actually suspended and expelled compared to the number of students who reportedly left school to march.[76] Former student activist Mary Moore explained that because teachers feared losing their jobs, they sometimes supported her and her classmates by acting as if they were reading a book, to indicate, "I don't see what's going on."[77] Willie A. Casey recalled skipping out on a test to participate in the demonstrations after his teacher assured him and his classmates in "a roundabout way" that he supported their actions.[78] Former student activist Gwendolyn Sanders Gamble summed up Birmingham educators' involvement in this way:

> We had some teachers that were afraid. Then we had some teachers that believed in it and wanted to do more than what they were actually doing. I know a few teachers who actually turn[ed] their heads and look[ed] out the window [as if to say], "If you want out, I didn't give you permission, I didn't see, so go while my head is turned." Then we had some that said we were troublemakers. We were disturbing the school, disturbing their classrooms, but the children went anyway.[79]

Annetta Streeter Gary recalled that student activism inspired her parents and other adults to get more involved in the movement. She noted that her former Ullman High School teacher, Odessa Woolfolk, "made her feel like a hero" for her participation in the movement.[80] Gary recalled that Woolfolk "would just casually turn her head and pretend she didn't know what was going on."[81] Similar to Gary, another student activist, James Stewart, remembered how Woolfolk used the classroom to inspire her students: "Miss Woolfolk challenged us to apply civics to everyday life."[82] Gary also noted that Cleopatra Goree was another teacher who "acted as if she did not see [us]."[83] According to Goree's oral history account, she attended mass meetings and referred to herself "not as [an] active, but a card-carrying member" of the NAACP.[84] She described her relationship with student activists as "neutral," noting that "I never stood in anybody's way," when students skipped school to participate in protest marches.[85] Goree also used classroom time to allow students to debrief about their civil rights involvement. As she described: "I was their confidant lady."[86]

Some former educators who were publicly involved in the movement recalled the courage and reticence of their fellow teachers. Famed civil rights musician and educator Carlton Reese acknowledged the effect that economic intimidation had on Black educators. He concluded, "In order to keep their jobs some people didn't want their names called [publicly] even though they were with it."[87] Former JeffCo educator Johnnie McKinstry Summerville recalled that she and a number of teachers participated in mass meetings and other civil rights activities. Although some expressed fear about losing their jobs, a number of them were willing to sacrifice their livelihood for the cause.

> [Some adults] were really afraid because a lot of times their livelihood and their support for their families depended on them keeping their jobs. Therefore, I felt like they said, "I have to keep my job and maybe let somebody else do it." That didn't frighten us. We still continued to go to the meetings and do whatever we could do. Whatever we needed to do to help the cause we did. When we saw those little children, that is what really inspired us.[88]

Lillie Fincher was also inspired by the bravery of the children and youth.[89] She recalled that some teachers tried to stop them from leaving school to participate in the Children's March but other teachers permitted them to walk out. In the academic year subsequent to the 1963 Children's March, Fincher noted that teachers' contracts had changed abruptly to include a clause that stipulated that they would not be paid if children were not in school. She insinuated that this change was instituted in retaliation for Black teachers' and administrators' inability or refusal to keep children from protesting during the school day. Fincher's account is supported by another source documenting that Alabama governor George Wallace engineered a resolution in 1965, in his role as ex-officio chair of the Alabama State Department of Education, to dock the pay of teachers and principals at schools with high absenteeism due to student protests. Wallace charged that the cause of these student protests was "teacher encouragement."[90] In response to this mandate, Fincher said that some teachers tried to divert subsequent student protests whereas others continued to permit students to leave their classrooms without punishment, even though they knew their paychecks would be impacted.

HBCUs Civil Rights Activism

Miles College's Selective Buying Campaign

Black educators and students at HBCUs also played a pivotal role in the civil rights struggle in Birmingham.[91] Miles College was a pivotal HBCU site for the Birmingham civil rights movement.[92] Miles College students were also joined by students from Daniel Payne College and Booker T. Washington Business College.[93] Not until recently has there been extensive media coverage of the role that educator- and student activists at Miles College played in the Birmingham civil rights movement.[94] Miles College is now credited as "a place where strategies were developed and hundreds of foot soldiers were recruited" to participate in the movement.[95] Some of the leading faculty and student activists included Miles faculty members Jonathan McPherson and Abraham Woods, and student activists Frank Dukes, Joe Dickson, and Willie Clyde Jones. Some leading women activists, including former educator Ruth Barefield-Pendleton, were affectionately referred to as "The Den Mothers of Miles," for their loyal support to Miles student activists.[96]

In 1962, Miles faculty and student activists strategized a campaign to "boycott" local stores without using this term explicitly since it was outlawed in the state at the time. The official name chosen was the "selective buying campaign," which was designed to stop the flow of Black dollars going to White merchants who refused to hire Black sales clerks or get rid of segregated bathrooms and water fountains.[97] Local residents were urged to spend their money selectively only in those business establishments where they would not be discriminated against. As one flier exhorted: "Join the fight for freedom. Let's celebrate a true Easter by not buying at stores which uphold segregation, discrimination, and inequality."[98]

The selective buying campaign had mixed results. Student bodies at the joint coalition of colleges had demanded hiring of Black retail workers, equal job opportunities in civil service careers, and desegregation of lunch counters, restrooms, and all drinking fountains.[99] On the positive side, the selective buying campaign was credited with engaging 90 percent of the Black community at the pinnacle of the campaign, putting a major dent in pre-Easter shopping with sales reportedly 12 percent lower than the previous years.[100] In response, Shuttlesworth used the selective buying campaign to persuade Martin Luther King and other SCLC members to select Birmingham as the site for "Project C," which stood for the "confrontation" that would ensue between activists and Bull Connor.[101] Although a significant number of Black citizens supported the campaign, Frank Dukes recalled that they had a little trouble convincing some teachers "who dressed sharp" to stop buying attire at their favorite shops.[102] In retaliation to the campaign, some of the few Black retail workers at White-owned stores were fired and segregated water fountain signs were placed back up.[103]

Lucius Pitts and HBCU Presidential Activism

There is a period in civil rights history characterized as "the era of the Black college president," wherein these higher education leaders were the acknowledged leaders in Black communities with HBCU sites.[104] Miles

College president Lucius Pitts was among a small cadre of educators who assumed a high-profile role in the Birmingham civil rights movement. Pitts was born into a sharecropping family and later became a CME preacher.[105] In the 1950s he became deeply involved in Atlanta's civil rights struggle, prompting King and Ella Baker to invite him to assume a leadership role in the SCLC. But Pitts declined their invitation in favor of working more deeply in the trenches.[106] He also served as the executive secretary of the Georgia Teachers and Educators Association and president of ATA. Pitts once stated, "I think a black college president has to encourage activism and create a climate where it can come out."[107] But doing so was easier said than done, especially for presidents of state-operated universities and colleges, who were at the behest of the Alabama legislature for job security and a lion's share of their institutional support. A case in point is H. Councill Trenholm, who in his role as president of Alabama State College (as well as research secretary for ASTA), refused to heed Alabama governor John Patterson's threat to cut off his state funding if he did not

Figure 3.3. Lucius Pitts, Miles College president, 1961–1971. Photo: Birmingham, Ala., Public Library Archives.

expel students who participated in a sit-in at the Montgomery County courthouse.[108] But ASTA, led by its Birmingham-based president Bessie Estell, stood by Trenholm by moving forward with holding its annual convention in Montgomery although they were dissuaded from doing so. Estell and ASTA's executive secretary, George Jones, wrote Governor Patterson to inform him that ASTA "reaffirms its confidence in the president of the college."[109] The fact that Pitts led a privately funded college gave him more leeway than his publicly funded peers to pursue activist aims but it did not shield him completely from retribution.

In contrast to some of his predecessors, by most accounts Pitts supported faculty and student activism and was deeply involved in his own activist pursuits through joint meetings between the ACMHR and the SCLC.[110] Former Miles College student activist U. W. Clemon noted that the president who preceded Pitts, William A. Bell, expelled students who were involved in civil rights demonstrations.[111] Bell's view was that "[you] can't fight and beg," noting that his job as a college president was to solicit money from Whites to keep Miles College afloat and on par with fulfilling its mission to educate Black students from all walks of life.[112] Yet Bell has also been characterized as a complex man who was skeptical of the salvific power of both accommodation and protest strategies.[113] In the 1940s, Bell advised and offered Miles as a home base to the radical Southern Negro Youth Congress (SNYC) but later parted ways with the group's communist contingent, especially in light of Bull Connor's public excoriation of the group.[114] Bell and Pitts were similar in their public and hands-on support for student-activist groups, but Pitts seemed to more eagerly encourage student, and even faculty, resistance. For example, he invited Miles faculty and students to his home to strategize the selective buying campaign. Former Miles faculty member Jonathan McPherson noted that he had Pitts' "blessings and encouragement" to advise student activists on the selective buying campaign, and that Miles "was an enclave for teachers who did not worry about losing their jobs because of their involvement in the Civil Rights Movement."[115] Former student activist Joe Dickson credited Pitts with bringing the idea for a selective buying campaign from Atlanta and initiating it at Miles.[116] Prior to the selective buying campaign's launch, Pitts permitted four Miles students to get arrested as test cases. He also allowed twenty-four students to take a year-long leave of absence to work on voter registration.[117] Under Pitts's leadership five hundred Miles College students conducted opinion surveys of residents in the all-Black Roosevelt City to get a pulse on "the anger and fear of these people and what they should do with their own power." His students' on-the-ground efforts, Pitts boasted, gave them invaluable field experience related to their college majors in law, social work, and political science.[118]

Although by many accounts Pitts was actively involved in advancing the civil rights cause, his characterization as an activist is not embraced universally.[119] By some accounts, Pitts is described as an overly cautious member of the Black bourgeoisie, who often opposed direct action during internal deliberations with Birmingham's civil rights organizations.[120] Similar to other larger-than-life figures, Pitts was "different things to different people."[121] His litany of competing roles included student protest mentor-leader, racial diplomat, college fundraiser, and politician.[122] Pitts was known to encourage and lead campus activism while alternately redirecting and stifling some efforts he deemed too radical. Toward the latter years of his presidency, some Black critics accused Pitts of being an "Uncle Tom," whereas uneasy White civic leaders suspected that he was an underground radical who "talk[ed] out of four sides of his mouth."[123] One example of his delicate negotiation of activism and diplomacy was his clash with a militant student group. He was known to favor and endorse campus groups that he believed would best represent the campus (e.g., the Voices of Harmony choir) over other groups he deemed overly militant (e.g., the African Singers choir).[124] Another example was his decision not to cave in to the demands of militant student groups that marched outside of his office and seized some campus buildings. Pitts stood his ground and demanded that the group's leaders meet with him in his office face to face, where he discreetly resolved the matter. Notably, he explicitly instructed the local police not to invade his campus or arrest any of the militant students without his express consent. A longtime member of both state and national Black teachers associations, during the early 1960s' deliberations around merging ATA with NEA, Pitts warned his fellow educators that ATA was the only organization that would authentically "represent the educational aspirations and strivings of the under-privileged rising people of color in America who teach Negro boys and girls."[125] In reflecting on his college presidency, Pitts described his role as "guiding from the rear."[126]

BIRMINGHAM SCHOOL DESEGREGATION ACTUALIZED: 1963–1983

While Black public school and higher educators negotiated their own civil rights involvement, school desegregation was finally underway in Birmingham. At the outset of *Brown*, the BPS student population was 57.9 percent White and 42.1 percent Black.[127] It was a dual (or racially segregated) system with respect to schools, students, teachers, staff, salary schedules, athletics, extracurricular activities, as well as in the separation of administrative forms, school directories, and data reports by race.[128] There were seven all-White high schools and forty-one all-White elementary schools as well as three all-Black high schools and thirty-three all-Black elementary schools.[129] As one former BPS educator described, "[Y]ou had a separate school system. We had a Director of Negro Education, and that was Dr. Carol W. Hayes . . . and so all of the Black teachers sort of reported to Dr. Hayes and the White teachers reported to the [White] superintendent. And when we had grade meetings, the grade meetings for Black teachers would be over at Parker High School and the grade meetings for White teachers would be over at Woodlawn [High School]."[130]

Four Phases of School Desegregation

Between 1963 and 1983, four phases of school desegregation were enacted in Birmingham and Alabama.[131] These included: the Freedom of Choice Plan (1967), which essentially subverted desegregation by permitting parents to opt in or out of desegregated schools; the Unitary System Plan (1970), which involved complex pupil placement laws; a modification of the Unitary System Plan (1976); and the Magnet School Plan (1980), which created racially balanced selective schools that drew academically competitive students from across the district away from their zoned neighborhood schools.[132]

Among these desegregation plans, the Freedom of Choice plan was the most disingenuous and accomplished the least in dismantling segregation. The Freedom of Choice plan feigned that all students had an equal opportunity to select their preferred school unencumbered by discrimination and retribution. A letter from JeffCo Public Schools' superintendent, Kermit A. Johnson, stated matter-of-factly that "[e]very student, white and Negro, must make a choice of schools."[133] The letter went on to say that "[n]o one is permitted to favor or penalize any student or other person because of a choice made."[134] Notably, the state-mandated pupil placement laws, which were amended shortly after *Brown* in an effort to undermine the Supreme Court's landmark decision, permitted the BPS and other public school districts throughout Alabama to enact "race-neutral" desegregation and assign students to schools according to highly subjective and complex psychological, academic, and behavioral criteria.[135] School superintendents had the discretion of interviewing students and their families. Some of the questions asked of parents were personal and subjective such as, "What does your child do in his leisure time?" "Do you regularly have your child's friends in the home?" and "Does your child seem to enjoy doing things in a group or is he inclined to be a 'lone wolf' type?"[136]

"Crossover Teacher" Transfers

The early phases of integration were characterized by violent resistance. Birmingham teachers such as Lillie Fincher recalled having to literally press past Ku Klux Klansmen in order to get to work.[137] Notably, Fincher and other teachers sometimes resisted court orders to integrate schools—and were often backed by their Black principals—in order to remain connected to Black students and anchored in Black communities as well as to mitigate inequities in "crossover-teacher" quality.[138] A Birmingham BOE survey of school staff tallied on July 12, 1968, reveals that the overwhelming majority of "Negro" and White respondents would not willingly accept a transfer or assignment to a school of the opposite race.[139] However, the "Negro" respondents were more likely to respond affirmatively to part two of the question, which asked if they would transfer "if the Board were ordered to make involuntary transfers and assignments?" In other words, neither Black or White school staff wholeheartedly embraced voluntary integration at that time, but the Black school staff felt it had the least liberty to defy BOE orders. BPS school desegregation documents between 1967 and 1969 confirm that Black educators bore the brunt of making desegregation a reality with thirty-one "Negro staff members assigned to White schools" and only three "White staff members assigned to Negro schools" in the first term of the 1967–68 school year.[140] In the following academic year, the numbers increased to 101 "Negro" staff and fifty-eight White staff transferring to opposite race schools.[141]

Some Black educators who were initially reluctant to leave their schools eventually embraced their new roles in integrated schools. One such teacher was Margaret Beard, who integrated the JeffCo public schools. As a result of the *Linda Stout v. Jefferson County Board of Education* desegregation ruling, Beard was ordered to leave Brighton School and report to McAdory High School in 1969.[142] She recalled that one of her former colleagues remarked that she was only selected because she was "yellow," referring to her fair-skinned complexion. Beard acknowledged that her remarks were hurtful especially given her deep love and affection for the all-Black Brighton School community.[143] Yet she came to view her mandated transfer as an opportunity to serve as an ambassador for racial integration. Beard attended integration training facilitated by university instructors from Georgia State at Brookley Air Force Base in Mobile, Alabama. She spent three to four weekends with an integrated group of participants learning how to adjust to a new environment and act as a change agent for racial relations. As Beard recalled, the participants went fishing together, dined together, and engaged in role-playing activities. "What they were really trying to find out is, 'are you going to be able to fit in'?," she concluded.[144] Beard took her charge to integrate McAdory School very seriously. Over time, she won the hearts of Black and White students alike by treating them fairly, encouraging them to exceed beyond their low academic and post–secondary school expectations, and inviting them to her home for weekend get-togethers as an alternative to engaging in delinquent behavior. Whenever she encountered racial animosity from White or Black students, she admonished them not to "bring that high-chair hate" into the school. Beard also established close ties with both Black and White parents.[145] "When parents find out that you are working for their children, and that you are interested in their children, they love you too," she reminisced.[146]

As noted previously, there is some speculation in the oral histories of Black teachers regarding teacher quality in desegregation transfer assignments to Black versus White school. By some accounts, teachers assigned to predominantly Black schools were not deemed as qualified as teachers assigned to predominantly White schools. As one former Birmingham-area teacher recalled, "I had watched . . . the best teachers that we had shipped out to White schools, and the worst that they had sent to our schools."[147] Former BPS teacher Willie Mae Crews recalled pleading with the administrators in her newly integrated school, "Please do not transfer the best black teachers to schools that are white and leave the black kids with what you deem [to be] the poorest black teachers and the poorest white teachers; that's totally unfair."[148] She politely refused to comply with a desegregation order to transfer her to an all-White school. When a White BPS school district official asked her if she would object to teaching "children of an opposite race," Crews replied, "No, I do not. Please send them to Hayes High School," which was the all-Black school to which she was already assigned.[149] BPS data on teacher quality during the school desegregation era is difficult to obtain, but one document indicated that among the forty White teachers assigned to "opposite race" (Black) high schools in 1968–69, ten had a rating of "excellent," three had a rating of "very good," fourteen had a rating of "satisfactory," four had a rating of "fair," one had a rating of "poor," and eight had a rating that was "not available."[150]

Accelerations and Reversals

Despite White resistance and violence, coupled with some instances of Black educators' refusal to comply with integration orders, desegregation slowly increased in the BPS between the mid-1960s and 1980.[151] Desegregation was accelerated by the *Lee v. Macon* case in 1967, in which the U.S. Middle District Court of Alabama mandated the ninety-nine school systems that had not been ordered previously to desegregate school staff and students, to now comply.[152] Furthermore, under U.S. president Lyndon B. Johnson's administration and pursuant to Title VI of the 1964 Civil Rights Act, Congress granted authority to the commissioner of education through the Secretary of Health, Education, and Welfare, to move forward with dissolving the dual system by withholding federal funds from public school systems that stonewalled Congress' policy.[153] Consequently, whereas in 1963–64 only five Black students attended previously all-White BPS, by 1967–68 this number had increased to 2,894 students.[154] Among the early integration test case schools, Graymont Elementary was reportedly 91 percent "Negro" by September 1967 and Woodlawn was nearly 60 percent "Negro" by 1979.[155] However, this heyday of desegregation did not last very long as the numbers of White residents living in the city limits subsequently became too few to enforce school desegregation due to White flight and a brief campaign to establish alternative all-White private schools to circumvent integration.[156]

Very often, desegregation resulted in "outergration" or "second-class integration" as freedom of choice plans reinforced the status quo, Black schools lost good teachers and gained some incompetent ones, Black teachers in previously all-White schools were relegated to certain subjects such as library science, physical education, and business education, and many Black teachers and principals were demoted or fired.[157] Since the 1970s, integration efforts across the U.S. South have been thwarted by conservative courts' reversals of integration decrees.[158] In Birmingham, these efforts have also been undermined by the splintering of larger, somewhat racially, ethnically, and economically heterogeneous school districts into smaller, independent, predominantly White middle-class districts.[159] In spite of these reversals, the courts eventually declared the BPS system unitary although the schools remained predominantly Black.[160]

BROWN'S PERIL AND PROMISE

There is no way to fully grasp how the fallout from *Brown* diminished the collective capacity for Black educators' activism in the post-*Brown* era. The detrimental long-term effects of *Brown* have been to divorce Black teachers and principals from their students and community members, and to reduce a talented pool of these educators in public schools.[161] According to one scholar, the loss of Black principals, "created a leadership vacuum in communities that has not since been recovered."[162] The caution and unease that members of Black teachers associations expressed at the dawn of the *Brown* decision proved to be well founded as many of their members lost jobs, tenure, and their prominent standing in their schools and communities. A telegram crafted by the ATA at its June 12, 1965, meeting in Atlanta outlined in painstaking detail the mighty blow that desegregation dealt to its association members.[163] These associations lost integral ties to and control of their professional organizations through mergers with White teachers associations.[164] These mergers typically resulted in the loss of visible and influential Black leadership in the newly integrated associations, which went hand in hand with a redirected focus away from prioritizing and addressing persistent problems and concerns endemic to Black education. The displacement of African American educators post-*Brown* was akin to "sociological shock" for many southern Black communities, as schools were closed, families were compelled to move, and many homes were foreclosed and abandoned.[165] These unintended consequences made the warning issued by the Alabama state school superintendent to Shuttlesworth in 1957 ironically prophetic: "I think you will destroy what you already have if you refuse to cooperate."[166]

Yet in the midst of its peril, *Brown* also ushered in a promising era of Black representation in school governance. The first Black Birmingham BOE member, Clyde Kirby, was appointed in 1970, followed by the appointments of Ossie Ware Mitchell (the first Black woman), Louis Dale (who replaced Kirby upon his untimely death), and Thomas L. Alexander, tilting the board toward a historic first Black majority.[167] In 1984, the first Black superintendent, Walter Harris, was appointed, followed by a second Black superintendent, Cleveland Hammonds, after Harris's tumultuous tenure and dismissal.[168] There was also a period of time preceding massive White flight when many BPS and JeffCo schools were desegregated and making some strides toward integration.

Although the extant primary and secondary sources on Black educators' involvement in the Birmingham civil rights movement are not as robust and ascertainable as sources available on high-profile civil rights leaders and organizations, revisiting this data from a different vantage point sheds considerable light on the significance of Black educators in the movement. Further augmentation of these sources, especially the creation of new oral history accounts that amplify the voices of relatively unknown educators born across distinctive phases of the long civil rights movement, go a long way in addressing critical gaps in the ever-morphing civil rights narrative. New accounts help to illuminate how past and present phases of this perpetual movement have ushered in both familiar and emergent problems, challenges, and promises for successive generations of Black educators in Birmingham, along with their students and families.

PART II

TRANSITIONING AND FORGING AHEAD

4

RELATIVE ACTIVISM

> I hear people call certain people "activist". . . . [Does that mean] pulling away from the norm? . . . Is it standing up for a belief that sometimes people don't understand? . . . Does the term change with generations? Does it change with activities [or] with a particular concern and struggle? I do see the word *act* there, and it means doing something extraordinary. But to me that's relative. . . . I think all of us are activists at some point.
>
> —"Doris," pre–Civil Rights Generation Educator

"Doris" was born in Birmingham's Black middle-class neighborhood of Titusville in 1942. She remembered her segregated neighborhood as an affirming and cohesive enclave akin to the communal first-century Christian church described in the Bible's New Testament. Titusville, she reminisced, "reminds me of Acts 2 where they talk about the forming of the first church where people just came together and wherever they were strongest, that's where they served." After graduating from A. H. Parker High School, Doris attended Alabama State University (ASU) in the early 1960s, where she made her foray into civil rights activism. She acknowledged that her contribution to the civil rights movement entailed supporting the involvement of her male college friends versus engaging publicly and directly, a role that she deemed to be "a vital position" to the movement. Doris was cautious about jeopardizing her standing as a college student in consideration of the sacrifices her parents made to send her to school. She rationalized that her contribution to the movement would need to be limited to supporting and affirming clandestinely the activities of her fellow male classmates, who felt inclined to directly challenge the system while she stayed focus on finishing school.

> My role was more of a supportive role, an uplifting role, because we had the opportunity to go to college. And [you] were encouraged . . . to do your very best to graduate on time so that you can help the others, because there were those who were making sacrifices for us.

Once she returned to Birmingham in the mid-1960s after completing a master's degree in the Midwest, Doris remained cautious about participating publicly in the civil rights movement. In her view, any direct confrontation would have jeopardized both her and her family's dreams for her to become a teacher, an achievement that would enable her to "help the others" in the long run. Doris's philosophy about the relative nature of activism characterizes the experiences of many other Black educators in her generation.

THE PRE–CIVIL RIGHTS AND CIVIL RIGHTS COHORTS

An examination of Black educators born on opposite sides of the classical phase of the Birmingham civil rights movement must take into account their divergent historical and generational experiences.[1] Black educators who were born between the 1920s and 1950s are referred to by demographers as the silent (1925–1945) and baby boomer (1945–1964) generations.[2] Members of the silent generation experienced the most rigid racial caste system compared to those associated with the baby boomer generation.[3] The childhood and adolescent experiences of Black educators in the silent generation predated the classical phase of the civil rights movement, which means most of them were novice or mid-career teachers in the 1950s and 1960s. In contrast, Black educators born during the early years of the baby boomer generation were youth and young adults in elementary, high school, and college during the height of social change in Birmingham. Their lives were linked together as they encountered unprecedented local and national watersheds, lived in segregated neighborhoods, attended and worked in segregated schools, and pioneered public school desegregation both as students and as educators.

National and Local Watersheds

Black educators in Birmingham who are identified with the silent and baby boomer generations recalled familiar national watersheds of the 1960s era

Table 4.1. Pre-Civil Rights Movement and Civil Rights Movement Cohort Demographics

Pseudonyms	*Birth Year*	*Professional Role*	*School Setting*
Hannah	1921	Retired Teacher	Urban Public
Claretha	1928	Retired Teacher	Urban Public
Wilma	1928	Retired Teacher	Urban Public
Lawrence	1936*	College Administrator**	Urban Public
Morgan	1935	Retired Teacher	Urban Public
Jerrie	1935	Retired Teacher	County Public
Francine	1937	Retired Teacher	Urban Public
Gloria	1937	College Administrator**	Urban Public
Sarah	1938	Retired Teacher	Urban Public
Dorene	1938	Retired School Manager	Urban Public
Isaac	1939	Retired Teacher	Urban Public
Abraham	1940*	Retired Teacher	Urban Public
Alvin	1942	Active Principal	Urban Public
Doris	1942	Retired Principal	Urban Public
Jemison	1943	Retired Principal	County Public
Joseph	1943	Retired Principal	County Public
Jacob	1944	Retired Counselor	Urban Public
Sheila	1944	Retired Teacher	County Public
Sherry	1950	Active Teacher	Urban Public
Tyler	1950	College Administrator**	County Public
Yvette	1950	Community Educator**	Urban Nonprofit Org.
Jeremy	1955	Community Educator	Urban Nonprofit Org.

*Approximate birth year

**Retired urban public school educator

such as the assassinations of John F. Kennedy, Martin Luther King Jr., and Robert F. Kennedy and the Vietnam War. But their most vivid memories were of triumphant and tragic local civil rights watersheds such as the Children's Crusade and the Sixteenth Street Baptist Church bombing.

"Jacob," a former BPS educator, made a poignant connection between his experiences as a Vietnam War veteran and his return home to "Bombingham" in the 1960s.[4]

> I had just gotten back from Vietnam and the bombing shook our house. I hit the floor, crawled, [and] looked out the win-

> dow. . . . It was Attorney [Arthur] Shores's house [that was bombed]. . . . They called out [Police Commissioner Eugene] "Bull" Connor, and they called out the [armored] tank, and they shot out the lights in our community . . . and we were restricted from leaving . . . and when nightfall came, they call[ed] out the [federal] troops.

Jacob disclosed that he had trouble trusting his surroundings upon returning to Birmingham after the war, and felt the need to keep a pistol near his bed until one of his parents discreetly removed it. Similar to the experiences of World War II Black veterans, Jacob grappled with fighting a war alongside White men yet returning home to racial hatred, violence, and second-class citizenship.

The most heinous of Birmingham's bombings occurred at church during Sunday morning worship services on September 15, 1963, killing four girls named Cynthia Wesley, Addie Mae Collins, Denise McNair, and Carole Rosamond Robertson.[5] Former BPS teacher "Francine" continues to be haunted by memories of the Sixteenth Street Church bombing. She lived on Sixteenth Street at the time and attended church on Seventeenth Street, which made her and her family proximate to the commotion that ensued after the bombing. Francine recalled how her family's ordinary Sunday morning routine was shattered by this abominable act of homegrown terrorism.

> My church was Macedonia Seventeenth Street Baptist Church. I had gotten my children ready, took them down to the Sunday School, and [planned on] going back to the church. I got back, and I was cooking my dinner so I wouldn't have to do that afterwards. I heard a BOOM, and I looked out my door. I didn't even try to find out what it was . . . I ran through that alley and got my babies out of church that day. Then about twelve o'clock [noon] the police was under my house. People from everywhere was on my front porch . . . and I guess about one o'clock or two o'clock the National Guard Armory was out there with guns . . . heading towards [my] door and trying to make people scatter.

The turbulent events of the classical phase of the Birmingham civil rights movement left an indelible imprint on Jacob's and Francine's lives. Because many members of their generation were young adults during this phase of the movement, they were very cognizant of significant events from the past and were able to recall details and associated emotions fairly vividly. In many respects, these watersheds distinguished their personal and professional lives from generations that both preceded and succeeded them.

Coming of Age in Birmingham and Alabama

Close-knit Families, Segregated Lives

Black educators in these two cohorts were products of two-parent working class, working poor, and lower-middle-class families in primarily urban segregated communities. Fathers typically labored in steel mills and mothers worked at home and in a variety of semiskilled professions. They described segregated, economically diverse, tight-knit communities where everyone supported one another. "Tyler" described segregated life in Alabama as a way of life, especially from the standpoint of being a child.

> Everything was segregated. . . . And being a child, you don't know the difference because you had your White/Colored water fountain. As a child it didn't have a real meaning to you. . . . You knew it was different [but] you felt that was just status quo and was just standard. It didn't arouse your consciousness enough to want to do something as a child during that time.

If the downside of segregation was restriction from full participation in American life, its upside was close-knit, economically diverse Black communities. As "Alvin" reminisced, "Segregation was the thing that brought the Blacks closer together in the schools and the communities." "Jeremy," a high school dropout counselor and GED instructor at a neighborhood nonprofit organization, also recalled the professional and socioeconomic diversity of his segregated Black community.

> In my neighborhood in Smithfield . . . there were people who were garbage collectors. There were people [who] were teachers. There were people [who] were lawyers. There were people [who] were doctors. And they all lived in a three or four block radius. So all of their children were able to be associated with one another, and we all knew each other.

When Birmingham's Black residents ventured beyond the familiar confines of their segregated neighborhoods, they had to be hypervigilant about the threat of racial violence. This threat was especially acute for young Black males. As Isaac recalled,

> Being a Black youngster [in Birmingham] was very difficult. . . . I was a big teenager and [when] I would go out, [my parents] were always concerned until I returned because . . . there were no Black policemen. All policemen were White. . . . You didn't have any rights. A policeman could have pulled you over and said that you tried to resist arrest or something. They could have shot and killed you, and they could have put a knife in your hand that they said you came at them with.

Most educators who were born in the 1920s through the 1940s experienced rural Southern life as children and adolescents and urban life as young adults, particularly as rural families across the U.S. South migrated to cities.[6] Urban life was not as harsh economically as rural life. Some of the participants grew up in Alabama's Black Belt region, which is named for its dark rich soils and home to several counties in the central part of the state. The Black Belt's legacy of Southern plantation culture has left it today in "a state of economic depression, underemployment, and poor social services."[7] According to "Wilma," who grew up in the Black Belt: "Oh, life was not easy . . . but there were wonderful times because home is home. And it's where you're loved, even in poverty, there is a place called home." Francine, who also grew up in the Black Belt, recalled the region as being a striking mid-twentieth-century holdover of slavery.

> It was from slavery in some parts of the Black Belt. . . . I didn't realize [it] but my Auntie had a guy that was . . . a little Black boss over the Big Man's slaves. [That is] if you like calling them slaves. . . . They used to say that they were "workers," but I've gotten in that truck, and rode down there with her, and they would be whipping workers. I really didn't realize this was slavery, but this is what I saw.[8]

HBCU Experiences

The parents of Black educators in the pre–civil rights and civil rights generations had high aspirations for their children, which translated into fulfilled dreams for first-generation college graduates. They labored painstakingly to support their children's college education. Sometimes they had a lot of say-so about which of the handful of available HBCUs in Alabama they would attend.

Most often, these educators attended HBCUs as undergraduates, and then ventured to predominantly White universities outside of the

Alabama and the U.S. South for graduate school due to segregation laws in higher education preventing Black students from attending all-White universities.[9] Ironically, the constraints of Jim Crow higher education laws opened the door for several of these educators to live outside of the U.S. South for the first and only time of their lives and attend competitive colleges and universities outside of the region. "Lawrence" recalled that after serving in the Korean War, he was well aware that pursuing a graduate degree in Alabama was not a viable option for him. In response to a UA admissions director's inquiry about why he was not attending graduate school at the university, Lawrence responded: "Well, [Governor] George Wallace had stood in the [UA schoolhouse] door, and I wasn't going to try to get him out of the door. [So] I came on up North." Consequently, Lawrence was rerouted from Wayne State University to UA by this same Alabama higher education official, who convinced him that Wallace's stand was more political ploy than reality.[10]

Even though HBCUs were the only viable higher education option for these educators, they did not see themselves as settling for them as a default choice. On the contrary, many credited HBCUs with instilling within them pride and knowledge about Black heritage. Furthermore, many HBCUs became centers of civil rights activism. "Yvette" recalled her experiences at what was then called, Tuskegee Institute.

> Tuskegee is a Black institution and they taught you about being Black. Growing [up] in the South we had no history of Alabama [and] we didn't talk about Black people, who were probably famous, who had done outstanding things. Tuskegee did that for me.

Tyler credited his experience at ASU with socializing him to become a consummate education professional. He recalled, "Something that was instilled in me at Alabama State University [was to] be a professional at all times because you never know who's watching you."

ACTIVIST TRAJECTORY

In an effort to move the dialogue beyond a discussion of conventional civil rights activism, I asked open-ended questions to ascertain participants' conceptualizations of the terms *activism* and *activist* rather than impose preconceived definitions on them. The fact that many of the educators were born, and all of them came of age professionally, in a city with a renowned civil rights history reinforced my decision to ask open-ended questions about their conceptualizations of activism. In response, these educators described activism in relative and flexible terms. They distinguished between the activism commonly portrayed in historical media, archival, and museum footage of the 1950s and 1960s (e.g., marches, sit-ins, organized protests) and the lesser-known activism that took place clandestinely in segregated and desegregated schools and classrooms. Black educators born prior to and during the classical phase of the civil rights movement named a litany of heroes and heroines such as Martin Luther King, Rosa Parks, and Fred Shuttlesworth. But quite often they noted the contributions of "ordinary" people. As Doris described, the activism of many Black educators during her day was "relative" to the traditional protests of Birmingham's foot soldiers but important in its own right.

The relative activism of latter-born pre–civil rights generation and early-born civil rights generation educators, in particular, manifested itself as direct and indirect involvement during their young adulthood and college years. During their early professional life their activism transitioned to the more subtle and less transparent arenas of clandestine support and silent protest, student advocacy in segregated and desegregated schools, "liberatory education and pedagogy," and preparing White students for a new racial order.[11] These practices are exemplary of Patricia Hill Collins's conceptualization of *struggles for group survival,* whereby Black women, in particular, create their own spheres of influence.[12]

Direct and Indirect Involvement in Young Adulthood and College

Some Black educators were actively involved in civil rights at Alabama's HBCUs, particularly Miles College, as well as ASU and Alabama A&M University. In many instances, the nature of their involvement reflected prevailing gender norms, which relegated Black men to paid work outside of the home and Black women to both paid and unpaid work in domestic spheres.[13]

The majority of men in this study (seven out of ten) indicated that they participated in conventional civil rights activities, primarily as college students, although a few were young enough to participate as late elementary and high school students. These men's participation included sit-ins, mass meetings, marches, civil rights organization membership, and transporting civil rights leaders to activities. Most of them made a point of noting that their conventional civil rights activism ended once they were employed as teachers. "Joseph" and Isaac were candid about their circumspect civil rights involvement. Joseph noted: "I was not one of them to participate in protest because I was getting ready to graduate." Isaac recalled his close call with losing military promotion due to his civil rights involvement, which deterred him from future involvement as a teacher.

> Being a teacher in the Birmingham Public Schools, I could not get out and march. Now when I was [a college student] in Tallahassee [Florida], I did take part in the marching. I almost wasn't going to get my promotion into the military because I demonstrated.

Isaac also expressed trepidation about his resolve to maintain a nonviolent stance in the midst of human denigration and violence. He recalled an incident that prompted him to put up his marching shoes.

> I found out that [civil rights protest] was something I wasn't going to be good at because I almost kind of got into it with a little White guy because [he] came up and spat on my young lady, who was marching there with me. And my demonstration was over then. You know, it wasn't going to be peaceful anymore.

"Jemison" was a standout among his cohort. He was by far the most actively involved in the civil rights movement. In fact, a few other participants recommended that I interview him because his activism was renowned at his college campus during that time. He noted that his father and siblings were also actively involved in the Birmingham civil rights movement to his mother's fearful dismay. Jemison's brave sit-in demonstration captured the attention of his local HBCU college town in Huntsville, Alabama.

> I was a sophomore and seven of us got dressed well and we went to Shoney's Big Boy [Restaurant] to integrate. We walked in and plates were clattering, clattering, clattering. All of a sudden it got real quiet, and we told the guy we wanted a table. He was from New York, and he said, "Man, I know what you're doing but you can't do it here." Somebody said, "You get the tall one, we'll get the [other] fellas, and we'll get these niggas

> out of here." So we turned around and looked at them. The goal was to make the community aware that we were there.

The women in this study were less likely to report direct involvement in conventional civil rights activism (only four out of ten). An additional two out of ten were ambivalent about their role and settled on describing themselves similar to "Sherry": "I participated [in the civil rights movement] but I was more like a silent participant." Sherry was one of the first Black students to attend Jacksonville State University in Alabama in the late 1960s. She recalled her experience integrating the freshman dorm room as her first cognizance of racial prejudice.

> At that time when I arrived at Jacksonville State University there were only ten Blacks on campus. We were the first to integrate the dorms. That in itself was an experience. I'll shall never forget my freshman year walking into the dorm, and you had no idea who was going to be your roommate. . . . I arrived first, and then all of a sudden . . . somebody knocked on the door. It was a White girl. She saw me, and she took off. She had her room changed because she was not going to stay in a room with a Black person. My first experience ever with prejudice.

Sherry remembered that the small contingent of ten Black students stuck together first and foremost "for protection." During her junior year, all of the Black students were joined by a few White students to form a racial reconciliation organization called "SARUE" sponsored by the Baptist Student Union. Although Sherry was more reticent about openly participating in campus civil rights activism, she noted that a fellow student, who would later become her husband, was quite "vocal."

"Dorene" was one among a few women who acknowledged being publicly involved in civil rights activism during young adulthood. Prior to embarking on a career in school food service management, she recalled her mother-in-law and a family friend encouraging her to participate in the Birmingham civil rights movement.

> My mother-in-law and I, and a man named Mister Willis were going to the [mass] meeting. . . . He would pick us up every Monday, and we would go down there. Then when we got to the place . . . they were skeeting [*sic*] the water down there [in

> Kelly Ingram Park] with the hose pipe. We were down there. But I ain't going to lie. I was scared, you know, I was scared. I backed [away]. . . . But when they went to Montgomery, my mother-in-law and Mister Willis, all of us went on the bus. They had a bus to go down to walk in [the] Montgomery [Bus Boycott].

Clandestine Support and Silent Protest during Professional Years

Black women born prior to and during the classical phase of the civil rights movement were least likely among all four groups (i.e., pre–civil rights and civil rights generation African American men and women and post–civil rights generation African American men and women) in my life story study to self-identify unreservedly as being activist, perhaps because of their limited involvement in conventional civil rights protests. For these women educators, the professional risks were much higher for their visible participation in formally organized civil rights activities (i.e., marching, boycotting, and attending meetings). Similar to their male counterparts, some of these same educators were active in or supportive of civil rights protests as college students; however, based on their interview responses, they did not deem it economically prudent to continue these activities once they were employed by their school districts. As was the case with the men, very few of these women reported participating in the civil rights movement beyond college. They were well aware of the damaging consequences of participating as a public school educator. "Gloria" recounted her mother's experience as an activist teacher in Wilcox County, Alabama, as both a proud and cautionary tale.

> My mother was fired because of her role. She was a teacher in Wilcox County, and the teachers and all the other professionals had been told not to participate or else they would lose their jobs. And several of them did. I think there were about seven or eight of them who did participate. And my mother did. . . . She attended mass meetings. She would take other people with her to the meetings so they would have a nice crowd. And she allowed the civil rights workers who . . . lived up North and came [down] South . . . to live in her home because [her adult children] were all gone then. . . . And they would get put in jail, and she would bond them out because she owned property. So she did lose her job, and she sued the

> Wilcox Board of Education, and it was held up, I believe, in the Mobile Circuit Court. . . . And the Alabama State Teachers Association came to her rescue and those of other teachers.

According to the *History of ASTA*, the organization defended the rights of ten Black teachers in Wilcox County who were fired allegedly because state funds were lost due to low average daily attendance in the 1964–65 school year.[14] However, these teachers did not have the least seniority and they also happened to have all been involved in civil rights and voter registration activities.[15] As a result of ASTA's advocacy, the state's Teacher Tenure Commission ruled that the Wilcox County BOE had usurped the teacher's rights, and therefore ordered that they be reinstated.[16]

"Hannah" was forthcoming about her fear of being involved publicly in civil rights protests, citing the professional repercussions encountered by other activist educators.

> I myself did not participate in any of the movement because I was afraid. . . . At that time, Ruby Jackson Gainer . . . was one of the first people that I know [who] openly protested for the movement. They fired her from her [teaching] job because she had participated in the movement. I was a Chicken Little. I wanted to be a part of it. My father was very diligent, dedicated, [and] devoted to the movement. . . . I knew everything that happened, but I was not there in person.

Although by her own admission, Hannah was afraid to participate publicly in civil rights protest, she acknowledged that she contributed to the movement by supporting her father's involvement, donating money privately to local churches that were involved, and on a few occasions, transporting civil rights activists who arrived to Birmingham from out of town. "Sandra," who was a young wife, mother, and elementary school teacher during the 1960s, also gave an economic rationale for her reticence about participating:

> I was not [involved in the civil rights movement]. No. I was not. I was a young working mother and really I was not. . . . You had a job. You knew you had to work. You could not go and get another job that was comparable to your teaching job. Even though we made nothing, but still, hey, we had a job. That was always a fear—of what would happen to you as a result of tak-

> ing part in things like that. And of course the principals were more conservative than we were. They were because they were elitists . . . they made more money than we made [Laughter].

Tyler, who grew up in Selma, Alabama, but moved to Birmingham as a young adult, described the behind-the-scenes support of the Black women teachers with whom he had grown up and worked side by side.

> What teachers did [is that] they worked behind the scenes. They went down to the church and they prepared food. [My teachers] would go down at night and make sandwiches for the marchers and . . . some of them perhaps took some of them into their homes to stay.

Unlike most of the older members in her cohort, who were teaching in Birmingham during the 1960s, Claretha participated in mass meetings after school hours. In fact, she recalled that as her students departed the classroom to protest, she would tell them, "I'll see you tonight." She recalled:

> [My students] knew I would see them that night because I went to all of the mass meetings. Once Doctor King came to town. I did not miss a mass meeting or anywhere I thought he was. Well, does that make you an activist? Yes, it does because even though you can't do nothin' but count one [person], if you're one in a million of thousands of people, you're there. You leave your job going there.

If the activism of these educators was judged solely by their participation in conventional civil rights activities, then these educators' contributions would be viewed dubiously. Only a slim majority reported varying degrees of conventional civil rights involvement, but even this involvement was often described as behind the scenes. For the most part, they were very tepid about engaging in public protest, particularly if they were on track to graduate from college or recently employed as a teacher, with the exception of a few outliers such as Jemison, Dorene, and Claretha. These descriptions of Black women's supportive role are consistent with Patricia Hill Collins's framework for understanding Black women's activism.[17] Many Black women, and a number of Black men, decided to contribute to the classical phase of the civil rights movement within the confines of "seemingly invisible spheres of social life and organization."[18] But a closer examination of the teaching and educational leadership practices employed by Black educators of this generation belies their reticent civil rights involvement.

Resistance and Adjustment to Brown Deferred

Brown was not often referenced explicitly in the life stories of these educators, no doubt, because school desegregation did not come to pass until nine years after this decision in Birmingham's civil rights watershed year of 1963. However, educators had vivid memories of *Brown*'s eventual impact on their job statuses, identities as Black teachers, and relationships with their students. Some educators resisted desegregation orders to transfer to all-White schools for as long as they could. Others acquiesced more readily but questioned the colorism and associated teacher competency assumptions that surfaced in the teacher transfer process.[19]

Jemison, who integrated a JeffCo school in the early 1970s, described his resistance to the very slow local implementation of *Brown* in Birmingham and Jefferson County.

> In seventy-three there were court orders integrating schools. And it seemed as if the White teachers they were transferring to the Black schools were not necessarily the best teachers. And they selected our best teachers to be sent to the White schools. My first transfer offer was to leave [the Black school] and go to [the White] junior high. I refused to go. I told my principal that I was not going because they were sending our better teachers to the White schools, and I wanted to stay at [the Black school]. So he undoubtedly took me off the list. I don't know what happened, but I didn't go.

Jemison eventually felt compelled to comply with a subsequent desegregation order when his supervisor conveyed in no uncertain terms that his only options were to transfer or lose his job. He later became the first Black principal of a junior high school in his school district.

"Abraham" recalled that he was not at all enthusiastic about receiving his desegregation orders, and like Jemison, he refused to transfer. He was especially perturbed about the fact that Black educators had no say-so in the transfers whereas White educators were permitted to shop around before committing to an all-Black school.

> I had no option. "You go. Here, come sign here; here's your contract." And Monday when school began, you report to [school]. [Whites] had an option. "Go out there and see if you like it."

Isaac remembered his dismay when he learned he would be transferred from the all-Black Western Olin to the formerly all-White West End High School. He reflected on how much he had invested in perfecting his teaching craft during the summer prior to the school year in order to teach Black students at his high school alma mater.

> I was going to different colleges and universities during the summer taking [teacher] institutes . . . and I was just really becoming profound in my [subject matter] area. That's why I was really hurt when I was transferred to West End [High School] during the integration process because I had prepared myself for *my* kids. I was a graduate of Western Olin myself, and so when I got the job to teach at my school. Oh! It was like hog heaven. . . . When they told me I was going to be transferred that really, really upset me.

"Jessie," a retired teacher from the JeffCo school system, reflected on the blatant colorism in teacher assignments circa the late 1960s, noting how she and other teachers were favored by it.

> Basically, at that time they were looking for the light-skinned teachers. And they were the first ones who were accosted. And then they said we want "light-plus-best" teachers; and that's how many of us ended up in the desegregation program.

Tyler also reflected on the colorism that appeared to dictate desegregation transfer assignments.

> I remember when they integrated the school system they took all the fair-skinned teachers and put them in the White schools. The interesting thing is that the Black teachers were better qualified than the White teachers because they had degrees. But the White teachers may have [only] gone three years or two years [to college].

Once Black teachers were reassigned to White schools, irrespective of skin tone favoritism, they confronted prejudiced assumptions about their professional competency. "Doris" recalled being demoted to teaching basic rather than advanced math classes at the formerly all-White school to which she was transferred in 1970.

> Upon receiving my teaching assignments initially—it's funny now, [but] I was assigned *basic* math classes. . . . Well, I enjoyed teaching basic math classes but I had [previously] taught Algebra I, Geometry, and Algebra II, and had six years teaching experience. But I was one of the teachers from [an all-Black high school]; and so I was assigned four basic math classes and one Algebra class.

Doris recounted that once her White principal observed the poor performance of her White counterpart, who had been assigned the advanced math classes, compared to her noteworthy instruction, he decided to reassign the White teacher's advanced math classes to her.

In retrospect, a few teachers lamented that Black educators did not do enough to fight for Black schools by joining ranks to refuse desegregation transfers. Jerrie reflected, "I don't know why we stood by and allowed our good teachers to be placed in all-White schools. . . . And you know we had the nerve to think we were special, [at least] some of us."

Abraham echoed this sentiment: "[Black teachers] were sent to Ramsay [High School], Phillips [High School] [and viewed it] like a promotion." But even with their reservations, many Black teachers who were transferred to formerly all-White schools eventually settled in and focused on teaching and supporting all of their students irrespective of race.

Student Advocacy in Segregated and Desegregated Schools

Another way these cohorts of Black educators contributed to the movement was to advocate for Black students, especially during the turbulent school desegregation period, which ensued in Birmingham between 1963 and 1983. A notable act of resistance, which was highlighted in the extant literature on Birmingham civil rights movement in chapter 3, was their subtle encouragement of student involvement in and refusal to report student absences during The Children's Crusade/March, which could have cost them their jobs and eventually impacted their salaries due to a state mandate penalizing them for massive student absences.

"Yvette," who was an elementary school student during The Children's Crusade but was forbidden by her parents from marching, paid express homage to "Birmingham teachers who turned their backs and allowed the children to walk out of the classroom." She credited the brave children who marched in place of their parents, teachers, and school administrators, many of whom felt that they could not afford to risk their tenuous livelihood with the threat of being fired for their participation. But she also acknowledged that Birmingham teachers strove to provide their students with an intellectual understanding of their nascent civil rights involvement.

Wilma recalled that she was not involved in the Birmingham civil rights movement "directly" but that she "did more in [terms of] teaching students methods of thinking about the United States, making choices, making decisions, and allowing them the opportunity to respond and to raise questions and issues to fortify them to prepare for whatever stand they needed to take." Wilma explained that when the children left their classrooms in droves in 1963 to march, her and her colleagues' contribution to this protest was to protect them from suspension and expulsion. She recounted:

> When students reached the point of leaving the school to participate, fortunately we had a principal who stood with us [and agreed] that we would not mark the children absent so they would not be expelled. We simply did not see them. So sometimes there's a silent voice [of protest].

Isaac recalled admonishing a group of students, who remained in his classroom after their classmates departed to attend The Children's March, to join their peers.

> I was at Western [Olin] [and] there were about two or three kids who came, and when they got to class I told them . . . "Now, you don't need to be here. You don't have anything to lose but a lot to gain." I said, "I don't know why you're here [but] you need to go and join the other young people." So they slipped out, and they left.

As noted previously, Claretha was one of the most actively involved women in her cohort. She taught in an all-Black high school during the Children's March, and acknowledged that she was "one of those persons who did not make one effort to stop [students] from leaving out of the room." Claretha took great pride in the contributions her students made to the Birmingham civil rights movement, noting that they have not received due recognition for their sacrifices: "[People] don't look [enough] at the children who paid the price in jail. That's why they call it 'The Children's March.' They paid the price." Claretha reported that she chaperoned the children involved in the Children's March by being "on hand when the children were down in [Kelly Ingram] Park." Some teachers resisted the mandate to suspend and expel student marchers from school by simply turning their backs to the classroom and pretending not to see them leave. Once she became a part of an integrated teaching staff, Claretha believed it was important not to reveal too much information about Black students that could be used against them by her White colleagues.

> One thing I learned early on [about] White faculty: They never talked about their White students [in front of Black faculty]. So therefore, I could not go to them about the problems of Black students. I never discussed the Black student, regardless of how rebellious or how resentful he or she might have been. That was not my job to talk about the Black students.

Hannah, who admittedly was fearful about being involved publicly in the civil rights movement, mustered up the courage to challenge a White teacher for using the *Jeopardy* television game show to make exam questions when most of her students did not have access to a television. "Dorene," who broke the glass ceiling in school food service management in the early 1970s, believed it was her duty to bend the rules regarding serving size and add extra food to the plates of poor Black students. She was reprimanded by her White principal and co-workers for her decisions, but she continued her practices anyway.

Tyler, in his role as assistant principal of a previously all-White high school that was undergoing integration in the early to mid-1980s, instituted diversity training workshops. He also intervened in school club decisions, which were hotly contested racial sites in newly desegregated schools.

> The dance team [and] the cheerleaders [were] predominantly White. So we had to encourage the Black students to try out. The rumor sort of got back to me that they had to have long hair. I said, "Hair is not the qualification to be a cheerleader." . . . They had to pay so much money [to become a

> cheerleader], so I rallied some of the Black teachers [and said], "If this kid makes it, and she needs some money, will you all be able to help me sponsor this child?" So I got commitment from some of them to do that because you know it was an outrageous amount of money they had to pay.

Claretha also described a desegregated school context at Woodlawn High School in the late 1960s, where Black students had little to no opportunity to participate in school clubs and organizations.

> The school was ninety-nine percent White when I went in. White children had all of the [school club officer] positions and extracurricular activities . . . it was hard for the Black children to enter into the curricular activities. Cheerleaders had to make it as best they could. Choir members, hand-picked. . . . White children were student council members and you would have thought they were faculty members, they had so much authority.

In an effort to change the decidedly White-privileged culture that prevailed in the Birmingham area during school integration, Jemison used his position as a principal in a racially transitioning JeffCo school to advocate for Black students.

> I made sure that my Black students were participants in everything. I had an unwritten code that was not legal: there will be no all-White cheerleaders. There will be no all-White dancers. There will be no all-White bands. And what I would do—and it was just fair, and I explained [it] to the staff—if we had . . . twenty cheerleaders (okay, everybody would try out, I mean we would have tryouts and judges), and then the sponsor would bring the list to my office. I said, "How many cheerleaders are we going to have?" And she said, "Twenty." I said, "There will be fourteen Whites and there will be six Blacks." I said, "Give me your list. . . . Give me your top ten Blacks and your top twenty Whites." And she handed me the list. I drew a line at fourteen for Whites, and I said, "One, two, three, four, five, six. Put them on this page, go out there, and announce the cheerleaders!" That was the only way that those little [Black] girls could ever be cheerleaders . . . by me penciling in equality.

As a career technology teacher, "Morgan" used his position to help Black students gain entry into the auto mechanic business in Birmingham. Consequently, some of the first Black-owned automotive shop owners hailed from his classroom. He took pride in helping White and Black students, but he emphasized his important affirmative action role for Black students in particular.

> My mission was to make the kids better than they were. . . . I wanted to make all kids better, but the Blacks were really the ones I was aiming at because when I started in auto body [mechanics], there weren't hardly [any] Blacks.

Black teachers believed it was incumbent upon them to advocate for their students in both segregated and desegregated contexts. In segregated contexts, several of them subversively encouraged their students to defy school rules to fight for their rights whereas in desegregated contexts they worked behind the scenes to ensure that they could take full advantage of the rights and privileges afforded by their new interracial contexts.

Liberatory Education and Pedagogy

Another common contribution to the Birmingham civil rights movement was the promotion of liberatory education and pedagogy.[20] Black educators in this study cited their teaching and leadership practices as activist contributions in their own right. They believed it was important for their students to understand the rationale behind civil rights protests, particularly their own budding involvement in the movement.

Teaching for Liberation

When asked what it meant to be an activist teacher, Jerrie recalled her efforts to educate her students about segregationist laws, with the goal of inspiring them to do their part in contributing to the civil rights movement.

> [I] let the students know that there are many laws on the books that denigrate people. . . . [I] showed the difference between de facto segregation, [de jure] segregation, and integration. And once we worked through the terminology . . . then the kids got a chance to really see . . . that the laws we have on

> our books are . . . unjust laws; and they're called Jim Crow-ism. We also had to talk from the activist standpoint and let the kids know that you need to be involved. . . . You do not accept what you . . . know to be an injustice. You speak up; but do it in such a manner that people will respect you. You don't have to get loud and boisterous. . . . The result is that they could react to the movement in a manner that was conducive for change. And they became change agents as a result of that.

Jacob described his experiences as an elementary teacher in an integrated BPS school in the late 1960s. He believed it was important to convey his commitment to the struggle for Black liberation not only through his pedagogy but also by his demeanor and attire. He recalled encountering some unspoken disapproval from White school district administrators, but he was not intimidated or deterred.

> My whole bulletin board had the [Black heritage] pictures . . . and some of the people from Central Office, they did not say anything but they came down and kind of looked me up and down. You know, I had the big afro, I had the bulletin board, and I was constantly telling the class about equality for all.

Jerrie's and Jacob's perspectives on the role they both played as educators in Birmingham's civil rights movement capture the sentiment of many of their cohort members. They believed that it was imperative to help their students understand why they were marching in the streets and going to jail, and their obligation to continue to struggle for freedom beyond the 1960s.

Debunking the Myth of Black Inferiority

In the wake of desegregation, educators in the pre–civil rights movement and civil rights movement cohorts often found themselves defending the intellectual capacity of Black students and faculty alike. These educators confronted the internalized "badge of inferiority," which undermined the self-esteem and self-worth of Black students.[21] For example, as she recounted her experiences in her desegregated county school in the late 1960s and early 1970s, Jerrie noted that she launched her school's first Black History Program. But to her dismay, the Black students were reluctant to participate.

> I incorporated Black history along with everything I taught. . . . So when I would teach the Black faces of history . . . I noticed that the few Blacks we had . . . would take their head and [shake it in disagreement] or they would put them on the desk. The first time I showed a filmstrip of Booker T. Washington and Tuskegee Institute, [the Black students] didn't want any parts of it. But it was the White kids who [raised their hands and inquired], "Where is the school?!" So many things that were introduced to [White children] . . . about Black culture, they eagerly learned—more than our kids wanted to know.

Jerrie lamented that even her grandson was not interested in learning about Black History when he was in high school. Now a college-educated young adult, her grandson has thanked her for exposing him to Black History because he learned that his White college peers knew more about it than he would have without her insistence.

As a Social Studies teacher, Claretha used the classroom to challenge her students' preconceived notions about the contributions of Africans to the advancement of world civilization. She recalled a history lesson where she set the record straight about the geographical positioning of Egypt in relation to the African continent.

> [I taught that] the first form of writing took place in Egypt. They gave us our first form of writing. And Egypt is in Africa. [My students' response was] "Huh?" [I reiterated]: Egypt is in Africa and Black folks came from Africa. . . . You can't take Egypt out of Africa and send it over there. Where you gon' send it?!

Black educators in desegregated schools were often confronted with racist assumptions about Black students' intellectual capacity. Isaac recalled attending a faculty meeting at West End High School in the late 1960s where a White principal, who was fearful about the pending transfer of new Black students, announced to the faculty, "We need to see how we can lower the grading system so that the Black kids will be able to make the honor roll." After composing himself, Isaac countered with, "Wait a minute. I don't think you need to change your system . . . just because some people are putting Black kids down. If you go into the Black schools, Black kids can learn just as well as White kids." Isaac noted that other Black teachers began to speak up after he took a stand.

Similar to Isaac, Wilma recalled fighting a contentious battle against the presumption of Black intellectual inferiority insinuated by her White colleagues in a newly desegregated school circa 1969. She was delegated to attend a meeting where the newly integrated staff discussed school policy, curriculum, and climate issues. When the question of maintaining academic standards arose, which she viewed as thinly veiled condescension about the intellectual capabilities of Black students and faculty, Wilma recalled her righteous indignation:

> During the session, I suppose I can say that I swallowed all I could at that point . . . after teacher after teacher after teacher—[all of them] White—stood up and expressed their concerns about possibly having to lower their standards . . . I just rose deliberately to my feet . . . because I wanted to know what made them think that they would have to lower their standards? Possibly, they'd have to raise them!

Years after her stance at the desegregated faculty meeting, Wilma found herself embroiled in another battle related to academic standards within her national professional organization. She and other Black teachers joined ranks to insist that Zora Neale Hurston's novel, *Their Eyes Were Watching God*, become a part of the national high school English canon. She recalled,

> That's the novel we chose and people raised issues about that [saying] we can't teach that because . . . [and I interrupted] "Well, why can't you teach it?! I guess the relationship between Teacake and Janie. I could not find objections for it. But maybe just because it was Zora Neale Hurston or it was a novel with Black characters.

But not all of Wilma's contemporaries felt comfortable challenging this myth through their pedagogy. For example, "Sheila" was a Social Studies teacher in a desegregated rural JeffCo school during the civil rights era, where she was one of the first Black teachers in a community with a strong Ku Klux Klan presence. I inquired about whether she taught Black history, to which she replied, "Oh! We didn't dare! You've got to understand the times and the places. You didn't dare!" But shortly after making this assertion, she recalled challenging a White colleague about her idyllic portrayal of slavery during a classroom lecture.

> This [Social Studies] teacher told them that slaves had a good life, that they had roofs over their head, they had clothes on their backs and food to eat. And when it got back to me . . . I had to confront her. . . . So I spoke my mind—Klan or no Klan!

Preparing White Students for a New Racial Order

Black educators often found themselves challenging the deeply ingrained racism that their White students brought to the classroom. They viewed it as their duty to prepare White students to participate in a racially integrated school and society. For example, as Yvette settled into her new role as a Black teacher in a desegregated school, she began to see her purpose in helping White students adjust to a new racial world order. Many of her students self-identified as having family members who were Klansmen. In response, Yvette used a history lesson to convey to her young White students the disparagement of the Ku Klux Klan.

> I'll never forget a little part in the Alabama History book on the KKK. Some of the babies would raise their hands and tell me their Dad used to be one, and we would . . . talk about it a little and say, "You know, well, we don't want to do that anymore."

Some Black educators established close ties with their White students and adopted a colorblind approach to teaching. Yvette recalled,

> When I came back home in seventy-one from Tuskegee and integration being fairly fresh, well, the majority of my kids were and would be White. But you know what? I tell people I don't care if they were powder blue. I just wanted to teach.

Similarly, Jemison developed a bond with White students whom he felt needed an extra dose of care from their administrators. He recalled,

> I had White kids that needed to believe in themselves. . . . Right now I have White "sons" that I "adopted" through school. . . . My thinking was . . . the color of your skin does not dictate what's within your mind, your head, and your soul.

Similar to the extant archival and oral history data, these life stories revealed that Black educators' contributions to the Birmingham civil rights movement entailed: participating in mass meetings and public protests; providing financial support through civil rights organizations; defying school policy by refusing to deter their students from participating, and thereby protecting them from suspension and expulsion; employing pedagogical strategies to prepare students both emotionally and intellectually for their own civil rights involvement; and advocating for Black students in both segregated and desegregated schools. An extension of their contributions entailed preparing White students to participate in a newly integrated society.

This is the largely untold story of Black educators' contributions to the Birmingham civil rights movement. Their contributions should be considered in light of their generally accommodationist or muted portrayal in civil rights history. The conceptualizations of activism articulated by the educators in the pre–civil rights movement and civil rights movement cohorts were flexible and broad enough to encompass those subtle and clandestine acts of pedagogical resistance that occurred behind schoolhouse doors. Although these educators revered the civil disobedience practiced by their contemporaries and predecessors, they offered new ways of thinking about activism that validated their daily practices as educators. A few of these educators combined their activist educational practices with traditional forms of civil rights activism (e.g., Jemison's sit-ins and Claretha's mass meetings), but the majority forfeited participation in public protests to protect their family's economic livelihood and guard their lifelong dreams to become college graduates and educators.

ENCOUNTERING A NEW GENERATION OF STUDENTS

Black educators who began their teaching careers before and during the classical phase of the Birmingham civil rights movement encountered successively younger generations of students during their professional tenure. These educators noted some concerns about their relationships with students and their relatively young parents, who were born after the height of the movement. Their concerns foreshadowed some of the challenges encountered by a new generation of post-civil-rights-born educators, who would have still been in school or college during the latter part of their older counterparts' careers.

Some veteran Black educators began to notice a change in Birmingham's student and community demographics in the 1990s. During the time of our interview, a few of them were mentoring and tutoring students during postretirement, so they had fresh contact with the post-hip-hop generation. They expressed some concerns about their students' low academic achievement and materialistic priorities, particularly what they deemed to be the negative influence of hip-hop culture in urban students' lives. Critical references to cultural styles and idiosyncrasies attributed to the hip-hop generation were notable in the life stories of educators born prior to and during the classical phase of the Birmingham civil rights movement, who witnessed the resegregation of their schools during the course of their careers.

Yvette captured the sentiments of many of her cohort members as she described the changes she began to see near her retirement. She described how the intersection of generational and social class differences distinguished her early versus latter experiences with her urban students and their families.

> At first it seemed like it was an integration thing when I first started thirty-one years [ago] but on down the line it got to be a socioeconomic type thing. I noticed a difference. It was like day and night. Instead of children learning how to get along with each other it was children learning how to survive. Their grandmothers are raising them. Their young parents are trying to raise them. They're used to parents in a skull cap and [fathers wearing] earrings and sagging pants and tattoos and [mothers wearing] miniskirts. This is what these children recognize as mom and dad now—poor, young, and impatient. And if they don't have that, it's grandma because mom and dad are not capable of taking care of them so the children have a hard way to go now.

Isaac was especially troubled by the status of today's African American youth in Birmingham.

> I think Doctor [Martin Luther] King would really be in tears to see how some of us have been affected by [integration]. . . . Things have become kind of easy for us. . . . The youngsters . . . feel that everything is going to be easy, folks going to give you something and that's a false concept. . . . My Daddy would say, "Son, you got to work hard, it will pay off for you later on." You don't hardly hear that in the younger generations now. It is [instead] try to find the easy [way] and shortcut, and you can make it.[22]

"Dorene," who retired after breaking ground as the first Black lunchroom manager in her school district in the early 1970s, placed blame squarely on the Black community, particularly parents, for what she viewed as a cultural regression among the hip-hop generation.[23]

> White folks don't be buying those high price tennis [shoes] for them. We buying the high price [tennis shoes] . . . we letting them wear their pants down here, and when they walk . . . they messing up their leg walking that way. They can't walk so good they showing they [under]shorts and things like that.

Drawing her young niece's attention to a clairvoyant yet sobering historical parallel between hip-hop culture and slavery, Dorene expressed dismay about what she viewed as a generation's misguided attempt to set cultural trends.

> Back [during slavery] they was putting tattoos on all them folks 'cause they [wanted to] know who their animal was and who the Black folks was . . . they was they property. I [told my niece]: "And ya'll think ya'll got something new."

Dorene's admonitions to her niece reveal her concerns about African Americans' failure in transmitting a knowledge and understanding of the historical experiences of slavery and oppression to younger African Americans. In her view, this failure has contributed to younger generations of African Americans unwittingly perpetuating symbolic practices of oppression under the guise of cultural trendsetting.

As older generations of Black educators retired in the 1980s, 1990s, and the early millennium, new generations of educators worked alongside them for a brief season and eventually replaced many of them. These "generation X/hip-hop generation" educators only have secondhand knowledge about the Birmingham civil rights movement and the experiences of their predecessors. Yet they encounter the daunting challenge of building bridges between the experiences of older and younger generations of African American educators along with their students and the students' relatively young parents.

5

INTERGENERATIONAL BRIDGE BUILDING

> I have a picture in my classroom. It says, "Courageous," and it has the people that were hosed down in the streets of Birmingham. I keep that up there for a reason. I was telling my husband, "You know what? It seems like I'm teaching in the nineteen sixties but it's two thousand seven. He said, "Why do you say that?" I said, "Because now it seems like we're worst off in terms of education than we were [back] then because we have so many young people that can't read."
>
> —Winifred, post–civil rights generation high school teacher

"Winifred" is a history teacher who was born in 1974. At the time of her interview she taught at a JeffCo high school undergoing a racial transition that tilted its student population toward being predominantly African American. Winifred is a self-proclaimed "activist" who made a point of utilizing her classroom and pedagogy to build bridges between her high school students and the civil rights generation. She expressed angst about her students' lack of knowledge about Birmingham's civil rights movement and their weak academic skills. Prior to her current school assignment, she taught at a predominantly White JeffCo high school in the late 1990s where students were permitted to display and sell Confederate flag memorabilia on the school grounds. At her previous school, she noted that many of her White students had never had an African American teacher or any encounter with African American professionals. Over the course of her relatively short career, she found it quite challenging to penetrate her White students' overt racism and her African American students' internalized racism. Similar to many of her predecessors in the pre- and post–civil rights generation, Winifred's perspectives on the future of younger generations of African American students and their relatively young parents vacillated between the polarities of hope and despair. Her experiences growing up and working in racially transitory neighborhoods and schools, coupled with her tentativeness about the future of African American youth, are characteristic of the post–civil rights movement cohort.

THE POST–CIVIL RIGHTS MOVEMENT COHORT

The post–civil rights movement cohort is distinctive from the pre–civil rights and civil rights movement cohorts in several respects, beginning most notably with their memories of significant historical events in the 1980s and 1990s. Their memories are marked by a few passing references to national and local political events such as the presidency of William Jefferson "Bill" Clinton (1992–2000), the end of the Cold War (1991), and the election and tenure of Birmingham's first African American mayor, Richard Arrington Jr. (1979–1999). More often, however, they expounded on events that were immediate to their daily lives, for example, the emergence of hip-hop culture, racial transitions in their schools and neighborhoods, the rise of the crack cocaine epidemic and gang violence, and the escalation of African American male homicides. Memories of Jim Crow are notably sparse or absent in their narratives as most members of this cohort were born several years after this era. However, a litany of new inter- and intraracial concerns was on the horizons as this cohort came of age in Birmingham.

New Problems for a New Generation

Given their generational location, very few educators born around or after the classical phase of the Birmingham civil rights movement experienced the full brunt of Jim Crow, although a few early-born cohort members experienced the vestiges of Jim Crow vicariously through the lived experiences of their parents and older siblings. These educators, who were typically the youngest of multiple siblings, were largely shielded from the harsh realities of Jim Crow, due partly to their age but also to their families' attempts to shield them from painful memories. For example, "Murphy," a suburban high school administrator who was born in 1966, could only recollect racial strife through the experiences of his older brother and sister.

> Growing up I saw some things with my brother. . . . He was the oldest in the family . . . [and] several years older than me. . . . I think he faced more racial issues than I did because I can

Table 5.1. Post-Civil Rights Movement Cohort Demographics

Pseudonyms	*Birth Year*	*Professional Role*	*School Setting*
Murphy	1966	Assistant Principal	Suburban Public
Jonathan	1967	Assistant Principal	Urban Public
Debbie	1968	Assistant Principal	Suburban Public
Tisha	1969	Teacher	Suburban Public
Wilona	1971	Teacher	Urban Public
Crawford	1973	Teacher	Urban Public
Justin	1973	Assistant Principal	Suburban Public
Mitchell	1974	College Professor	Urban Public
Tammy	1974	Teacher	Urban Public
Tiffany	1974	Teacher	Urban Public
Winifred	1974	Teacher	County Public
Lorenzo	1976	College Professor	Urban Public
Courtney	1977	Community Educator	Urban Nonprofit Org.
Brandon	1978	Teacher	Urban Public
Nichelle	1978	Teacher	Urban Public
Alisha	1979	Teacher	Urban Public
April	1980	Teacher	Urban Public
Rick	1981	Teacher	Urban Public
Sybil	1981	Community Educator	Urban Nonprofit Org.
Marshall	1983	Community Educator	Urban Nonprofit Org.

> remember vividly him getting into a fight. . . . I don't remember the fight [but] my mother was telling me about it. . . . He beat up this White boy who called him a nigger. . . . So I assumed he faced more racial issues . . . than I did growing up. And so did my sister. She faced similar things. She was several years older than I am.

"Debbie," a suburban elementary school administrator, who was born in 1968, recalled an incident where her mother chastised her for attempting to board a Birmingham transit bus through the back door in the early 1970s.

> I remember one day the bus pulled up, and I wanted to hop on [at] the back [door] and [my mother] almost snatched a knot in me. She said, "No ma'am, we always enter the front." I

> was a little girl [so] I didn't know the story at that time. As I grew older she explained to me why she told me those things: [that] she couldn't go through that door . . . and how many people fought so that we could go to the front [door] so we could sit at the front of the bus. . . . It became painfully clear to me that my mother had gone through a lot because I was the last of five [children], so you know they tried to protect me from all of those things.

Although memories of Birmingham's notorious interracial violence were not prominent in the narratives of the post–civil rights movement cohort, a disconcerting escalation of intraracial violence (i.e., "Black-on-Black crime"), exacerbated by a growing crack cocaine epidemic in the late 1980s and early 1990s, is notable in several of the narratives, especially among male educators. For example, Murphy recalled an intensification of school violence in urban schools, particularly as he reflected on his early career as a high school administrator in the 1990s.

> What I remember most . . . is a lot of violence in schools going on during this time. . . . There wasn't any major thing happening yet but there was violence starting to happen throughout the inner-city schools. That's one thing I noticed. I would see it on television. . . . I didn't see anything that was addressing those issues. . . . There was a lot of gang activity and it started spreading over into the schools.

In contrast to the pre–civil rights and civil rights movement cohorts, the post–civil rights movement cohort spoke very little about personal encounters with overt racism. Their concerns focused more on problems and challenges internal to African American neighborhoods and schools. Their unique positioning as generation X/hip-hop generation educators set the stage for framing and seeking new solutions for addressing unprecedented post–civil rights dilemmas.

Family and Community Transition

In the midst of rapid and dynamic societal changes, the African American family and community were strong anchors for post–civil rights movement educators. Their parents and grandparents strived daily to keep them safe and buffer them from negative influences. Post–civil rights movement educators grew up in primarily tight-knit African American urban neighborhoods. Similar to some members of the pre–civil rights and civil rights movement cohorts, a few grew up in rural neighborhoods, which even as late as the 1970s and 1980s were encased in the yesteryear of Jim Crow society. During their early childhood and elementary school years, the participants recalled segregated neighborhoods and schools. However, as they progressed to middle and high school, some of their parents moved their families to adjacent municipalities in search of better public schools for their children. Consequently, many post–civil rights movement educators experienced racially transitory neighborhoods and schools during their early life trajectory.

Post–civil rights movement educators described their families as ranging from lower-to-middle-income to working-class and low-income. Slightly over one-quarter of the cohort described its family status as solidly middle-class whereas only one-tenth described the span of their childhood experiences as poor. The remaining members described their family status as working-class and lower-middle-class with increasing upward mobility between their late-elementary and high school matriculation.

The family structures of this cohort were notably different from those of older cohorts, who were typically raised in two-parent nuclear households; and if there was the loss of a parent among members of older cohorts, then it was usually due to early death rather than to divorce. In contrast, divorce was more prevalent among the parents of the post–civil rights movement cohort. Moreover, single-female-headed households were more common along with absentee biological fathers, actively involved stepfathers, and blended and intergenerational families. The single mothers of some post–civil rights movement educators moved back in with their elderly parents to manage childrearing, work, and school. Some cohort members were latchkey children, who assumed responsibility for letting themselves into their houses after school until their parent(s) arrived home from work.

"Lorenzo," who was a doctoral candidate and adjunct professor born in 1976, recalled his experiences growing up in a working-class community in western Birmingham in the late 1980s and early 1990s.

> I was coming up right at the end of the manufacturing age in the United States where households could be supported by the father working at a factory job. . . . I saw where that family did not want the same type of industrial life for their kids, and they impressed upon their kids the importance of

> an education. Or maybe the children saw the hardships that were involved in working in a factory. They saw the downsizing . . . and they thought of education as something that could release them from that type of lifestyle.

"Tammy," an urban elementary school teacher born in 1974, described childhood family and community experiences that were typical of cohort members who came from middle-class backgrounds. She grew up in one of Birmingham's historically Black neighborhoods, which, by the time she was born, had become well established by its middle-class professional residents.

> I grew up in the Smithfield area—College Hills. We were always in a quiet neighborhood. The neighborhood was filled with professionals: doctors and lawyers, educators, business owners, entrepreneurs. So I thought that's what the whole world was made of. . . . My parents were [there] . . . if I needed help with anything. . . . And my grandparents and my mother were always nurturing. And I came home to eating dinner at the table. And my grandmother would pick me up from school [accompanied by] my grandfather. And she would have dinner waiting. And my parents would pick me up. . . . They would check over my homework. . . . So I would say that—without bragging—I think we [were] better than the [Cosby Show's] Huxtables![1]

"Courtney," a nonprofit community educator born in 1977, is one of the few participants who described the span of his childhood experiences as working poor. But even in the midst of the harsh inner-city environment he described, he noted his parents' protective childrearing.

> I was born and raised in Birmingham, Alabama. I grew up in Fountain Heights. . . . And I always tell my students, "I grew up in the same 'hood y'all grew up in." You know, the same atmosphere. . . . And I tell them [about] the neighborhood I grew up in. . . . When we first moved out there in 1986 . . . I remember [there were] a lot of women walking down the street [with a] purse in the middle of the night. And over time it transferred into a drug zone. You know, a lot of drugs, a lot of violence . . . seeing the police kick in a couple of doors coming

> home from school, sometimes guys lined up on the sidewalk. And when I was little, people used to talk about us because we never came outside. And I was kind of mad because I didn't get to go outside. . . . But the main people that my parents were trying to keep us from were the main people we wanted to be around because they were cool; [or] so we thought.

Overall, post–civil rights movement educators described themselves as growing up in predominantly lower-middle and middle-class African American communities. However, a few, such as Courtney, described themselves as growing up in communities that had transitioned from working-class to poor in the 1980s and 1990s, particularly as African American families began to venture to previously segregated neighborhoods within or proximate to Birmingham's city limits. Although Courtney's neighborhood is an outlier among his cohort, he shares more in common socioeconomically with successive generations of students who entered BCS during the first decade of the new millennium. Ironically, compared to parents in the 1950s and 1960s, the parents of children in the 1980s and 1990s were not so much afraid about what could happen to their children outside of the confines of their segregated neighborhoods as they were about their children's safety within African American communities that were becoming increasingly plagued with drugs, vice, and crime.

From Segregation to Integration to Resegregation

Similar to their older counterparts, post–civil rights movement educators described their early childhood and elementary school experiences as being racially segregated. However, in contrast to the older cohorts, nearly two-thirds of the post–civil rights movement cohort attended integrated schools during their elementary and secondary educational trajectory. Many encountered White Americans for the first time during upper elementary, middle or junior high, and high school. As discussed in chapter 3, these integrated schooling opportunities were created by federally mandated integration plans enacted several decades after the 1954 *Brown* case. The Birmingham BOE's enactment of a racially balanced magnet school policy in 1980, which was designed to circumvent controversial across-town busing, had a significant impact on the educational trajectories of this cohort. For virtually all members of this cohort, school was the only racially integrated dimension of their lives. They generally described their integrated schooling experiences as being positive or "neutral" with respect to race relations. In some instances, they were pleasantly surprised to have White peers befriend them. But retrospectively, some of them expressed reservations about being isolated from their African American neighborhood schools and peers. Not only is this cohort unique compared to preceding generations, it is also unique compared to the post-hip-hop generation students whom they teach. Most students attending urban schools in today's Birmingham metropolitan area have classmates of the same race and live in both racially and economically segregated neighborhoods due to resegregation.[2]

Debbie recalled her decision not to attend the historically Black A. H. Parker High School to which she and her family had been zoned for years. Prior to attending an integrated magnet public high school, Debbie's direct encounters with White Americans were virtually nonexistent. Her decision to attend Ramsay High School in the 1980s signaled a critical turning point in her life, which no doubt, prepared her to be hired as one of the first African American administrators in her suburban school district in the early 2000s.

> I was supposed to go to Parker [High School]. It was family tradition. But something just said, "No don't do that." And I went to Ramsay. And that was my first experience of ever seeing people who were different from me. First time ever. You know I kind of saw those [White] people downtown but it was surreal. But here I am sitting in class with [White] people and talking to [White] people, you know becoming friends with [White] people.

Tiffany recalled attending a predominantly White high school in northern rural Jefferson County in the early 1990s. It was a school where White students proudly displayed Confederate flag insignia on their pickup trucks and attire. Referring to the school culture as exuding an "us versus them mentality," she recalled that African American students "retaliated" by wearing red, black, and green African medallions and "Malcolm, Martin, and Me" T-shirts. She noted that the African American students were forbidden by the administrator from wearing Afrocentric insignia to school whereas the White students who donned Confederate memorabilia were not mandated accordingly. Tiffany reflected:

> I guess my first touches of just realizing that racism existed in my immediate world were [in] junior high and high school. And it wasn't, you know, just any[thing] outlandish, but you

> just started being more cognizant of social differences that were made.

Tiffany also remembered encountering intraracial tension as it related to developing interracial friendships. She recalled her caution about getting too close to her White friends in order to avoid intraracial conflicts with her African American peers.

> In elementary [school] I had friends of different races but in high school . . . you were considered a sell-out if you hung too much [with White students]. You know it was okay to do it but [not] if you did it too much; and you wanted to fit in with the people that you live with, because when you go home . . . you want to play and you want to be invited to social things. So you started having to choose and . . . pick.

Tiffany's parents were uncomfortable with her desire to attend interracial activities at the homes of her White friends. She recalled that her parents forbid her to attend a slumber party at her White elementary school friend's house. Describing her parents as "liberal" and "not racist," Tiffany explained that her parents felt like a sleepover was crossing a taboo line with which they were uncomfortable given their experiences growing up in the Jim Crow South.

Lorenzo believed his integrated elementary school experiences at a "gifted magnet school" prepared him to succeed in an integrated society. But after being taunted by African American male peers who lived in and attended the predominantly African American neighborhood school, Lorenzo opted to attend his zoned neighborhood high school, which was predominantly African American and low-income. In his words, this school was "rough . . . an entirely different situation than [I] had been used to." But he believed it was good for him to be exposed to a school that was "run by African Americans." He recalled that the curriculum "was weak," but he supplemented it with "outside sources and outside activities." He went on to attend a HBCU, but he later transferred to a predominantly White but relatively racially diverse state public university in Alabama.

Tisha expressed similar concerns about feeling isolated from her African American neighborhood peers when she began attending a BCS magnet high school. Although she was satisfied with her academic preparation, she shared a critique about the negative impact that the magnet school policy had on African American peer relationships in the 1980s and 1990s.

> I felt like my academic experiences were good. Again, social life seemed a little disconnected because we were all pulled from different neighborhoods . . . so therefore, you tried to come back in your community and assimilate with other students who you didn't have a lot of connection with because you did not spend a lot of time with them. And then sometimes it seemed like the other kids resented children who went to Ramsay [High School]. You know, we got labeled, and they were false labels.

Similar to the class of 1980 graduates of integrated schools in Amy Stuart Wells's *Both Sides Now*, post–civil rights movement educators who attended an integrated school at some point in their trajectory viewed their experience as a mixed blessing.[3] Although they attested to receiving a quality academic experience, it came at the expense of being isolated from African American neighborhood peers and being viewed as elitist. This isolation did not foster the same sense of solidarity with their peers that characterized the experiences of pre–civil rights and civil rights movement educators who grew up during de jure segregation.

ACTIVISM OF THE POST–CIVIL RIGHTS MOVEMENT COHORT

From the perspectives of the hip-hop commentary and educational scholarship and Black Feminist Thought, it is critical to engage younger generations of African Americans in a dialogue about their views on activism rather than to impose on them global definitions of this concept. Toward this end, I sought post–civil rights movement educators' personal conceptions of activism. Similar to educators in the pre–civil rights and civil rights movement cohorts, younger educators described activism in broad and relative terms, yet they are distinctive in their assumption that a new activism is needed for a new generation of African Americans to confront relatively novel iterations of racism.

Conceptualizations of Activism

The post–civil rights movement cohort described activism as taking an action or a stand either for or against a cause. Similar to the pre–civil rights and civil rights movement cohorts, they associated activism with courage and boldness, often naming legendary figures such as Martin Luther King and Malcolm X as examples. For example, "Winifred" described activism as:

> Being radical, being able to stand up for what you believe in regardless of the consequences. Activism is like a revolutionary. . . . A true revolutionary is willing to stand up and do whatever it takes even if it means losing something dear to you. If it's something that you believe in, you're going to fight for what you believe in.

Lorenzo named familiar activist figures but extended traditional definitions of activism to encompass unresolved and emergent contemporary generational challenges in the post–civil rights era.

> I think that [W. E. B.] Du Bois was an activist. He's a different type of activist than Doctor King or Malcolm X or Marcus Garvey, all of whom I respect to a large degree. But . . . in the context of the new millennium, I think of activism as something that is *internal.* I think that before—especially during the civil rights movement . . . and the Jim Crow period [and] right after slavery—activism was an external practice where we . . . reacted against oppression that was given to us from the [White] mainstream. . . . But I think that now activism involves us internally, and what we do to help each other out as a community.

Lorenzo's articulation of activism as "internal" in many ways captures the essence of his cohort members' theorizing about contemporary problems confronting their students, families, and community members. The pressing issues confronting this generation were generally not articulated as interracial problems—although they acknowledged experiences with covert racism—but more so as intraracial, generational, or social class problems.

Self-Identification as "Activist"

The majority of post–civil rights movement cohort members were unequivocal about their self-identification as activist. Notably, more of them readily identified themselves as activist compared to members of the pre–civil rights and civil rights movement cohorts. For example, men in the post–civil rights movement cohort were most likely to self-identify as being activist, followed by women in the post–civil rights movement cohort, men in the pre–civil rights and civil rights movement cohorts, and finally, women in the pre–civil rights and civil rights movement cohorts. The activist identity of post–civil rights cohort members was expressed almost exclusively in unconventional ways, particularly through cultural expressions such as attire, physical demeanor, and artifacts displayed in their homes and classrooms. For example, Winifred made a point of wearing her hair natural, displaying African American heritage-themed artwork in her home, and raising her sons to be proud of their heritage.

> My house is decorated with African sculptures and books and everything. So [family members] tease me about my boys: "You're going to have little militant boys." And I was like, "Well, no, I want them to be confident . . . in who they are and their identity, even with the books they read. . . . You know, I always felt like if you're going to buy me a book, make sure they're African American children's books.

"Mitchell" believes he embodies activism by his "mere presence" as a professional African American man on a predominantly White university campus where others may not expect him to carry himself in this way.

> Every day I walk down the hall, and by my mere presence, [I see it] as activism. . . . So I work out in the gym across the street. . . . And I had my suit on . . . I'm sure no one [typically] walks to the gym with a suit on and just goes on out the door. . . . So that's an episode of activism because I think White people don't see Black people in suits. And . . . when they do see Black people in suits they have a certain idea about what Black people ought to be doing in the suits. So I . . . feel I have to show that we do other things other than what you think. You know, every Black man who has a tie [on] is not a preacher. . . . And when I wear a shirt and tie or a suit, I'm not here to preach unless you call what I teach preaching.

There were a few post–civil rights movement educators who were ambivalent about self-identifying as activists, among whom were included three women and two men. The three women, who worked in urban educational settings, acknowledged that although they would like to be viewed as activist, they believe they fall short of this revered identification given their relatively young age and limited life experiences. Notably, both of the "nonactivist" men hail from the small cadre of suburban educators represented in this study.

Wilona was reluctant to self-identify as an activist but noted that her tireless efforts to garner resources for her urban school might be categorized as a form of activism. In the tradition of Black teachers who worked in segregated schools during the Jim Crow era, Wilona was always on a quest to pool together resources for her students.

> I guess in some aspects as far as [obtaining] resources for my students . . . making sure they have everything they need to pass the test so therefore, they can go on and graduate. In that aspect I guess I am an activist because I go . . . over and beyond to find the resources.

"Sybil," a nonprofit community educator, was reluctant to self-identify as activist because she did not feel that she had paid enough dues, especially in light of the sacrifices of the local foot soldiers with whom she partnered to expose students to Birmingham's civil rights movement history. She reflected:

> I would like to see [myself as an activist]. I wish I was. I don't think I'm there yet. [Laugh]. I don't think I'm there yet. I think this is the youth piece. I'm twenty-five. So I'm not comfortable yet with that title. But I want to be.

"Alisha," a doctoral candidate and urban public university researcher, stated that she has "always tried to do [her] own little thing, make my own little contributions." But she stopped short of referring to herself as an activist due to her distinction between the terms *activism* and *volunteerism*. "I still don't see [my contribution] as [being] activist. I see it as volunteering and doing it because I want to do it."

She added: "I see activists as grand leaders who have visibility whereas I just try to do my little contribution and call it a day." The examples of activists she shared included Reverend Jesse Jackson Sr., Reverend Al Sharpton, and recent presidents of the NAACP. She eventually conceded that she considers herself to be "an activist for women when it comes to [being] pro-choice [on abortion issues]." Alisha's distinction between activism and volunteerism is similar to comparisons made by public intellectual and hip-hop commentator Michael Eric Dyson, who cautioned against blurring the lines between charitable acts and social service projects versus social activism that addresses systemic inequities in U.S. and global society. Dyson argued that younger generations of high-profile African American athletes fall prey to lending their personal name brand and clout to corporate charitable efforts without critically examining how these corporations reinforce societal inequities through their policies and practices.[4]

The two male suburban administrators, Justin and Murphy, were the least comfortable with identifying themselves as activists. Throughout his narrative, Justin grappled with his decision to teach in a predominantly White middle-class suburban school when his family and peers tried to dissuade him. Their view of an educator "giving back" was to work in an African American urban school. But Justin reconciled his decision by considering that he is a role model to the small but emerging number of students of color in his school, some of whom transferred from nearby BCS and JeffCo districts. He also felt his presence was important for White students and families that had very little direct contact with African American professionals. Justin reflected:

> I never really thought about seeing myself any kind of way because I . . . don't like to focus on me so much. That's just not me. But I guess I could be [an activist educator], and it's simply because of the path that I chose to take. And again I'll allude to the "road less traveled" that describes the route that I have taken in my life.

Murphy's narrative conveys little evidence that he has confronted overt racism in his personal or professional life. I wrote previously about his secondhand accounts of the racism his older siblings experienced in his segregated rural hometown. Even as the only African American administrator at his suburban school, he said he did not encounter what he considered to be overt racism. He did, however, allude to feeling that his disciplinary decisions were scrutinized more closely than those of his White colleagues. Sometimes African American students accused him of being easier on White students and, conversely, White students sometimes charged that he showed favoritism to African American students. Murphy's resolution to these disparate perceptions was to present himself as a neutral, even "colorblind" administrator who serves as a positive role model to all of his students. In response to my question about whether he would describe himself as being an activist educator, Murphy stated:

> I don't think so . . . I just try to do my job as best I can. I want to try and impact people. I realize my role now. I'm looked upon as a leader and as someone to admire by some of these young people. . . . So I try to be the best role model I possibly can for them.

Overall, post–civil rights movement educators self-identified as being activist although a few were not comfortable comparing themselves to traditional Birmingham civil rights foot soldiers. Those who identified themselves unequivocally as being activists described consistently throughout their narratives their efforts to effect change professionally, communally, and, in one instance, on the home front.

Family Socialization and Activism

Post–civil rights movement educators often learned about Birmingham's role in the movement through their families. Many recalled stories their parents and grandparents shared as they were growing up. These stories shaped their perspectives on activism and their role as educators. For example, "Nichelle" recalled the influence of her grandmother on her activist socialization.

> My grandmother was at Alabama State [University] during the civil rights era. . . . She actually would babysit for a couple of Doctor [Martin Luther] King's kids. . . . So when we were growing up, she'd always throw in these references [about] how things were when she was at Alabama State.

Nichelle's grandmother, who was also a teacher, not only influenced her personal decision to become a teacher but also her pedagogy.

> My grandmother was a teacher. And she would always talk about [how] she did Black history throughout the year. And even though she never pushed me to teach, some kind of way I got that.

Brandon used his mother's experiences in the civil rights movement as a reference point for examining his generation's progress in realizing King's dream.

> My mom . . . was arrested [during the civil rights movement] at the age of six for standing with her mom, my grandmother. . . . I guess just like a mother compares her generation to our generation . . . I do it with her [generation] as well. There's going to be massive differences but there are massive similarities as well. The difference, I guess, would be, of course, [what] they went through. She was going through the actual struggle of trying to get things changed. My generation, we're supposedly in that change. We're supposed to be, I guess, keeping that change ongoing. But it doesn't seem like we're doing it. It seems like we're still in Doctor Martin Luther King's dream. It's like his dream [but] nobody woke up yet.[5]

Not everyone was exposed to the civil rights movement through their family. Winifred, who unreservedly self-identified as being activist, acknowledged that she learned very little about Birmingham's civil rights movement from her middle-class family members.

> It was funny [that] in my household I never was really exposed to a lot of civil rights. Like we knew Martin Luther King, but it was never an issue. . . . I didn't grow up in an "activism-type" household where people were radical or something like that. It was kind of take whatever they give you and just don't go against the grain.

Generativity

Closely related to post–civil rights movement educators' activist identity is their *generative* identity. Even though a few were reluctant to identify as activist, all of them showed evidence of being generative. According to psychology scholar Dan McAdams, "generativity is an adult's concern for and commitment to promoting the development and well-being of future generations."[6] Generativity is exuded time and time again in historical footage of the classical phase of the civil rights movement, where participants disclose their motivation for fighting for equal rights. A sentiment commonly expressed is the sense that: I am not fighting for myself but for my children and my children's children. Courtney captured this sentiment succinctly in his articulation of his professional mission: "My work is basically impacting people's future." Generativity is also closely associated with spiritual values and principles for young adults.[7] For example, Lorenzo viewed the classroom as a place to impact lives, which, in turn, was his way of heeding a religious calling.

> I always wanted to have a positive impact on individuals, and one of the best ways to do that is to have them in the classroom where I can share knowledge with them. I've always believed that knowledge was one of the keys to progress and growth. So if I'm able to confer knowledge to individuals, then I feel as if I have in some way fulfilled my Godly purpose.

"Marshall's" narrative was consistently characterized by generative motives. However, he grappled with the authenticity of his activist pursuits. As a college student, he was responsible for reviving a local chapter of a national civil rights organization. He also worked as a community educator, exposing Birmingham's youth to African American heritage and civil rights issues. He reflected on unassuming legendary activists compared to famous contemporary activists, and considered where he is situated within this activist trajectory.

> Malcolm [X], Stokely [Carmichael], all of them took the front lines seriously. [They] took their leadership roles seriously. They weren't in it for the fame. I don't think any of them realized how famous they had become . . . [until] years after death. Whereas I think the Tavises [Smiley], the Cornell West's, Doctor [Michael] Dyson, even Bill Cosby. They have fame. I think they recognize and realize their fame even though it's an "activist kind of fame." So that's what troubles me too because I . . . think about the things that I want to do . . . and I question myself: "Well, am I doing this for the people or am I doing this for myself?"

Marshall's critical self-examination of both his and contemporary activists' motives for publicly representing African American issues and platforms brings to mind scholar Houston A. Baker's scathing critique of African American leaders in the post–civil rights era, which includes some of the activists whom Marshall identified above.[8] Baker proposed that self-proclaimed activist public intellectuals (and neoconservatives) are hijacking the ideals of Martin Luther King for personal acclaim and gain.[9] According to Baker, these activists use the twenty-four-hour cable news circuit to keep their faces and viewpoints in the public's consciousness but their real motives are self- versus communally promoting. Baker's critique helps to contextualize Marshall's caution about following in the footsteps of his activist heroes.[10]

Liberatory Education and Pedagogy

Similar to their older counterparts, post–civil rights movement educators viewed their professional practice—whether it be teaching, leading, counseling, developing educational programs, or fostering partnerships—as constituting activist practice in its own right. As discussed in chapter 1, African American educators have produced a robust tradition of Black intellectual thought, which undergirded their fight for justice and equality. The contributions of intellectual elites have been crucial to the success of national and global revolutions, notably those of nineteenth- and early-twentieth-century African American intellectuals and educators such as Alexander Crummell, Anna Julia Cooper, Booker T. Washington, W. E. B. Du Bois, Carter G. Woodson, Mary McLeod Bethune, and Charles S. Johnson.[11] In a similar vein, Lorenzo philosophized about how intellectual elites have played an integral role in mobilizing national and global social movements.

> I always tell my students that every revolution started with intellectuals. I mean, the peasants, they fought; but the intellectuals, they produced . . . the foundation, the ideology, for why we should even be fighting. . . . [T]he intellectuals play an important part on the front end. And then during the actual revolution they justify why the revolution is going on. And then afterward, they still have a part.

Along this same line of thought, Jonathan made a direct link between Birmingham educators as essential "scholars" of the civil rights movement: "The role of educators in the movement [was] to be the primary scholars in the lives of students, helping them to realize they [could] soar, and they [could] ride with the stars."

Winifred also made connections between education and social change, stating that "education is a revolution within itself. . . . We don't realize it, but teachers . . . can be true revolutionaries and true activists if we realize our calling." Reflecting on the contributions of educators during the classical phase of the Birmingham civil rights movement, Winifred concluded:

> I've done a lot of research and talked to a lot of educators who taught during segregation and integration. They give me so much power. And I feel like as teachers, they played a very visible role. They were the intellectuals. They were the voice. They were the ones encouraging the students to go out there, even though they could not go because they had families, and they had different things on the line.

Post–civil rights movement educators enacted liberatory education and pedagogy through their role as "intergenerational bridge builders," and by choosing to teach either in urban or suburban schools to serve as role models to younger generations.[12]

Intergenerational Bridge Builders

The challenge for post–civil rights movement educators is to bridge the liberatory educational tradition of their predecessors to their current pedagogical and leadership context. Toward this end, post–civil rights movement educators position themselves as "intergenerational bridge builders" between educators born prior to and during the civil rights movement and their post-hip-hop generation students.[13] They grappled with finding ways to bridge a legacy of activism to which they did not contribute but are the beneficiaries of, while perpetuating this legacy in a new and relevant way. This generation is caught between the proverbial rock and a hard place of encountering critiques from older generations about not having yet paid its dues, and confronting the sometimes wayward, cavalier, and self- and communally destructive behaviors and attitudes of their younger post-hip-hop-generation K–12 students and community members. In light of this context, these educators pushed the envelope of redefining activism even further than the pre–civil rights movement and civil rights movement cohorts, noting that contemporary challenges confronting the African American community must be addressed and rectified in new ways.

In an effort to help her students appreciate their educational opportunities, Wilona often focused her history lessons on the African American struggle for liberation.

> [I tell my students] we were taken from our homeland and brought here . . . forced into slavery and subjected to all types of abuse through Jim Crow. . . . Even though I didn't live during that time period I always try to instill [this lesson] in my students: "You just don't understand how far we have come as a race." . . . I even invite older teachers who lived during that time to come in and talk to my students.

As mentioned previously, Sybil's role as a nonprofit educator involved establishing partnerships between her organization and schools and individuals across the city, state, country, and even the globe, to expose them to the city's and region's civil rights movement history. She worked closely with local activists, inviting them to speak to local, national, and global audiences of students and educators about their experiences. Sybil viewed her mission as being uniquely oriented to the younger generation.

> You have to start young with [teaching civil rights movement history]. . . . [This teaching] is still required because the problem won't go away until you face it. . . . I think that the things that happened [in Birmingham occurred] to be able to heal the world, to be able to heal this city. And so it's important that people share.

Courtney made use of Birmingham's unique historical sites to enrich the general equivalency diploma (GED) courses that he taught low-income youth who lived in public housing. He reflected on a visit to the historic Fourth Avenue Civil Rights District, which is home to the BCRI, Sixteenth Street Baptist Church, and Kelly Ingram Park, and also where schoolchildren and college students were savagely assaulted with fire hoses and police dogs, under the orders of notorious public safety commissioner Eugene "Bull" Connor. He reflected:

> Birmingham is one of the most . . . historical cities in the world when it comes to civil rights. I mean basically just living in Birmingham makes you a part of the civil rights movement. Like Friday [our GED class] was at the Sixteenth Street Baptist Church commemorating the church bombing. And just about anywhere you go in downtown. . . . Birmingham, especially in

> the Civil Rights District, you can't help but kind of feel the mood or the atmosphere. It's like, "Man!" And that's what I'm telling my students about: People died for the right to do what y'all are doing here. You know it's up to us to keep the dream going.

Tisha captured the sentiments of her cohort members most poignantly and succinctly in one aspirational statement: "I want my children to understand that they are also expected to be . . . agents of change."

However, some post–civil rights movement educators acknowledged roadblocks to assuming the role of intergenerational bridge builders, especially related to communication and a mutual willingness to empathize across generation. Jonathan explained:

> I think the challenge is being able to bridge the gap between my generation and the generations before me. And I think that one of the main problems . . . is that there is not enough dialogue. . . . And then you also have situations where . . . as generations get older, they become more stubborn. . . . I just think we need more communication and more interaction between generations.

Echoing Jonathan's sentiment, Rick shared his dilemma with collaborating with older teachers to reach younger generations of students.

> When I first got into the profession [there were] a lot of older teachers . . . I was willing to listen and learn some of the things they've learned. But I wanted to have my little way of getting over to the kids. And it didn't [go] over real well at first because . . . you're doing it a different way. . . . But I'm able to relate to my students . . . I might be able to use music or a TV show, something that . . . an older person . . . may not be [up to] date [on] or relate to the [younger] generation.

At times, post–civil rights movement educators expressed bewilderment that their older colleagues were still bitter and angry about the past. Murphy, in particular, felt that an older male teacher's unwillingness to make amends with Birmingham's past kept him from cultivating interracial collegiality, which he deemed critical to being successful in an integrated suburban school.

> I guess I know of one person who lived during that time of civil rights. I worked with him for a couple of years, and immediately I could see the animosity he has towards White people in general. . . . He seemed to have issues with [Whites], and I couldn't quite understand why. He went into some details about some things that were happening back during the nineteen sixties. . . . You know, not being able to go into certain restaurants, and having to drink out of a fountain that had "colored" on it. . . . He remembered being mistreated by other White males simply because he was a Black male. And I think some of that stayed with him over the years. . . . He's been teaching for twenty plus years—and he still has issues with Whites! I've been to several conferences with him and there always seems to be some tension whenever White people try to add their input about how they feel something should happen in this meeting. He seems to kind of disregard it, or just have a real problem with it, or [he] tries to go the opposite way even though he may agree. But simply because that White person said it [he's like], "I'm going to disagree because I know what's best for a Black child," so to speak. I don't know. I had issues with that, and I tried to address it with him; but he would just refuse to change. He was just adamant that he wasn't going to change the way he was. You know I think it all stems from during that time when he felt like he was mistreated by Whites growing up.

Murphy admitted that he did not have a frame of reference for empathizing with his older African American male colleague whom he viewed as bitter, angry, and self-defeating in his behavior toward their White colleagues. He said he made several attempts to help his older colleague relate better to White colleagues, but was not successful. Murphy seemed troubled by the fact that he and his older colleague could never really see eye to eye about how to negotiate race relations in their integrated school.

Choosing "Urban" Schools

The civil rights movement paved the way for opening more professional opportunities for post–civil rights movement educators than had been afforded their predecessors. They now have the "option," albeit constrained given the realities of post–civil rights era racism, of deciding whether they want to work in urban or suburban schools.[14] Therefore, choosing to work in urban schools may be viewed as an activist practice in light of the challenging contexts they described. In some respects, post–civil rights movement educators who choose urban schools are similar to their predecessors, who resisted integration for as long as they could and opted instead to serve as role models for their students in all-Black schools. The overwhelming majority of post–civil rights movement educators (75 percent) worked in urban educational settings at the time of the interview, most typically in urban public K–12 schools. Their experiences were distinctive from suburban public educators in this study who worked in predominantly White—and in some cases, virtually all-White—middle- to upper-middle-class schools. However, both urban and suburban educators encountered urban public school students and families either by rezoning or transfer enrollment, in some instances, due to longstanding school desegregation consent decrees. The diverse professional contexts they encountered provide an informative framework for interpreting their perspectives on activism.

Wilona reflected on her conscious decision to teach in a low-income, predominantly African American urban district versus a well-resourced, predominantly White suburban district. Her decision was motivated by a sense of loyalty to her African American heritage and a commitment to serve students whom she deemed to be more disadvantaged than others.

> I didn't feel like I had to go to Mountain Brook or Hoover. . . . I just want to give something back to my culture. All students can learn if they have the necessary resources needed. . . . If I was going to go into teaching I would want to teach in [an urban] setting, but not in a setting . . . where everything is provided for them already per se.[15]

Tammy viewed her role as a teacher in an impoverished urban school nested within a public housing development as a divine appointment.

> Coming here to [an urban school], I find myself really believing every day that I've been placed here for a reason, and it's to help my children understand that where they are, they can grow, and they can be whatever it is that they want to be as long as they put the work into it.

Tiffany once thought her days in urban schools were over, until she transferred to a suburban school and decided within one year to return to her former urban school district.

> I stayed in Birmingham [City Schools] for nine years. And I went to Hoover City [Schools] my tenth year. And I worked in that system for one year. I thought I wanted a change, and I thought that I wanted to do something beyond an urban school setting. But when I got to that situation, I just felt a void, and I just felt like somehow I had neglected the students that I left behind because I feel that I just bring something different to the table that is a good attribute in the suburban system, but it's needed more in an urban school system.

K–12 educators employed in the BCS and JeffCo Schools, in particular, expressed concerns about an urban school crisis and their responsibility to combat it. They disclosed that they were up against challenges such as scarce resources, declining test scores in an era of heightened accountability under the 2001 No Child Left Behind Act, low teacher morale, apathetic parents, discipline problems, and negative media coverage.[16] The alumni of Birmingham-area urban schools were especially disheartened by what they perceived to be a marked decline in the quality of schooling since their matriculation. For example, "Crawford" drew sobering contrasts between his experiences growing up in the same neighborhood where he was teaching.

> This neighborhood used to be my neighborhood. . . . It is was a lot different then, though. I grew up primarily with my grandparents. Mom was working a lot so I spent a lot of time with them, and the neighborhood . . . was very safe. It was family-oriented because everybody was related to me on the block it seems. . . . From the front to the back of that block were kinfolk. . . . Everybody was concerned because we were all kin. If I needed anything, I knew where I could go. I knew I wasn't cuttin' up because it was so many eyes on me. [The] [l] ast thing you want to happen is to get caught doing something wrong because everybody has permission to beat your butt.

In contrast to his experiences as a student in an urban school, which are reminiscent of the experiences of pre–civil rights and civil rights movement cohorts in this study, Crawford described the changing demographics and milieu of his current school's community.

> I've run into a lot of young parents. I've run into more single-family situations where mother is just the sole provider or protector or responsible for rearing. And sometimes you deal with kids . . . who act just as grown as the mama and daddy. . . . So there is a difference in that regard of what I saw when I was growing up [compared] to twenty years later.

Similar to Crawford, "Wilona" described how her urban high school students' experiences seemed very different from her previous experiences in the BCS. She attributed her previous experience working in a juvenile residential center as an eye-opening preparation for working as an urban high school teacher.

> I don't want to say [urban students] are not normal, but you know they have problems coming in. I mean . . . some of them work because I have a student who . . . leaves school and works until about one to two o'clock in the morning. But they have to in order to provide money to the family. . . . And other issues . . . you know parents may be on drugs, some children may be wards of the State where they're living in residential homes. . . . You have foster children on occasion. You have children who are wearing ankle bracelets in your class who've been in the . . . juvenile system.

Urban educators sometimes contrasted their experiences with their suburban counterparts when they encountered them in cross-district competitions. For example, Rick frequently traveled with his integrated urban district's swim team to compete in swim meets in suburban school districts. He learned the hard way that some of his suburban competitors and their fans harbored derisive feelings about his urban students, especially his African American students.

> This past summer . . . as a swim coach . . . we had an undefeated season. . . . And we would go to different places in the suburbs . . . and things would be said—not to me, but to my White parents—that I never thought would happen in two thousand six, two thousand seven. But at the end of the season, they shared some of these things with me, [i.e.,] some of the racial comments that were made about African Americans.

"Jonathan" attempted to contextualize the stark disparities between underresourced urban school districts and well-resourced suburban districts in order to come to grips with his perceived second-class status as an urban educator. In his analysis, he attributed this disparity to deeply rooted and historic structural problems with Alabama's school finance system. These problems, he concluded, create a vicious cycle resulting in misinformed perceptions of urban schools that are bereft of a keen understanding of their socioeconomic context. Although he made a conscious decision to work in urban schools, he was well aware of how systemic inequities dramatically distinguish, and in many respects demean, his professional context and standing compared to his suburban counterparts.

> We still have a disparity when it comes to resources [and] when it comes to the type of instruction that students receive in some areas as opposed to the instruction they receive in other areas. And a lot of that has to do with law. You know in the state of Alabama schools are financed according to property tax. . . . So that means I didn't choose my parents. I didn't choose the circumference of our home. I didn't choose the neighborhood we live in. So that means I'm living in this household that I have no choice [but] to live in and other houses around me are only forty, fifty thousand dollars. Then that means that there's not much coming in through property tax[es]. Whereas this other child, who also can't help who his parents are, is living in a house where the average house is two hundred to two hundred fifty thousand dollars. So that means there's a lot of property tax coming into that particular area of the state. So that means the more money, the better the facility I can purchase. The more money, the more I can pay my teachers, the more I can pay my administrators. The more money I can [invest] into athletics, the more I can [invest] into the cultural arts. The more I can [invest] into security of the school. So that means it gives the perception that the school is better. It probably is better, but is it better because those people are better or is it better because of the resources financially that are put in place by way of what the law states?

Pioneering in Upper-class Suburban Schools

Post–civil rights movement educators who taught in predominantly White middle- and upper-class suburban schools (20 percent of this cohort) described a racial context that was strikingly different than their cohort members who taught in urban public schools. There were some African American "firsts" in suburban schools who acknowledged feeling as if they had to be twice as good as their White colleagues, which, in turn, made them feel lonely and isolated. Their psychic responses to isolation, covert racism, and discrimination sometimes entailed engaging in the "politics of respectability," which historian Evelyn Brooks Higginbotham described as "disavow[ing], in often repressive ways, much of the expressive culture of the 'folk,' for example, sexual behavior, dress style, leisure activity, music, speech patterns, and religious worship patterns."[17]

"Justin" was the first assistant principal hired at his predominantly middle-class White suburban school. He reflected on what he described as a covert form of racism that has emerged in the post–civil rights movement era, which he referred to as "professional racism."

> I don't think [racism is] as overt [today]. And I don't know if I'm coining the term but there's more of a *professional racism*. Things are done that you cannot necessarily pinpoint, but you know certain things are being done. You know that certain eyes are watching, and you know that despite your best efforts . . . there are some persons who are looking for something negative to say. You can do the job as well as your contemporary, who may be of a different cultural background, but because you did it in a certain way, [the] scrutiny is going to be harder.

Justin went on to describe the chilly reception he received when he first accepted his position as an assistant principal in the early 2000s. He recalled that he received vocal opposition from members of his family and social network because they did not believe he belonged in a White suburban school district, but rather in an African American urban public school. But the reception he received at his first parent meeting was especially unsettling for him.

> My introduction here—I can remember, it was a parent night. And when my principal introduced me to go up to the stage there was a deafening silence. Now I had a few [parents] afterwards to come and welcome me, and some said they prayed for me to be here. And I was appreciative of that. I think that will always stick with me because I felt . . . alone. And I felt as if I needed to see somebody [African American] . . . even

> though I saw a few [African American] faces it was almost as if they weren't sure it was okay to welcome me.

Tisha was the first African American teacher hired at her upper-to-middle-class suburban school in the mid-1990s. She experienced "professional racism" that made her feel hypervigilant about the way she carried herself as a teacher both in her school and its surrounding community.

> I try to think back and say, "What were their thoughts when I first came to [this school]?" You know what did the faculty think? They were very careful in their conversations with me because they didn't want to offend me. They didn't know what to expect. I had some teachers saying, "You really have to know what you're doing out here because the parents will really look at you closely." . . . It was as if [they were thinking], "I wonder if she's going to be able to rise to the occasion?"

Tisha attempted to temper her colleagues' concerns about her professional competency by being especially cautious about her verbal articulation and professional demeanor. She suggested that her effort to set the bar higher than what her colleagues, students, and parents expected, particularly as an African American teacher, helped her prove herself in the school and community, but did not remove her from the "fishbowl."

> In my first class, I remember I taught fourth grade. And I've always put forth the effort to be very conscious about the way that I communicate. So in any classrooms that I've taught in, I try to be very articulate. I try to make sure that when I speak, it's not redundant and I bring in some rich vocabulary, just for my benefit and for the kids' benefit. So I had some parents that came in for a conference one day and said, "Do you think you could talk down a little bit because the way that you're speaking, it's just a little bit above what our children can really process?" And I think that once they started seeing my expectations and how high they were, I think they were a little stunned. But they were very willing to give me what I needed. They wanted to support me but they were still watching very carefully just to see if I really knew what I was doing.

Debbie was also a "first" at her suburban school when she was hired as an assistant principal. She described the "professional racism" she has encountered in trying to get promoted.

> There was an opening one time, and while my experience—I've been an administrator in different settings—would count for someone else, that wouldn't count for me. And they chose a person who had years and years of experience, but in my opinion, it was the same year over and over again. . . . But that person was selected . . . and that was okay, that was fine but someone whom I had a lot of respect for said to me that by the time another opening arose, I would be through with my doctorate, and then maybe they would consider me. . . . And I said, "You know I read that job description and that's not the requirement. So why is there a different requirement for me?"

The experiences of post–civil rights movement educators working in predominantly White suburban schools is similar in some respects to their pre–civil rights movement and civil rights movement cohorts who integrated schools post-*Brown*. Both groups experienced isolation and elements of covert racism that they found elusive to pinpoint. This racism was not expressed through racist pickets, epithets, intimidation, obstruction, and mob violence but rather through "deafening silence," hyperscrutiny, and other subtleties. In one instance, an educator alluded to African American suburban parents' reservations about openly embracing African American school staff in schools with all- or predominantly White professional personnel, which further exacerbated his feelings of isolation as the first African American administrator at his suburban school. In addition, the African Americans who were "firsts" in their suburban schools did so by choice versus mandate, which sometimes prompted wariness and critiques from their family and community members.

HOPE AND DESPAIR FOR THE POST-HIP-HOP GENERATION

From a life course perspective, it is critical to examine intergenerational encounters between successive cohorts of educators and students in order to gain a better grasp of continuities and discontinuities in the tradition of African American educational activism. Pre–civil rights movement, civil rights movement, and post–civil rights movement educators encountered successively younger generations of students during their professional tenure. Although some pre–civil rights and civil rights movement educators noted concerns about their relationships with post-hip-hop generation (i.e., those born after 1984) students and their relatively young parents, the most pointed critiques of this generation emerged from post–civil rights movement educators. Perhaps the proximate age and generational statuses between post–civil rights movement educators and their students and parents contributed to their concerns. Post–civil rights movement educators also have more direct and prolonged exposure to successive generations of younger African American youth as older educators retire. Interviewer dynamics may have also contributed to these candid disclosures. The fact that I, as an interviewer, am more closely identified with the post–civil rights movement cohort in terms of age, generation, race, and profession may have made these participants feel more comfortable about disclosing what they sometimes qualified as being "politically incorrect" commentary about their students and parents.

In their role as intergenerational bridge builders, post–civil rights movement educators, namely those who work in predominantly or solely African American urban schools, shared insightful perspectives about post-hip-hop generation students and their primarily generation X/hip-hop generation parents. Post–civil rights movement educators' critiques of the post-hip-hop generation were dominant in the life stories of men (eight out of ten). These critiques were also notable in the life stories of women (five out of ten). Post–civil rights movement educators were concerned about what they deemed to be the negative influence of hip-hop culture in urban African American youth's lives. At times there was a sense of hopelessness and despair in their reflections, but notably these educators were employing or seeking strategies, sometimes beyond the classroom and school, to address low academic achievement, low self-esteem, and the need for more positive male role models in their schools.[18]

Lorenzo theorized that members of his generation created hip hop as a counterculture in response to racism around the 1960s and 1970s. He credited the early history of hip-hop culture as being a positive force in African American youth culture: "KRS One, Chuck D, Public Enemy, Sister Souljah, these people represented positive aspects of rap." Lorenzo stated that these early rappers filled a void in the music industry by presenting thoughtful and edgy critiques of American society. But he concluded that some aspects of hip-hop culture, namely "the objectifying of

African American women, and essentially reducing them to sex objects" have been detrimental to African Americans.

> I had the luxury of growing up or being around during the duration of the hip-hop era. And what I've seen is hip hop go from being a . . . positive voice of the African American community, to being more of . . . the voice [that] is being controlled by powers that are not interested in Black folks. I think that we have lost our grip on what emits from hip hop. I think now [hip hop] has had terrible effects, very detrimental effects in our community.

Lorenzo went on to say:

> In my lifetime. . . . maybe in the early seventies, late sixties . . . growing up in an all–African American community and just having peers that were African American, a lot of times it wasn't cool to be intellectual. And I think that during this time . . . African Americans developed a different type of subculture that was rebellious against some of the more mainstream vehicles for success. . . . We became more polarized, where we saw certain activities as "being White" and certain activities as "being Black". . . . And we rebelled against the so-called White activities because of the history of what people have inflicted upon us in the form of oppression. And so I think with hip hop coming out, with African Americans developing a new voice . . . we rebelled against a lot of the things that we considered to be White or mainstream.

Sybil was forthright in attributing blame to hip-hop entertainment moguls for what she deemed to be self-denigrating African American youth culture. Making a distinction between "old school" and "new school" hip hop, she chronicled a regression in the lyrics of the early rap artists who presented what she considered to be a more enlightened view of urban realities compared to more recent rap artists and entertainment moguls, who she said denigrate women and African American culture. Sybil also expressed concerns about hip-hop moguls' exploitation of urban youth.

> I think that the way that people with little money in the Black community, and people with little money in the associated

> hip-hop community are being caricatured is very negative. And Russell Simmons and P. Diddy have had a role in that.[19]

Winifred expressed concerns regarding what she considered to be the misguided priorities of her students and their parents. Her critique implicates hip-hop culture and relatively young mothers, whom she deemed as not quite capable of raising their children to be successful in high school.

> The only problems I'm having at [my school is] that the people that look like me don't accept the things that I'm telling them, you know, young students. It's like they're living in a time warp. They don't realize how far behind they are. And I see a lot of young mothers, and nothing against the young mothers, but parents that are my age. I'm thirty-two. I have parents [of my high school students] that are my age and younger . . . they're not doing the things that they are supposed to do for their children. And one of the issues that I have with our kids is that when they come to school, they look good, you know, they have on the latest Jags, the "J's and the grills."[20] But you ask them to spell certain things; they're behind. You ask them about current issues; they're behind. You ask them about historical issues about us; they don't know. They don't grasp the material. You know . . . I'm speaking of a certain segment of these students—not all the students are like that. . . . But it's enough where it has made a mark on me; you know, to realize that something is wrong.

"Nichelle" was ambivalent about criticizing African American youth, but she did not withhold her genuine viewpoints. Similar to Winifred, she implicated premature parenting as a contributing factor to what she deemed to be the misguided priorities of her students and their parents.

> The things I would like to address are just very touchy. How do you say . . . materialism is bad or the media is bad . . . don't let your kids watch this, don't let them listen to this . . . don't spend all your money on [Michael] Jordan products? And at first I was like, I don't want to be stereotypical by saying that; but now I see it. You know, I really do see that's a problem.

"Marshall" was forthcoming about implicating himself in his critique of the hip-hop generation. He also noted that his students sometimes challenged his penchant for frequenting nightclubs where hip-hop music was being played while chastising them for their identification with hip-hop culture. He reflected critically on how believes his generation has been too uncritical about the denigrating aspects of hip-hop culture.

> I think too many times, myself and others in our generation, have let others influence our decisions, [and] influence our value system. You know, I remember I would never use the "N-word," especially when I was getting to high school. My best friend of nine years, when . . . he used to greet me, [it was] you know, "Hey 'N.'" And I would tell him then [that] I was convicted. I would say, "I'm not a nigger." They laughed at me but I did say it. I stood my ground. Nine years later, it's like, "Hey, what's up my nig?" We're using the words [again]. And then you have all of these issues cropping up here lately about artists and other hip-hop [people] using these same terms, and it's kind of like, "Wow, I wish I had [ceased using the word]" because it's much harder to stop now because it's embedded in my lexicon, my everyday language, unfortunately.

Educators born during the early bracket of the post–civil rights movement cohort tended to be especially critical of the post-hip-hop generation. In response to a question about his views on Bill Cosby's critique of the African American community in a book he co-authored in 2007 with his longtime collaborator, African American psychologist Alvin Poussaint, Jonathan, who was born in 1967, expressed these views about the younger generation:

> Well, personally speaking, the media is quite consistent in that area. I have to give it up to them. I mean there's nothing that they're saying that I can't go in the Black community and see. I was looking on MSNBC [cable news network] and the news [anchor] was talking about how it's no excuse in two thousand seven for a large contingency of our society saying [that] education doesn't pay. . . . Then he said you go to a White school and these kids are carrying books, and they can't hardly walk. Then you go to [a] Black school and these

> kids don't have books. That means that there's a missing link as far as the value system. . . . So I don't think the data is oversensitized I just think that we need more examples of Bill Cosby. More examples of *Time* magazine [coming] out with the "Plight of the Black Man" to look us dead in the face and tell us, "You're not getting the job done."[21]

I contend that social class and relative age differences both within and across the hip-hop and post-hip-hop generations are at play in these critiques. Birmingham's population is predominantly African American and increasingly poor, and akin to cities across the United States, there is an intensifying social and geographic distance between the poor and the middle class as higher-income African American residents move farther out of the city limits.[22] In turn, hip-hop generation and youth culture scholars and commentators have observed a distinctive difference in the tenor of rap artists' critiques of American society over time as well as the public's reaction to this music, particularly the controversial "gangsta rap" genre, which became popular in the late 1980s and early 1990s.[23] All of these factors undoubtedly contribute to the Black value-system dissonance conveyed in the post–civil rights movement cohort's life stories.[24]

Historian Charles Payne warned about the dire consequences of producing a younger generation of African Americans that does not know, or care to know, its history and heritage.[25] He cautioned that if young African Americans continue down the destructive path described by many of the post–civil rights movement educators in this study,

> [t]he result could be the adoption of an individualistic ethos that makes it harder to pass on the norms that once held the racial community together and a simultaneous weakening of the mutual respect and self-confidence that undergirds democratic participation.[26]

ARRESTED DEVELOPMENT OF COLLECTIVE STRUGGLES FOR INSTITUTIONAL TRANSFORMATION

Reminiscent of the nineteenth- and twentieth-century self-help programs and teachers associations established by African American educators, only a few members of the post–civil rights movement cohort acknowledged their efforts to address aforementioned concerns through the sponsorship of mentoring programs, which were typically launched and funded in collaboration with their professional and personal peer networks. Two rare examples of initiatives that I would characterize as examples of "struggles for institutional transformation" were elaborated by Debbie and Lorenzo.[27] Notably, both initiatives are targeted to African American males, although one was launched in a predominantly White middle-class school and the other in predominantly African American working-class and low-income communities. Both initiatives respond either indirectly or directly to the post-hip-hop generation critiques discussed previously with a targeted emphasis on African American males.

Debbie expressed concerns about what she perceived to be an increasing lack of respect for education among African American students in her suburban school. This lack of respect was incongruent with her and her peers' attitudes toward schooling when she was growing up in 1980s Birmingham. Debbie felt obligated to come up with affirming resolutions to address student discipline problems, particularly in a middle-class White suburban school where these problems were routinely portrayed as being "Black [male] student problems." Rather than to follow the typical role of strict disciplinarian, she opted to address what she perceived to be a pronounced discipline problem among African American male students in a proactive and edifying manner.

> We need to be sure that we secure enough [African Americans] so that we can let our voices be heard. One of the things that we've been able to do here is to address discipline issues. I don't have a lot of [these issues] so I don't want to exaggerate. But they were usually, you know, our African American children—mostly African American male children. So we started to see this pattern emerge and we decided we needed to do something; so we decided to start a mentorship program. And so we got men from the [Birmingham] community to come out and to actually spend time with them, you know, to tell them, "I once was where you are. I had a difficult upbringing. I . . . had a single mother."

Even though she was successful in launching an African American male mentoring program, Debbie admitted encountering roadblocks. The most notable roadblock was the minuscule number of African Americans in administrative and teaching positions at her suburban school and district. Her school hired its "first" African American male teacher in

2007, and she was successful in getting him on board with the mentoring program. Although she noted the support of her White principal, Debbie indicated that the paucity of African American staff in her school and district hindered her from mobilizing the critical mass of African American adults she felt she needed to advocate more strongly on behalf of African American students. She was especially concerned about those students who encountered cultural shock and stereotyping as they transferred from urban to suburban school districts and neighborhoods. In response, Debbie corralled African American men citywide to serve as mentors for boys at her school. As a result of her leadership efforts, she has noted a significant decline in punitive disciplinary practices toward African American males.

Lorenzo also grappled with teaching and mentoring post-hip-hop generation youth. His philosophy about his role as an African American educator may be summed up in his self-professed philosophy: "As an African American I don't think that I have the luxury to be ivory tower. And I think that it is incumbent upon me to share what I have in the form of resources, whether they be material or abstract, in the form of intellectual resources." His philosophy is what drove his "activist dissertation" topic.

> [My dissertation] is definitely an activist dissertation. . . . I want to discover different factors that actually keep resourceful African Americans in the ghetto. Because if we look at low-income African American neighborhoods before, let's say, de facto desegregation, what happened was you would have a different mix of African Americans in one community. You would have poor African Americans, middle-class, and wealthy Black folks living in the same neighborhood. . . . I mean . . . don't get me wrong, there were barriers. But these resources, were still for the most part kept within the community. I mean, a lot of our businesses were thriving. And there were a lot of good things also associated with that. But now what has happened, and [sociologists] Douglas Massey and William Julius Wilson make this point, [is] that when middle-class African Americans started leaving the . . . inner city neighborhoods, and when the social isolation of poverty began . . . ghetto conditions intensified and when these ghetto conditions intensified, we saw a lot of destructive things beginning to happen. . . . It is

> my hope that my dissertation is the first step in reversing some of these negative trends.

As a graduate student and college instructor, Lorenzo launched a nonprofit organization dedicated to mentoring African American males. He enlisted the support of young African Americans in his personal and professional network to assist him. In fact, another post–civil rights movement educator (Winifred) made a passing reference to Lorenzo in her interview, noting that her husband collaborates with him in this mentoring program. Lorenzo has a vision to expand his program to effect systemic changes in the African American community.

> I would . . . like to continue my work in the community as an activist and attempt to develop some programs and activities and institutions that actually benefit the [African American] community. . . . Now, some of the things that I want to accomplish, or some of the things that I would like to see accomplished, is definitely a reduction in Black-on-Black homicides. I think that is a terrible thing that is going on right now and it really contradicts the whole idea of [an African] village. I would also like to see . . . African Americans take a more vested interest in . . . the education of our children. As you know and as I know, after slavery, we as a people . . . really took a serious interest in education. I mean, we overcame some unbelievable obstacles just to learn how to read. And now it's as if these things are not as important to us. I mean we're not willing to go the extra mile . . . to pursue the knowledge that we need to be progressive.

FROM CONTINUITY TO DISCONTINUITY?

Post–civil rights movement educators described themselves as having a very positive sense of their heritage as African Americans. These educators referred to the enduring influence that family, community, schools, and Birmingham's civil rights movement foot soldiers played in shaping their values and worldviews. Yet they expressed vacillating feelings of hope and despair for urban African American youth and their parents, even though they occupy a proximate or similar generational location with them. They were conflicted by what they perceived to be a divergent value system among their urban students as well as their parents, who represent latter-born members of the hip-hop generation. On the one hand, they stressed promoting racial solidarity with their students while on the other hand, they expressed discomfort with behavior, attitudes, and cultural styles that they associated either directly or by inference to socioeconomic class, cultural, and generational differences. In contrast to the proud memories their predecessors recounted of their own students' bravery during the height of the Birmingham civil rights movement, educators in the post–civil rights movement cohort were tentative at best about the capacity of their early—twenty-first-century students to take up this activist mantle. In fact, they were not fully persuaded that they, as a collective of post–civil rights generation educators, could perpetuate the social change propelled by their predecessors. Most of these educators opted to teach in urban schools in hopes of making a difference in their students' lives whereas others pursued positions in suburban schools to serve as role models for the small but burgeoning population of African American students resulting from urban-to-suburban African American family migration trends in the Birmingham metropolitan area. Notably, very few of these educators discussed collective efforts to impact their schools and communities through formal organizations that characterized the experiences of their predecessors in the pre- and immediately post-*Brown* eras. Yet they coveted the bravery, tenacity, and solidarity that characterized generations of educators and students in Birmingham's yesteryear.

6

RESURGENT ACTIVISM?

> Now if I were a teacher in this school, or any Negro school, and I was dealing with Negro children, who were in my care only a few hours of every day and would then return to their homes and to the streets, children who have an apprehension of their future which with every hour grows grimmer and darker, I would try to teach them—I would try to make them know—that those streets, those houses, those dangers, those agonies by which they are surrounded, are criminal.
>
> ****
>
> If America is going to become a nation, she must find a way—and this child must help her to find a way to use the tremendous potential and tremendous energy which this child represents. If this country does not find a way to use that energy, it will be destroyed by that energy.
>
> —James Baldwin, "A Talk to Teachers"

Through newly applied theoretical and conceptual lenses, this book has reexamined the salience of activism in the lives of African American educators in Birmingham who came of age professionally in the years preceding, encompassing, and following the classical phase of the civil rights movement. These lenses grant broader and more flexible consideration of what it means to be an activist, allowing educators to self-identify as being activist (or not) in their own right, particularly in a city where civil rights activism has been conventionally defined and its images perpetually broadcast through modern media and texts. Based on this analysis, some educators were reluctant to self-identify as activist and acknowledged that their contributions have been minimized or discounted because pedagogical and leadership practices do not constitute legitimate acts of resistance within the context of Birmingham's civil rights movement. In other words, conventional activism in Birmingham, which is often canonized as marching in the streets and getting arrested for civil disobedience, trumps teaching students about the philosophical underpinnings of the civil rights movement and transforming the institutional culture of newly desegregated schools into enclaves of interracial equality.

This book highlights the unconventional activism of a multigenerational segment of Birmingham educators, which entailed: preparing student activists to understand why they were participating in the movement; not impeding students' involvement or jeopardizing their futures with suspensions and expulsions; promoting liberatory education and pedagogy; and debunking the myth of Black inferiority. These educators were the early pioneers of school desegregation, serving as ardent advocates for African American students and paving the way for them to gain their intellectual and social footing within newly desegregated schools. They advocated for them while simultaneously fighting for their own rights for respect and equitable pay as educators. In addition, they challenged White students to rethink the ways of the "old South" in order to embrace an interracial society.

As a continuation of this legacy, educators who were born and came of age during the post–civil rights movement have assumed responsibility for perpetuating the mission of their predecessors. They are privileged to have many more career and employment options than the older cohorts could have imagined in their day. Yet, following in the footsteps of their predecessors, some have opted to teach in all- or predominantly African American urban schools even though they must contend with the pernicious persistence of separate but (un)equal schooling whereas others have chosen to pioneer unfamiliar terrain in predominantly White middle- to upper-class suburban schools. Many embrace the role of intergenerational bridge builders charged with teaching younger generations about Birmingham's civil rights history. They often express hope and despair for a younger generation of students and parents, whom they believe are being exploited by hip-hop culture and a capitalistic society.

Across cohort, Birmingham educators spoke with clarity about the roles they have enacted as individual teachers and leaders within the confines of their respective classrooms and schools. In fact, younger educators more readily self-identified as being activist even though to date they have not participated in a social movement that rivals the civil rights movement. However, very few of the educators across cohort acknowledged joining ranks with other educators and community members to address concerns they observed in contemporary urban and metropolitan schools. Their life stories are filled with notable examples of what Patricia Hill Collins labeled "struggles for group survival."[1] Far less prominent are "struggles for institutional transformation" beyond the historical recollections of Birmingham civil rights movement participation. In addition, a few small-scale initiatives launched by educators in the post–civil rights movement cohort reflect the interdependency of struggles for group survival and struggles for institutional transformation.[2] For example, some post–civil rights movement educators mentioned that they were engaged in self-help programs targeted to African American males that entailed mentoring and tutoring. They sponsored these programs in collaboration with African American members of their professional and personal networks, and in one instance, the program's express purpose was to transform school-wide overly punitive discipline toward African American males. But they admitted that much more needs to be done. This finding underscores V. P. Franklin's observation that contemporary African American educators have failed *as a collective* to perpetuate the longstanding tradition of educational activism.[3]

HOPE FOR THE FUTURE

I believe two potential nexus points for educators born during the pre–civil rights, civil rights, and post–civil rights movement are: (1) their shared conviction that teaching and leading constitute legitimate and necessary activist strategies; and (2) their deep-seated concerns about the arrested transmission of communal values from their respective generations to the post-hip-hop generation. Young people have always been at the forefront of important social movements, but the hip-hop generation must navigate uncharted waters in a post–civil rights "colorblind racist" context.[4] The challenge for younger generations is to craft "a new language for analyzing the new color-blind racism of contemporary American society that has stymied its efforts to live up to the promise of American democracy."[5] In turn, the hip-hop generation necessitates new forms of public engagement within American social institutions, such as schools, to address pervasive disparities in public education.[6] Furthermore, their teachers must come up with new strategies for helping their students confront multiple domains of racism ("structural, cultural, disciplinary, and interpersonal"), which may be unique to their post–civil rights context.[7] These strategies include "creating safe and free learning spaces," establishing "classrooms as political spaces," and enacting "teaching and learning as subversive activities" for confronting racism.[8]

How can generation X/hip-hop generation educators assume this challenge effectively, when they, too, are grappling with how to confront post–civil rights colorblind racism? Notably, pre–civil rights and civil rights movement educators confronted a similar yet distinctive context when they desegregated schools between the 1960s and the 1980s. In solidarity with Black teachers associations, students, parents, and community members, they found ways to challenge Jim Crow through the courts and civil disobedience, teach Black history, institute cultural heritage programs, create safe spaces for students to discuss their budding involvement in the civil rights movement, and advocate for Black students to be recognized as intellectual equals and full participants in school organizations. Many of these strategies are actually quite similar to what Patricia Hill Collins and other scholars have proposed for younger generations of teachers and students but the post-*Brown* fallout has drastically altered and undermined their collective capacity to affect transformative changes.[9]

Recent perspectives from hip-hop educational researchers call for a more serious commitment to scholarship and research to explore these issues. Derrick Alridge and Petro Dagbovie, in particular, have advocated for pedagogical strategies that bridge nineteenth- and twentieth-century Black intellectual thought and practice with the contemporary realities of African American youth.[10] Engaging urban youth in critical dialogues about educational inequity would go a long way in helping educators understand their students' unique generational and contemporary location.[11] Furthermore, engaging urban youth in formal activist activities, particularly in their schools and communities, shows promising signs for mitigating their alienation[12] and promoting "radical healing."[13] In fact, there's evidence that today's young activists view schools as uniquely critical sites for activist socialization in contrast to the direct confrontations and experiences that politicized previous generations of African Americans.[14] But are contemporary educators maximizing this potential for public schools to be transformed into activist sites? If this transformation is untenable in traditional public schools, then how might educators seek other venues for engaging their students in dialogue and collective action to promote social change?

In 2007, I convened a community symposium at the BCRI, which was my first attempt to bring together a multigenerational panel of participants from my life story study.[15] It was a microcosm of synergistic dialogue and collective thought that I believe can be mobilized among a much larger multigenerational group of educators committed to spurring transformative change in schools and communities. The opportunity to exchange ideas, critiques, and strategies for change was invaluable especially in light of the dearth of *realized* opportunities for authentic dialogue between the civil rights movement and generation X/hip-hop generations.[16] As the convener, I posed a number of questions, but two have the most immediacy and relevancy for this book:

1. How can educators born during the pre- and post–civil rights eras build bridges to advance the education of African American youth?
2. What do you see as the potential for today's youth to lead a civil rights movement that is relevant to their generation?

The four panelists, along with audience members, raised a number of concerns, but I was struck by their perception of a waning commitment to the education profession among generation X/hip-hop teachers and successively younger generations of teachers. They intimated that younger African American educators no longer view teaching and leading as high professional callings, and that this view is contradictory to the historic mission of "education as racial uplift." The post–civil rights generation female panelist (Winifred) lamented that she has observed a decline in professionalism among her age-peer colleagues, which digresses from the example modeled by her veteran teachers. At one point, both she and the pre–civil rights generation female panelist (Wilma) shared an exchange, where Wilma gave Winifred accolades for embodying the quality of excellence that she felt Black teachers demanded in her day. Wilma also conveyed her concern about local school districts neglecting to tap into a rich reservoir of retired teachers as mentors for younger teachers. During the panel's dialogue, the post–civil rights generation male panelist (Jonathan) exclaimed: "We need to mandate intergenerational mentoring!" The panel members' consensus was that bringing together educators across the pre- and post–civil rights generational divide is critical to improving schools and advancing progress in the African American community.

Six years after this panel, the city commemorated the fiftieth anniversary of the watershed civil rights year of 1963, which revealed a few bright spots of youth activism in Birmingham. In April 2013, the BCRI convened a conference titled "Lessons of the Birmingham Movement: Youth, Activism and the Struggle for Human Rights," which drew local and national speakers and participants.[17] The following month an estimated 1,400 students representing nine Birmingham-area high schools and three colleges marched on May 2, 2013, to commemorate the fiftieth anniversary of the Children's March.[18] Also during this same month, an interracial group of youth convened a high-tech forum titled "Next Movement," where they shared their efforts to lead a new generation of activists to address persistent racism, sexism, homophobia, and ethnocentrism, particularly in relation to recent controversial anti-immigration laws in Alabama, Arizona, and across the country.[19] Notably, a small multigenerational crowd of residents organized by the Birmingham NAACP and local community activists led a peaceful protest in the civil rights landmark of Kelly Ingram Park to protest the highly publicized not-guilty verdict rendered to George Zimmerman in the murder of unarmed teenager Trayvon Martin, in Sanford, Florida. Yet it remains to be seen whether these pockets of youth activist dialogues and community protest will be mobilized into larger-scale social change. A case in point is the series of high-profile murders of young African Americans that have occurred subsequent to Trayvon Martin's murder. Most recently, the killings of two young African American males by White police officers in the St. Louis metropolitan area have set off a new firestorm of both volatile and peaceful protests and public debate about police brutality and the devaluation of African American humanity in the United States. Some old guard civil rights leaders and African American organizations have been at the forefront of these protests, often making connections between past murders of Black youth, such as the 1955 murder of thirteen-year-old Emmett Till at the hands of White racists in Money, Mississippi, and the present-day murders of Trayvon Martin and eighteen-year-old Michael Brown in Ferguson, Missouri.[20] Yet even with these efforts to make intergenerational connections, the Ferguson conflict has exposed a generational and social class fault line within the African American community.[21] According to one commentary, when a young African American man from St. Louis was asked to identify the leader of the ongoing protests in Ferguson, which prompted Missouri's governor to declare a state of emergency and curfew, he replied, "Do we have a leader? No."[22] The young man determined that the real leader was the gunned-down Michael Brown, who represented the angst of enraged and alienated African American youth.[23]

SO, WHERE TO?

I have written previously about the need for more research that explores the extent to which generational divergences may impede the mobilization of grassroots social change in contemporary African American education.[24] I continue to propose that generation is a critical yet underexplored variable in the scholarship on African American education. Recent calls for teacher education reform, particularly to address the needs of African American teachers and students,[25] should take into account generational (and social class) tensions inherent in relationships between contemporary African American educators and their students and parents.[26] Some generation X/hip-hop generation educators believe that their efforts to effect changes in their schools and communities are undermined by older educators and community members who do not feel that they have paid their dues.[27] This perspective is disconcerting in light of recent data highlighting a resurgent activism among African American youth and young adults, especially surrounding the 2008 election of Barack Obama as the first African American president of the United States.[28]

Future research is needed to explore the extent to which generational differences impede efforts to mobilize grassroots change in the public education arena. Extant literature concerning the home-school cultural gap in education has primarily emphasized the White teacher–Black student cultural gap. Generation, in relation to other social identity variables such as race, ethnicity, gender, social class, etc., is yet another crucial variable that should be factored into these analyses, especially in all-Black urban schools. National survey data on teachers across race and region suggest possible generational differences about policy matters of great significance to teachers such as tenure, evaluations, and merit pay.[29]

At the national level, more long-term, comprehensive, intergenerational collaborations are desperately needed to redress the persistent and systemic disparities in predominantly and exclusively African American schools and communities. One consideration would be to elevate the visibility of the few existing national professional organizations dedicated to advancing the causes of African American education. A notable organization is the National Alliance of Black School Educators (NABSE), which was birthed out of a vision to shift African American superintendents from isolation to collaboration. In 1973, under the leadership of Ulysses Byas, whose legacy is chronicled by him and Vanessa Siddle Walker in *Hello Professor*, NABSE was officially established as an organization that would include not only superintendents, but also school administrators and other personnel. Similarly, Carter G. Woodson's legacy organization, now named the Association for the Study of African American Life and History (ASALH) is embarking on its centennial celebration in 2015. Organizations such as these might very well hold the key for reclaiming the influence wielded by Black professional teacher associations established in the pre-*Brown* era.

Mainstream national professional teachers associations and teachers unions are reexamining their missions and agendas, especially in light of their diminishing enrollment, due partly to public perception that teachers unions are prioritizing professional survival over students' needs and interests.[30] Recent school governance controversies and massive school personnel layoffs in Birmingham have brought to the surface divided loyalties between African American parents and community members on the one hand and teachers union leaders and their rank and file members on the other hand. School governance has been a major point of contention in Birmingham in recent years. Several years of acrimony between the (African American) school superintendent and (predominantly African American) elected Birmingham BOE led to a state takeover and an accreditation warning.[31] In response, Birmingham's voters virtually revamped the entire board.[32] The new Birmingham BOE is decidedly multigenerational compared to previous boards, with three out of nine members who are in their early to mid thirties. Yet lingering intraracial tensions hinder coalition building between and among African American school personnel and parents, all of whom are left behind to grapple with the fallout of the post-*Brown* urban school context.[33] Modern-day foes of the BCS are no longer cast as White racist anti-integrationists. Today they are portrayed as primarily African American school bureaucrats who impede progress. When school leaders threaten to close schools or are perceived to be jeopardizing student interests, parents show up in droves at Birmingham BOE and local district meetings to voice their concerns.[34] However, when school personnel cuts are proposed, particularly in the central office, primarily, teachers unions and their constituents are left to fend for their own professional fates.[35]

In post–civil rights Birmingham, rarely has there been a generationally and economically diverse coalition of African American parents, community members, *and* educators advocating publicly and concertedly on behalf of public education. One rare exception is a multiracial and cross-municipal grassroots coalition spearheaded by a nonprofit organization along with local educational civic, business, and community leaders.[36] Although this initiative is viewed as successful by several local leaders, it remains to be seen whether it is viewed by the local African American community as a viable solution for public school problems.[37] The lack of visible multigenerational coalition building among contemporary African American educators, parents, and community members runs counter, historically, to the coalitions that fought for educational equity in the nineteenth and twentieth centuries. The "disintegration" or "splintering of Black America" is a particularly disconcerting fallout of the postintegration era.[38]

Intergenerational conversations between contemporary African American educators concerning the advancement of the aims of African American education are essential to fostering "audacious hope in action."[39] Gathering together multigenerational groups of educators and students will help orient these groups to the unique social realities each confronts and, hopefully, foster more social trust, empathy, and understanding between the two groups. Social trust, in particular, is a critical factor in motivating young people of color to participate in civic activities such as voting and community service.[40] Sharing stories about resilience in the face of formidable odds might help older and younger generations appreciate the respective social realities they confront, with the ultimate goal of jointly crafting new strategies to address formidable problems in education.

EDUCATIONAL EQUITY: THE CIVIL RIGHTS ISSUE OF THE TWENTY-FIRST CENTURY

The civil rights issue for the current generation is often touted as the fight for quality public education for all students.[41] Birmingham residents recently commemorated the fiftieth anniversary of the height of the Birmingham civil rights movement as well as the sixtieth anniversary of *Brown*. These two commemorations highlighted how public education continues to be bound by the problem of the color line and exacerbated by poverty, leading some scholars to question whether it would have been better for African Americans to aim for a well-implemented *Plessy v. Ferguson* (i.e., segregated schools that are actually equal with respect to resources) or a poorly enacted *Brown* given the current status of public education.[42] Do today's educators have the wherewithal to join ranks with local community members, including their post-hip-hop generation students, to break *Plessy's* stronghold on American education? Or has the post–civil rights era ushered in a smaller-scale, piecemeal approach to addressing public education's ills heralded by salvific educators such as Chicago Preparatory Schools founder Marva Collins and, more recently, Harlem Children's Zone founder Geoffrey Canada and Capital Prep Magnet School founder Steve Perry?[43] The answers to these questions still remain to be seen, but I remain hopeful that we will witness, and even more importantly, take part in, a resurgence of educational activism in this century to finally address the unfinished business of *Brown*.

APPENDIX

NOTES ON METHODOLOGY

RESEARCH STUDY

Data Sources

The primary data sources for this study include the following: forty-three life story interviews of Birmingham-area educators; two community forums, the first of which featured a four-member multigenerational subsample of the aforementioned life story participants, and the second of which featured a five-member panel of urban educators who pioneered desegregation in Birmingham-area K–12 public schools and universities (one of whom was also featured in the life story study); and oral histories and documents accessed from several local, state, and national archives noted previously in this book's Acknowledgements and Abbreviations sections.[1]

Participants and Settings

The life story participants include current and former teachers, administrators, and school personnel primarily from the BCS (58 percent) as well as adjacent county and suburban school districts (22 percent). A notable number (20 percent) of participants work in non-K–12 school settings that partner with BCS (e.g., nonprofit educational organizations and a local university). These percentages should be viewed fluidly given that some participants worked across urban and metropolitan K–12 and non-K–12 school settings over the course of their careers.

Birmingham's single school district (BCS) is predominantly African American (98 percent) with nearly 90 percent of its students enrolled in the federal government's free or reduced lunch program, and the student population has steeply declined since the 1970s (from 70,000 to around 25,000) due to both White and African American middle class flight.[2] According to a 2012 Birmingham Education Foundation report, the teaching staff of 1,500 is 79 percent African American and 81 percent female with 93 percent of these teachers meeting the federal designation of "highly qualified" under NCLB.[3] Notably, 61 percent of the district's teachers have a Master's degree and 121 are National Board Certified.[4]

It is difficult to ascertain reliable racial/ethnic student and staff data on the JeffCo Schools from school district and state education department websites, although I know from experience that the district is predominantly White with a large representation of African American and small but growing number of Hispanic/Latino students. The 2013 U.S. Census reported the JeffCo *municipal area* is 54.2 percent White, 42.8 percent African American, 3.8 percent Hispanic/Latino, and a very small percentage of Asian, Pacific Islander, and Native American populations.[5] According to the Alabama State Department of Education (ALSDE), a little over 56 percent of JeffCo students are enrolled in the federal government's free or reduced lunch program.[6] The most recent publicly accessible data for teachers indicates that among the 2,422 teachers, 53 percent have a Master's degree and a little over 7 percent have a doctoral degree.[7]

In Tables 1 and 2, which describe cohort demographics, the terms *urban public, county public, suburban public* are used to refer to schools in the BCS, Jeffco Schools, and contiguous public municipalities respectively. The term *urban public* is also used to refer to public higher education institutions located in the Birmingham city limits. Urban nonprofit organizations refer to 501(c)3 organizations located in the Birmingham city limits.

Study Design

The life story study is configured as a multiple-cohort design that encompasses pre–civil rights, civil rights, and post–civil rights movement cohorts. Participants in the pre–civil rights and civil rights movement cohorts were born between 1921 and 1955, which, with the exception of one outlier (born in 1921), encompasses two generations described by demographers as the "silent generation" and the "baby boomers."[8] In contrast, participants in the post–civil rights movement cohort were born between 1966 and 1983, which encompasses the generally agreed upon birth period for groups identified as being members of the hip-hop generation and generation X.[9] The pre–civil rights and civil rights movement cohorts are made up primarily of retired BCS educators whereas the post–civil rights movement cohort is fairly evenly distributed across city, county, suburban, and non-K–12 settings. The cohort difference in professional settings reflects, in part, the contrasting opportunity structures for employment in the education profession before, during, and after the classical phase of the civil rights movement.

Data Collection and Analysis

Each participant in the life story study was interviewed at least once for one to two hours between the 2005 and 2009. The two community panels were convened in 2007 and 2013, and each lasted approximately ninety minutes. I also interviewed an additional educator (Margaret Z. Beard) individually in 2014 for approximately forty-five minutes to round out my understanding of the JeffCo School desegregation era.

A purposive and community nomination sample was recruited through personal and professional networks based on the criteria of: age and generational status; current or former employment as an educator, which I defined broadly as a K–12 public school teacher or school administrator, an urban public university faculty member, or a staff member responsible for education in an urban nonprofit educational organization in the Birmingham metropolitan area; and gender.[10] Prior to recruiting participants, I initiated conversations with local "memory elites" (e.g., museum archivists and curators and civil rights historians) and guest speakers invited to participate in a Birmingham civil rights movement course I co-taught between 2004–06, to assess general perceptions of educators' involvement in the Birmingham movement. I learned from these conversations that Birmingham educators as a professional class are not viewed as significant contributors to the civil rights movement. However, the names of a select few activist educators continued to surface during my conversations. In response, I either approached these educators about participating in the study or sought archival data about their lives, particularly if they were deceased. The overwhelming majority of educators selected for this study were not identified by these informants, but rather through my intensive recruitment efforts, which were supported by my research assistants. I circulated fliers throughout my campus and electronically to colleagues, students, local K–12 educators, family, church, and community members. Therefore, my general sense is that the study sample, namely pre–civil rights and civil rights movement cohorts, is reflective of Black educators who taught in Birmingham-area schools during the civil rights movement.

For the sake of full disclosure, during the course of the study I learned that three of my forty-three life story participants had been interviewed previously by local and national archival staff. Once I discovered these interview transcripts, I compared them to my own transcripts for consistency. In instances where I covered similar ground (e.g., interview questions about the Birmingham civil rights movement and school desegregation), the narratives were highly consistent. Of course, I asked a number of questions that were not asked by other interviewers, and these new data are included in chapter 4 of this book. Based on permissions ascertained from archives, these three participants agreed to waive their right to anonymity in their previous interviews but not all of them agreed to do so in my life story study, which is why I have opted to use pseudonyms instead of their actual names in Part II of this book.

I hired an African American male undergraduate research assistant in his early twenties, who helped me recruit some of the post–civil rights movement participants, especially male educators. His background was in African American Studies, and he was a former teaching assistant in the "Birmingham Civil Rights Movement" teacher education course that I previously co-taught. I enlisted him to interview and analyze data on three participants in the post–civil rights movement male cohort. He also videotaped the 2007 intergenerational community panel at the BCRI. I also hired an African American female undergraduate research assistant in her early twenties. She was referred to me by a UAB filmmaking professor to provide short-term assistance on the project, which included offering valuable insights on the life stories of the younger cohort. Both research assistants completed UAB's Internal Review Board (IRB) training and requirements.

All interviews were audiotaped, and the two community symposia were videorecorded. All interview and panel participants completed IRB-approved consent forms. I employed methods to ensure data reliability such as member checking (i.e., sending transcripts to participants for review and feedback) and interrater reliability techniques (i.e., independent and interdependent analysis, discussion, and coding of the transcriptions by the author and research assistants).[11]

I conducted most of the interviews with women in the pre–civil rights and civil rights movement at their homes by their invitation. The other interviews were conducted at university campus locations or public schools at the end of the school day when the buildings were generally quiet. As a generational and professional courtesy, during the interviews I addressed pre–civil rights and civil rights movement educators by their last name and title (Mr. or Dr. Doe) although I am on a first-name basis with some of them.

Following the conventions of historical research, I use the full names of individuals whose oral histories or archival data are publicly accessible through archives, or who consented to participate in public interview panels that I convened (chapters 1 through 3). However, as noted previously, I use first-name pseudonyms for participants in my life story study (chapters 4 and 5) to honor my agreement with some of them who opted not to have their identities made public. The selection of first-name pseudonyms also facilitates readability and name recall for a large qualitative sample.

Protocols

The life story project protocols included an in-depth interview and a demographic profile sheet. The interview questions addressed participants' early socialization, reflections on the civil rights movement and activism, teaching and administrative experiences and settings, training and philosophy, and school and community context. The demographic profile documented birth year, age, current employment site, personal contact information, interview date, and location. The protocol for the community interview panels was derived from a condensed version of the life story protocol.

RESEARCH METHODS

"Methodological pluralism" was employed throughout this book (e.g., life course methods, narrative research, archives, and other documentary sources) to tell a more robust story about the Birmingham civil rights movement from the perspective of African American educators.[12] Each of these methods is discussed in detail below.

Life Course Methods

The study's methodology is guided by a life course perspective, which is a multidisciplinary framework for examining the interplay among human lives, structural contexts, and social change.[13] This perspective encompasses ideas and observations from a range of disciplines, notably history, sociology, demography, and developmental psychology. Life course scholars view lives as unfolding within a changing social context and interdependency of lives and social institutions.[14]

There are several key life course concepts that are central to understanding this study. The concept of *watersheds*, defined by life course scholars as dramatic periods of social change, markedly distinguish the life experiences and life chances of individuals who were born on either side of them.[15] A *generation* is closely associated with an understanding of watersheds, and has been described as "similarly located contemporaries [who] participate in a common destiny and in the ideas and concepts which are in some way bound up with its unfolding."[16] The concept of *cohort,* which refers to the socially shared experiences of age peers, helps life course scholars further delineate generations in their research.[17] Finally, *trajectories,* which "depict long-term patterns of behavior marked by a sequence of transitions" (i.e., events and roles) that may be analyzed at individual or "group-based" levels, are also critical to understanding the life course.[18]

In this study, I employ life course perspectives to parse the ways in which multiple cohorts of African American educators, whose lives are distinguished by being born prior to, during, or after the watershed classical phase of the Birmingham civil rights movement, conceptualize the term *activism* and enact (or avoid enacting) it over time. As noted in chapter 1, I also attempt to *extrapolate* an "activist trajectory" inclusive of past and present generations of African American educators in order to *deduce* whether this trajectory has increased or declined over time. I choose my verbs very carefully because I recognize both the limitations of my qualitative methodology and the considerable speculation about the activist participation of African American educators predating (and even including) the time frame when more archival data about their roles was produced and made available.

An analysis of African American educators born on opposite sides of the classical phase of the Birmingham civil rights movement should be considered in light of Mannheim's articulation of a *problem of generations.* Mannheim proposed that subjective awareness, or a shared consciousness, is the critical link between generational succession and social change.[19] Different generations live at the same time, yet their members experience and live in qualitatively distinctive subjective eras. In turn, the narratives of age peers are uniquely shaped by their generational identity. Therefore, it is critical for life course researchers at any given point in time to attempt to sort out the individual voices of the various generations. Studying cohort differences offers life course scholars suggestions about why change is occurring.[20] But Mannheim cautioned against the implicit assumption of intracohort homogeneity: "The fact that people are born at the same time . . . does not in itself involve similarity of location; what does create a similar location is that they are in a position to experience the same events."[21] Hence, there is the acknowledgment that within each cohort, variables such as race, class, gender, and regional location are likely to differentiate the experience of cohort members.

For Mannheim, age and place matter when examining the impact that watersheds have on generations.[22] Collective memories about significant events tend to be remembered most vividly by individuals who experienced them as young adults and adolescents. Participants in this study who were born in the pre–civil rights movement, civil rights movement, and post–civil rights movement eras share the same contemporary space as educators in Birmingham-area public schools and community educational settings, yet they occupy strikingly different subjective realities, which uniquely shape their worldviews. Mannheim also recognized that successive generations battle different internal and external opponents.[23] Whereas an older generation may be consumed with a particular adversary, a younger generation may view this adversary as immaterial relative to another opponent it is encountering. Occupying divergent subjective realities, and not being wholly cognizant of the threats and opportunities concomitant to these realities, may breed feelings of misunderstanding, distrust, and resentment between older and younger generations. One resolution to this tension is the "intergenerational transmission of cultural heritage," where the teacher educates the pupil and likewise the pupil educates the teacher, thereby keeping successive generations in a constant state of engagement.[24]

Notably, not every generation will be distinctive in taking up major social causes. Those generations that experience "an accelerated tempo of social change" are more likely to give rise to "generation units," that is to say, subgroups within the generation that are especially attuned to the changing times and necessity for collective action (e.g., conventional activists of the civil rights movement cohort).[25]

Narrative Research

The study's methods are grounded primarily in narrative research, which broadly encompasses oral histories, life stories, autobiographies, biographies, qualitative interviews, and many more approaches. For this study, the narrative forms included oral histories (chapters 1 through 3), life stories (chapters 4 and 5), and public interview panels (chapters 3 through 6).

Oral historians document personal recollections and commentaries of historical significance through recorded interviews.[26] Life stories are similar to oral histories in many respects, and they are often used in life course research. The distinction between oral (or life) histories and life stories is that the life story documents a person's subjective account of his or her life whereas the oral (or life) history extends this account with other corroborating sources.[27] I find life course scholar John Clausen's perspectives on the life story (or life review) to be quite useful. He defined the life story as an individual's retrospective report of past experiences and their meaning to that person.[28] According to Clausen, the life story "reflects how the person views particular aspects of the past now, not necessarily how the past was seen previously or how an observer might have interpreted its effects."[29] Furthermore, individuals change in many ways over the life course and these changes are reflected in "modified memories and modified senses of identity" even though they may not be cognizant of this change.[30]

Memories about the civil rights movement, in particular, are shaped by generation, race, and region.[31] Collective memories of civil rights events have been appropriated by political leaders to mobilize collective action.[32] There is also evidence of a compelling link between collective memory and collective activism. Notably, the sheer memory of watershed civil rights events, such as the 1955 brutal murder of thirteen-year-old Emmett Till in Money, Mississippi, had enough potency to mobilize civil rights activism years after the tragedy.[33] Moreover, living in the U.S. South during the height of the classical phase of the civil rights movement has sharpened the memories of civil rights generation cohorts. For example, research indicates that for White U.S. Southerners, in particular, their social location distinguishes their recall of civil rights events from their age peers residing in other regions of the country.[34]

From both a life course and feminist perspective, life stories present the individual as simultaneously changed and a change agent.[35] Multigenerational life stories shed light on how the subjective meanings of significant life events are bound up in distinctive historical experiences that may only be fully understood or appreciated by an individual's generational contemporary.[36] Life stories also help us to understand the diversity of life experiences, particularly variations according to social class, race, and gender.[37]

Charlotte Linde's concept of explanatory systems in oral life stories offers a fitting framework for understanding how the life story participants featured in this book reflected on social change and their professional roles.[38] Explanatory systems are described as semi-expert systems that lie within the nexus of opinion and common sense and may be employed as a narrative device to establish coherence in life stories. According to this view, it is not only experts who offer theories to explain social problems, but "any adult has a wide variety of theories available that can be used to make sense of his or her life."[39] From this perspective, the African American educators featured in this book are akin to social scientists who theorize about how schools and communities have been impacted by social change.

Archival Research

Archival research is defined as locating, evaluating, analyzing, and interpreting sources of information found in archives.[40] Archival data reflect the institutional culture and practices of the entities in which they were created. Therefore, it is important for archival researchers to learn as much as they can about the social context of archival data and their associated institutions. Original sources and documents may be consulted and analyzed for purposes other than their original intent, but it is important to recognize that, on the surface, the people, events, and organizations referenced in archives may not always be what they appear to be.[41]

Archives reflect the social mores of the societies in which they are embedded, which means that social stratifications such as race, gender, and social class very often dictate what kind of information is preserved and made accessible over time.[42] As Michael R. Hill noted, "The papers of privileged and institutionally powerful people are far more likely to be accepted by archives than are the donations of 'lesser men and women.' "[43] In order to mitigate this problem, I consulted with archivists across local, state, regional, and national institutions and made a special effort to include smaller and lesser-known archives housed at HBCUs and online African American newspaper portals. Along these lines, there is much contention in civil rights history and community circles about who has a right to own or tell "*the* civil rights story."[44] Some Birmingham civil rights foot soldiers have voiced concerns about their experiences and stories being co-opted by memory elites, and even by some of their contemporaries, who they claim were not really involved in the movement. In recent years, some Birmingham foot soldiers have reclaimed their previously donated archives and used this information to publish their own memoirs and documents.[45] In consideration of these concerns, whenever I could, I made an intentional effort to consult primary and secondary sources produced by, as well as to attend public forums featuring, the individuals discussed in this book.

AUTHOR'S STANDPOINT AND REFLEXIVITY

The methods I have chosen to employ reflect my interdisciplinary academic and professional background and training. For the past twelve years I have taught in the Educational Foundations Program at UAB with an emphasis on Social Foundations, which rely heavily on the disciplines and methodologies of the humanities, particularly history and philosophy, and the social sciences, such as sociology and political science.[46] My undergraduate and graduate credentials are in the disciplines of Political Science, Urban Poverty and Public Policy, and Human Development and Social Policy. My academic preparation in a graduate seminar on conceptualizing innovative intergenerational social services (co-taught by Bernice Neugarten and Harold Richman) at The University of Chicago and throughout my doctoral studies at the Northwestern University School of Education and Social Policy (co-advised by Gunhild O. Hagestad and James Spillane) laid the foundation for my understanding of life course perspectives and their surprisingly limited applications in traditional schools and colleges of education. I believe wholeheartedly that life course perspectives should be applied more broadly in the field of education.

In addition to working with local educators, I have worked closely with a racially, socioeconomically, and generationally diverse coalition of parent, community, governmental, civic, educational, business, and corporate leaders on grassroots urban school reform such as the Yes We Can! Birmingham initiative, and its nonprofit organizational offshoot, the Birmingham Education Foundation as well as home-school relations' research with primarily African American parents.[47] Pre–civil rights and civil rights movement educators, who generally expressed a sense of pride and honor when asked to participate in this study, approached the interviews as an opportunity to instruct both me and younger generations about civil rights history whereas post–civil rights movement participants appeared to view me as a knowledgeable peer-colleague with whom they could be candid in voicing sometimes "politically incorrect" views about race, social class, and youth culture.[48]

CHRONOLOGY

NATIONAL TIMELINE

1. *Plessy v. Ferguson* Supreme Court Case (1896)
2. *Brown v. Board of Education* Supreme Court Cases (1954, 1955)
3. The Civil Rights Act of 1964
    a. Title IV prohibits discrimination in public schools and higher education institutions on the basis of race, color, sex, religion, and national origin, thereby authorizing the federal government to file school desegregation and antidiscrimination cases on these grounds.
    b. Title VI prohibits discrimination on basis of race and national origin in programs and activities, including schools, receiving financial assistance.
4. Supreme Court Orders Dismantling of Segregated School Systems "Root and Branch" in *Green v. School Board of New Kent County* (1968)

LOCAL TIMELINE

1. *William J. Bolden v. School Board of Jefferson County, Alabama* (1942)
2. *Brown* Noncompliance (1954–1963)
3. *Ruby Jackson Gainer v. School Board of Jefferson County, Alabama* (1955)
4. *Ruby Fredericka Shuttlesworth v. Birmingham Board of Education* (1957)
5. *Dwight Armstrong et al. v. Birmingham Board of Education* (Case filed in 1962 and decided on May 28, 1963)
6. *Lee v. Macon County Board of Education* (Case filed January 28, 1963)
7. Vivian Malone and James Hood Integrate University of Alabama/ George Wallace's "Stand in Schoolhouse Door" (June 11, 1963)

8. *U.S. v. Jefferson County Board of Education* (March 29, 1967)
9. Birmingham Board of Education Freedom of Choice Plan (May 8, 1967)
10. Birmingham Board of Education Unitary System Plan (1970)
11. Birmingham Board of Education Modification of Unitary System Plan (1976)
12. Birmingham Board of Education Magnet School Plan (1980)

NOTES

PREFACE

1. For more information about the SOHP's oral history project, see http://sohp.org/research/the-long-civil-rights-movement-initiative/.

2. There is much debate about using the prefix "post" to delineate a discreet beginning and ending point of eras viewed by some as perpetual. During a March 2013 speech commemorating the Birmingham civil rights movement, freedom rights activist and former Birmingham native Angela Davis critiqued the use of the term "post–civil rights movement," noting that the struggle for African American freedom in the United States is complex, perpetual, and incomplete. While I agree with Davis's assessment and fully acknowledge the term's limitations (as well as others with the "post" prefix, e.g., "postracial" or Molefi Asante Jr.'s reference to a "post-hip-hop generation"), I use it to aid readers in distinguishing between multiple eras and generations discussed in this book.

3. Rustin, "From Protest to Politics," 25.

4. Hall, "Long Civil Rights Movement," 1733; and Georgia Senator Hank Johnson quoted in Murray, "Black Leaders Divided," ¶ 8.

5. See discussions in Patricia Hill Collins, *Black Feminist Thought*, 222–25; Payne, "More Than a Symbol"; and Wenger, *Rising African American Leaders*.

6. In her book *Call to Home*, Carol Stack chronicled the reverse migration of African Americans originally from the U.S. South who had moved to the Northeast and Mideast during the Great Migration only to make their way back home in the 1970s and 1980s to rural communities in the U.S. South.

7. Christensen, Loder, Volker, and Fincher, "Historical Legacy of the Civil Rights Movement."

8. Thankfully, my colleague Lois Christensen interviewed Ms. Fincher before her death and published an article about her life titled, "Ms. Lillie M. H. Fincher: A Luminary African-American Educator." The SOHP at University of North Carolina at Chapel Hill also interviewed Ms. Fincher for "The Long Civil Rights Movement" project. In addition, Ms. Fincher's mother, deceased Birmingham educator Dr. Gertrude Sanders, was interviewed by the Duke University Behind the Veil oral history project. All three sources are referenced in this book.

9. Beyond the novel publication of Michele Foster's *Black Teachers on Teaching*, I have not run across a book focused exclusively on the juxtaposed life stories of successive generations of African American educators. *Schoolhouse Activists* is similar to Foster's work in that it focuses on a multigenerational sample of male and female African American educators and employs a narrative methodology. However, in contrast, this book presents a larger and more professionally diverse sample of educators from K–12 schools, higher education, and nonprofit organizations, and includes in-depth scholarly analysis and commentary throughout the book, linking the lives of Birmingham educators to broader social changes in U.S. public education.

10. Chapter 1 addresses numerous works in more detail but a few of the most notable histories of African American education related to this book's topic include James D. Anderson's *Education of Blacks in the South*, Fairclough's *Class of their Own*, and Walker's *Their Highest Potential*.

11. Wells, Slayton, and Scott, "Defining Democracy in Neoliberal Age." The authors address the recent prominence of market-based strategies such as charter schools and private school vouchers as reforms promising to provide equal educational opportunities to low-income students and families.

INTRODUCTION. ACTIVISTS OR ACCOMMODATIONISTS?

1. Eskew, *But for Birmingham*, 259–97; Fairclough, *Teaching Equality*, 45–46; McWhorter, *Carry Me Home*, 365–78; R. Hudson and Houston, *Mighty Times: The Children's March*; Levinson, *We've Got a Job*; and de Schweinitz, *If We Could Change the World*.

2. Dailey, Gilmore, and Simon, *Jumpin' Jim Crow*. Jim Crow is a nickname co-opted from White minstrelsy to describe the deeply entrenched system of White supremacy and Black oppression that permeated every sphere of life in the U.S. South from post-Reconstruction era through the classical phase of civil rights movement.

3. Eskew, *But for Birmingham*, 264; Fairclough, *Teaching Equality*, 45; and McWhorter, *Carry Me Home*, 366, 390. Former Parker High School principal R. C. Johnson is portrayed in Birmingham civil rights history as the prototypical "accommodationist" educator, who forbade students from skipping school to participate in protests. The history of A. H. Parker High School, formerly named Industrial High School, is discussed in chapter 2.

4. I have encountered a number of individuals in Birmingham who view educators as inconsequential to the civil rights movement. One of my most memorable exchanges was with a well-known author of Birmingham's civil rights history who inquired about my work during an archival visit. The author seemed intrigued with my thesis albeit a bit wary about its divergence from conventional thinking about Birmingham educators.

5. Branch, *Pillar of Fire*; Eskew, *But for Birmingham*; Garrow, *Birmingham, Alabama 1956–1963*; Huntley and McKerley, *Footsoldiers for Democracy*; Levinson, *We've Got a Job*; McWhorter, *Carry Me Home*; Aldon D. Morris, *Origins of Civil Rights Movement*, 229–74; White and McManis, *Birmingham Revolutionaries*; and Bobby M. Wilson, *Race and Place in Birmingham.*

6. Eskew, *But for Birmingham*, 264.

7. Fairclough, *Teaching Equality*, 57–63; Fairclough, *A Class of Their Own*, 307–53; James T. Patterson, *Brown v. Board of Education*; Tushnet, *NAACP Legal Strategy*, 18–19, 37, 42; and Walker, "Annual *Brown* Lecture."

8. Kirk, "NAACP Campaign for Teachers' Salary"; and Walker, "Annual Brown Lecture."

9. Fairclough, *Class of their Own*, 382.

10. Dittmer, *Local People*, 75.

11. Newby, *Black Carolinians*, 82–94, 102–11, 258–73.

12. Garrow, *Birmingham, Alabama 1956–1963*, 233.

13. Epps, "Race and School Desegregation," 40–41; Eskew, *But for Birmingham*, xi–xii; Fairclough, "Cost of *Brown*"; Fairclough, *Teaching Equality*; Fairclough, *Class of their Own*; and Fultz, "African American Teachers in the South."

14. James D. Anderson, *Education of Blacks in the South.*

15. Ibid., 2.

16. Walker, *Their Highest Potential*, 3.

17. Gaddis, *Landscape of History*, 119.

18. Fairclough, *Teaching Equality*, 48–51. Although Fairclough attests to limited archival data documenting daily classroom experiences, some historians, notably Vanessa Siddle Walker, have located difficult-to-ascertain documents about Black teacher associations during this period through their well-cultivated personal and professional networks.

19. Ibid.

20. Griffin and Bollen, "What Do These Memories Do?," 595; and Schwartz and Schumann, "History, Commemoration, and Belief."

21. Griffin and Bollen, "What Do These Memories Do?," 595.

22. Roth and Mehta, "The Rashomon Effect." Some scholars have taken hardline stances about how the history of African American education should be approached and portrayed, which at times, has prompted a strident discourse about this subject matter.

23. Fairclough, "Being in the Field of Education"; Fairclough, *Teaching Equality*; and Fairclough, *Class of their Own.*

24. Ibid.

25. Ibid.

26. Ibid.

27. Fairclough, "Being in the Field of Education"; and Gasman, "Perceptions of Black College Presidents."

28. Eskew, *But for Birmingham*, 264.

29. Alridge, "From Civil Rights to Hip Hop"; Patricia Hill Collins, *From Black Power to Hip Hop*; Dagbovie, "Strategies for Teaching African American History"; Loder-Jackson, "Bridging the Tradition of Activism"; and Loder-Jackson, "Hope and Despair."

30. Several education scholars and historians have documented African American education before, during, and shortly after *Brown*. Some notable publications include James D. Anderson, *Education of Blacks in the South*; Bond, *Negro Education in Alabama*; Butchart, *Schooling the Freed People*; Franklin, "They Rose or Fell Together"; Cecelski, *Along Freedom Road*; Fultz, "African American Teachers in the South"; Vivian G. Morris and Curtis L. Morris, *Creating Caring and Nurturing Educational Environments*; and several works by Walker that are referenced throughout this book, among which include, *Their Highest Potential.*

31. Fields-Smith, "African American Parents Before and After *Brown*"; Loder, "Dilemmas Confronting Urban Principals"; Loder-Jackson, Voltz, and Froning, "New Horizons for Urban Teacher Preparation and Parent Engagement"; and Patillo, *Black Picket Fences.*

32. Massey and Denton, *American Apartheid*; Reardon and Bischoff, "Income Inequality and Income Segregation"; William Julius Wilson, *Truly Disadvantaged*; and Robinson, *Disintegration.*

33. Allison Davis, Burleigh B. Gardner, and Mary R. Gardner, *Deep South*; Hansen, "Birmingham Changes as Blacks Move to Suburbs"; and Hansen and Leech, "City's Black Students Leaving."

34. Bositis, *Diverging Generations*; and Cose, *End of Anger.*

35. Alridge, "From Civil Rights to Hip Hop"; Alridge, Stewart, and Franklin, *Message in the Music*; Bynoe, "Connected but Distinct"; Dyson, *Know What I Mean?*; Patricia Hill Collins, *From Black Power to Hip Hop*; Ginwright, *Black in School*; Hill, *Beats, Rhymes, and Classroom Life*; Kitwana, *Hip Hop Generation*; Petchauer, "Framing and Reviewing Hip-Hop Educational Research"; and Rose, "Fear of a Black Planet."

36. Franklin, "They Rose or Fell Together"; Fultz, "Displacement of Black Educators Post-*Brown*"; Fultz, "Caught Between a Rock and a Hard Place"; Mildred J. Hudson and Holmes, "Missing Teachers, Impaired Communities"; Vivian G. Morris and Curtis L. Morris, *Creating Caring and Nurturing Educational Environments*; Tillman, "(Un)intended Consequences?"; Tillman, "African American Principals and Legacy of *Brown*"; Walker, "Annual *Brown* Lecture in Education Research"; and Walker, "Tolerated Tokenism, or the Injustice."

37. Franklin, "They Rose or Fell Together," 48.

38. Perlstein, "Minds Stayed on Freedom," 249; and Joseph, *Black Power Movement.* There is some debate among scholars about the extent to which Black power activism has waned since the 1970s. Perlstein concluded that there has been a marked decline in the cutting-edge vision of Black power schools whereas Joseph et al. contend that the Black power movement is still relevant although it has assumed new forms in modern times.

39. Ibid.

40. Beauboeuf-Lafontant, "A Movement Against and Beyond"; Beauboeuf-Lafontant, "Womanist Experience of Caring"; Beauboeuf-Lafontant, "Womanist Lessons for Reinventing"; Dixson, "Let's Do This!"; Jean-Marie, James, and Bynum, "Black Women Activists"; and Jerome E. Morris, *Troubling the Waters.*

41. Patricia Hill Collins, *Black Feminist Thought.* Collins uses the terms *Black* and *African-American* interchangeably.

42. Sabrina Hope King, "Limited Presence of African American Teachers"; and National Center for Education Statistics.

43. Patricia Hill Collins, *Black Feminist Thought*, 202.

44. Collier-Thomas and Franklin, *Sisters in the Struggle*; Angela Y. Davis, *Women, Race, and Class*; hooks, *Ain't I a Woman*; Payne, *I've Got the Light*, 265–83, 363–90; and Sartain, *Invisible Activists.*

45. Carter, *Everybody's Paid but the Teacher*; Collier-Thomas and Franklin, *Sisters in the Struggle*; Crawford, Rouse, and Woods, *Women in the Civil Rights Movement*; Crocco, Munro, and Weiler, *Pedagogies of Resistance*; Angela Y. Davis, *Women, Race, and Class*; Giddings, *When and Where I Enter*; Gilmore, *Gender and Jim Crow*; Greene, *Our Separate Ways*; Harris-Perry, *Sister Citizen*; Hine, *Black Women in America*; Hine, *Hine Sight*; McGuire, *At the Dark End of the Street*; Ransby, *Ella Baker*; and Ransby, *Eslanda.*

46. Barnett, "Invisible Southern Black Women," 162.

47. Ibid.

48. Gilmore, *Gender and Jim Crow*, 147–75.

49. Patricia Hill Collins, *Black Feminist Thought*, 204.

50. Ibid.

51. Ibid.

52. Ibid.

53. Huntley and McKerley, *Footsoldiers for Democracy*; and Nick Patterson, *Birmingham Foot Soldiers.* The term *foot soldiers* is a local color moniker for those individuals who fought on the front lines of the Birmingham civil rights movement.

54. Loder-Jackson, "Bridging the Tradition of Activism"; and Loder-Jackson, "Hope and Despair."

55. Charron, *Freedom's Teacher*; Christensen, "Ms. Lillie M. H. Fincher"; and Huntley and McKerley, *Footsoldiers for Democracy.*

56. Aldon D. Morris, *Origins of the Civil Rights Movement*; Fairclough, *Teaching Equality*; and Fairclough, *A Class of Their Own.* In addition, Vanessa Siddle Walker has authored several notable works: *Their Highest Potential*; "Valued Segregated Schools"; "The Architects of Black Schooling"; "Organized Resistance and Black Educators' Quest"; *Hello Professor;* and "The Annual *Brown* Lecture"; and "Tolerated Tokenism."

57. Beauboeuf-Lafontant, "A Movement Against and Beyond"; Beauboeuf-Lafontant, "Womanist Experience of Caring"; Beauboeuf-Lafontant," Womanist Lessons for Reinventing"; Dingus, "Doing the Best We Could"; Foster, *Black Teachers on Teaching*; Franklin, "They Rose or Fell Together"; Karen A. Johnson,

Pitre, and Kenneth L. Johnson, *African American Women Educators*; Hilton Kelly, "What Jim Crow's Teachers Could Do"; Hilton Kelly, *Race, Remembering, and Jim Crow's Teachers*; Hilton Kelly, "Just Something Gone"; Loder-Jackson, "Bridging the Tradition of Activism"; Loder-Jackson, "Hope and Despair"; Marshall and Amy L. Anderson, *Activist Educators*; Preston-Grimes, "Fulfilling the Promise"; Ramsey, "Caring is Activism"; and Ward Randolph, "It is Better to Light a Candle."

58. Bailey, "Teaching as Activism and Excuse," 125–26; James, *Transcending the Talented Tenth*, 141–42; and hooks, *Teaching to Transgress*, 52. Bailey noted a philosophical tension between feminist scholars hooks and James that is instructive for illuminating this assumption. hooks contended that her African American teachers' critical pedagogy influenced her own pedagogy as a college professor and prepared her to confront racism and White supremacy constructively. Conversely, James refuted the notion that teaching in and of itself constitutes activism. She argued that institutionalized teaching, which by design reinforces the status quo of those in power and control of schools, often undermines activist aims. In James's view, being an activist very often jeopardized the teaching careers of African American women.

59. Freire, *Pedagogy of the Oppressed*, 87.

60. Patricia Hill Collins, *Another Kind of Public Education*, 133; and Preston-Grimes, "Fulfilling the Promise," 41.

61. Baker, *Betrayal*; Chabot, "Framing, Transnational Diffusion"; and Aldon D. Morris, *Origins of Civil Rights Movement*.

62. Alridge, "African American Education"; James D. Anderson, *Education of Blacks in the South*; Joyce E. King, "Declaration of Intellectual Independence"; Carol D. Lee, "State of Knowledge about Education of African Americans"; Carol D. Lee and Slaughter-Defoe, "Historical and Cultural Influences," 352; Lomotey, *Encyclopedia of African American Education*; Theresa Perry, Steele, and Hilliard, *Young, Gifted, and Black*; and Tillman, *Sage Handbook of African American Education*.

63. Alridge, "African American Education."

64. Ibid., 24.

65. Alridge, "African American Education," 24; Carol D. Lee, "State of Knowledge about Education of African Americans"; Carol D. Lee and Slaughter-Defoe, "Historical and Cultural Influences," 352; Alridge, *Educational Thought of W. E. B. Du Bois*; and David Levering Lewis, *W. E. B. Du Bois*, 546–51. Education scholars Carol D. Lee and Slaughter-Defoe offer an insightful framework for delineating three distinctive historical models of Black intellectual thought that prevailed in the late nineteenth and early twentieth century: Euro-classical liberal; industrial education; and education for Black self-reliance. While I agree that these models dominated certain historical periods, the "supporters" of these models were often influenced by more than one educational philosophy. For example, Derrick Alridge and David Levering Lewis present complex portraits of Du Bois's educational philosophy in their respective biographies. Moreover, elements of

these three models identified by Lee and Slaughter-Defoe were commingled in a number of early-twentieth-century Black schools in the U.S. South.

66. Alridge, "African American Education," 25.

67. Ibid., 25; and Woodson, *Mis-education of the Negro*.

68. Alridge, "African American Education"; Bieze and Gasman, *Booker T. Washington Rediscovered*; Hilton Kelly, "Just Something Gone"; Loder-Jackson, "Mary McCleod Bethune"; McCluskey, 2014; and Karen A. Johnson, "On Classical versus Vocational Training." Some historians have noted that prominent late-nineteenth- and early-twentieth-century African American educators that are typically pigeonholed as accommodationist actually supported civil rights causes behind the scenes and often integrated strands of classical education and Black cultural heritage into their industrial education curricula.

69. Dingus, "Doing the Best We Could"; Harley, "Beyond the Classroom"; Karen A. Johnson, "On Classical versus Vocational Training"; Karen A. Johnson, "Cooper, Anna Julia Haywood"; Karen A. Johnson, Pitre, and Kenneth L. Johnson, *African American Women Educators*; Loder-Jackson, "Mary McCleod Bethune"; Neverdon-Morton, "Self-help Programs as Educative Activities"; Perkins, "Impact of 'Cult of True Womanhood"; Perkins, "The History of Blacks in Teaching"; Shaw, *What a Woman Ought to Be and to Do*; and Ward Randolph, "It Is Better to Light a Candle."

70. Charron, *Freedom's Teacher*; Collier-Thomas and Franklin, *Sisters in the Struggle*, 95–120; Karen A. Johnson, "Septima Poinsette Clark's Literacy Teaching"; and Aldon D. Morris, *Origins of the Civil Rights Movement*, 148–52, 237–39.

71. Crocco, Munro, and Weiler, *Pedagogies of Resistance*, 61–82; James T. Patterson, *Brown v. Board of Education*, 132–33, 136; and Roach, "Scholar-Activists."

72. Preston-Grimes, "Fulfilling the Promise"; and Ward Randolph, "It is Better to Light a Candle."

73. Hilton Kelly, "What Jim Crow's Teachers Could Do"; and Hilton Kelly, *Race, Remembering, and Jim Crow's Teachers*.

74. Mannheim, "Problem of Generations"; and Ryder, "Cohort as a Concept." Life course methods undergird the third assumption and are discussed in more detail in the appendix. Selected texts addressing contemporary African American generational tensions include: Patricia Hill Collins, *From Black Power to Hip Hop*; Ginwright, *Black Youth Rising*; Hamilton, "Activists for the New Millennium"; Kelley, *In the Fire*; Loder-Jackson, "Bridging the Tradition of Activism"; Loder-Jackson, "Hope and Despair"; and Taines, "Intervening in Alienation."

75. Carsen, *In Struggle*; Lewis, *Shadows of Youth*; Payne, *I've Got the Light of Freedom*, 338–62; Aldon D. Morris, *Origins of the Civil Rights Movement*, 239–50; and Juan Williams, *Eyes on the Prize*, 164–78.

76. Fairclough, *To Redeem the Soul of America*; Andrew B. Lewis, *Shadows of Youth*; Carsen, *In Struggle*; and Aldon D. Morris, *Origins of the Civil Rights Movement*, 233–35.

77. Shaw, *What a Woman Ought to Be*.

78. Strauss and Howe, *Generations*; Wellner, "Forgotten Baby Boom"; and Mannheim, "Problem of Generations." An analysis of African American educators born on opposite sides of the civil rights movement should be considered in light of Mannheim's articulation of a *problem of generations,* which is explicated in the Appendix.

79. Bynoe, "Connected but Distinct"; Ginwright, *Black in School*; Dyson, *Know What I Mean?*; Kitwana, *Hip Hop Generation;* and Rose, "Fear of a Black Planet."

80. Boyd, *New H.N.I.C.*, 7. Boyd proposed that the hip-hop generation should be judged in its own right apart from the designation "Generation X" because mainstream categorizations "have little to do with Black people because they were most appropriately terms used to understand dominant White youth culture, and, at best, lump Black youth in this flawed equation as an afterthought."

81. Alridge, "From Civil Rights to Hip Hop"; Bositis, *Diverging Generations*; Patricia Hill Collins, *From Black Power to Hip Hop*; Cose, *End of Anger;* Kelley, *Into the Fire*; Kitwana, *Hip Hop Generation*; Loder-Jackson, "Bridging the Tradition of Activism"; and Loder-Jackson, "Hope and Despair."

82. Kitwana, *Hip Hop Generation*, 147.

83. Tavernise, "Outside Cleveland, Snapshots of Poverty's Surge"; Michelle Alexander, *New Jim Crow*; Bositis, *Diverging Generations*; Patricia Hill Collins, *From Black Power to Hip Hop*; Dyson, *Know What I Mean?*; Kelley, *Into the Fire*; and William Julius Wilson, *Truly Disadvantaged.*

84. Kitwana, *Hip Hop Generation*, 3–24.

85. Ibid., 3–24.

86. Patricia Hill Collins, *Black Feminist Thought*, 223.

87. Ibid.

88. Bonvillian, "State Earns 'A' for Schools Teaching Civil Rights"; and Griffin and Bollen, "What Do These Memories Do?," 596.

89. Alridge, "From Civil Rights to Hip Hop," 238.

90. Ibid., 241.

91. Kitwana, *Hip Hop Generation*, 145–74; Patricia Hill Collins, *Black Feminist Thought*, 204; and Patricia Hill Collins, *From Black Power to Hip Hop*. I hesitate to take these comparisons too far given Collins's sociological critique of the sexism and sexual politics inherent in hip-hop culture.

92. Kitwana, *Hip Hop Generation*, 195–215; Patricia Hill Collins, *From Black Power to Hip Hop*; Rose, "Fear of a Black Planet"; and Jeff Johnson, "Young, Black and in Decline in the Obama Age?" In contrast to Kitwana's and other young activists' optimistic portrayal of hip-hop politics, Jeff Johnson, a journalist and social activist who served as vice president for the Hip Hop Summit Action Network and national youth director for the NAACP, expressed skepticism about the capacity for hip-hop politics to produce meaningful social change, noting its members' diminished visibility in the 2012 presidential election season compared to the historic 2008 election of Barack Obama as the first African American president of the United States.

93. Kitwana, *Hip Hop Generation*, 117.

94. Harris-Lacewell (now Harris-Perry) quoted in Moyers, "Interview with Melissa Harris-Lacewell."

95. Ibid.

96. Jeremy Gray, "Civil Rights Institute Honors Lowery," 8D.

97. Ibid.

98. Patricia Hill Collins, *Another Kind of Public Education*, 82–134; Knight, "Why Schools Must Talk about Trayvon Martin"; and Pratt-Harris, "Pedagogy and Trayvon Martin." George Zimmerman's exoneration in killing Trayvon Martin, an unarmed African American teenager in Sanford, Florida, on February 26, 2012, set off a firestorm of protest, public discourse, and curricular recommendations concerning race and criminal justice centered around the notorious state-level "stand your ground" laws, which remove the duty to retreat before using force in self-defense (see criminal.findlaw.com/criminal-law-basics/states-that-have-stand-your-ground-laws.html).

99. Hamilton, "Activists for the New Millennium," 21.

100. Franklin, "They Rose or Fell Together," 48.

101. Akrofi, Botchey, and Takyi, *An English Akan Ewe Dictionary.*

CHAPTER 1. PIONEERING BLACK SCHOOLS SECOND TO NONE

1. The racial descriptors "Black" and "African American" are used interchangeably throughout this book. However, Black is used consistently in chapters addressing historical content that predated the common use of the term African American.

2. Ex-slave narrative interview by Edward F. Harper, "They 'Hung' Mr. Lincoln," Box# SG022774, transcript, Ex-Slave Tales, Jefferson County Collection, Alabama Writers Project, Digital Collections, Alabama Department of Archives and History. digital.archives.alabama.gov/.

3. Ibid., 1.

4. Ibid., 3; and Blackmon, *Slavery by Another Name.*

5. Jerome A. Gray, Reed, and Walton, 16.

6. Dillon, *History of Birmingham Public Schools*; Ruth B. Lamonte, "Origin of an Urban School"; Edward S. Lamonte, *Politics and Welfare in Birmingham*; and Vaughn, "Historical Sketches of Birmingham Schools."

7. Jerome A. Gray, Reed, and Walton, *History of Alabama State Teachers Association*, 14; and Flynt, *Dixie's Forgotten People*, 8. One rare exception was in Mobile, Alabama, where some Blacks were educated during slavery. In *Education of Blacks in the South*, James D. Anderson estimated a 5 percent literacy rate among enslaved Africans, as illustrated in Esther King Casey's narrative.

8. Jefferson County Board of Education, "Elementary and Secondary Public Education, 1819–1868," 16. The city of Birmingham established a school district independent of the Jefferson County Schools in 1885.

9. James D. Anderson, *Education of Blacks in the South*, 5; Feldman, *Sense of Place*, 36, 112, 113, 140; Bond, *Negro Education in Alabama*, 82–84; Jerome A. Gray, Reed, and Walton, *History of ASTA*, 115–16; Sherer, *Subordination or Liberation?*, 114–48; and Schweninger, "American Missionary Association and Northern Philanthropy."

10. Jerome A. Gray, Reed, and Walton, *History of ASTA*, 15–17.

11. Ibid.

12. Jerome A. Gray, Reed, and Walton, *History of ASTA*, 15–17; Schweninger, "AMA and Northern Philanthropy"; and Sherer, *Subordination or Liberation?*, 2–3.

13. Ibid. According to Sherer, The Freedmen's Bureau, in conjunction with the AMA, began enlisting Black teachers and principals in 1866 "wherever possible." The bureau did so more so out of necessity because the enormous demand for Black education could not be met solely by White missionaries. There was also an exploitive motivation given that the bureau realized it could get away with paying Black teachers less than White teachers.

14. Feldman, *Sense of Place*; Ruth B. Lamonte, "Origin of an Urban School"; Dillon, *History of Birmingham Public Schools*; and Vaughn, "Historical Sketches of Birmingham Schools." Feldman has published the only book to date chronicling Birmingham's Black middle-class community's investment in schools and other institutions. A few other early histories of Birmingham education attribute the establishment of Birmingham's first Black schools primarily or solely to the efforts of White civic and school leaders such as John Herbert Phillips and Samuel Ullman.

15. Carl V. Harris, "Stability and Change in Discrimination," 376; and Jerome A. Gray, Reed, and Walton, 17–25.

16. James D. Anderson, *Education of Blacks in the South*; Ashmore, *Negro and the Schools*; Bond, "Negro Education"; Bond, *Negro Education in Alabama*; and Sherer, *Subordination or Liberation*. Sherer concluded that White Southerners were motivated to educate Blacks in the post–Civil War era for the following reasons: many were threatened by the prospect of White Northern missionaries and philanthropists educating Blacks for liberation; some poor Whites needed jobs as teachers in Black schools; many Whites were concerned about illiterate Blacks voting after 1867–68; and some White educators supported universal education for Blacks and Whites.

17. Bullock, *History of Negro Education*, 74.

18. Bond, *Negro Education in Alabama*; Jerome A. Gray, Reed, and Walton, *History of ASTA*, 17–25; and Sherer, *Subordination or Liberation?*, 3.

19. Ibid.

20. Ibid.

21. Ibid.

22. Ibid., "Stability and Change in Discrimination," 376.

23. Carl V. Harris; and Jerome A. Gray, Reed, and Walton, *History of ASTA*, 17–25.

24. Bond, *Negro Education in Alabama*; Carl V. Harris, "Stability and Change in Discrimination"; Jerome A. Gray, Reed, and Walton, *History of ASTA*, 17–25; and Sherer, *Subordination or Liberation?*.

25. *Birmingham News*, "Looking Back . . . First Public School"; Ruth B. Lamonte, "Origin of an Urban School," 6; and Edward S. Lamonte, *Politics and Welfare in Alabama*, 10.

26. Feldman, *Sense of Place*, 113–14; and Ruth B. Lamonte, "Origins of Urban School," 6–7.

27. Ibid. It should be emphasized that while Birmingham's Black residents strived arduously for publicly supported schools, in the interim they educated their children through private institutions including churches, homes, and civic organizations.

28. Ruth B. Lamonte, "Origins of an Urban School," 6–7. The race of the first teacher was not mentioned in this text, but according to Rabinowitz's "Half a Loaf" there was a shift from White to Black teachers in Black schools in the urban U.S. South between 1865 and 1890.

29. Feldman, *Sense of Place*, 113–14; and Ruth B. Lamonte, "Origins of Urban School," 6–7.

30. Dillon, *History of Birmingham Public Schools*, 3; Feldman, *Sense of Place*, 113–14; Ruth B. Lamonte, "Origins of an Urban School," 6–7; Phillips, "History of Public Schools in Birmingham," 107; and Vaughn, "Historical Sketches of Birmingham Schools," 6. Although Feldman and Ruth B. Lamonte credit Birmingham's Black community for initiating public school establishment for their children, Dillon and Vaughn either gloss over or omit their agency altogether.

31. Feldman, *Sense of Place*, 112–36; and Ruth B. Lamonte, "Origins of Urban School," 6–7. Early White supporters of Black education in Birmingham were typically not natives of the U.S. South. John Herbert Phillips was an English emigrant from Kentucky and Ohio, who became the school superintendent in 1883 until his death in 1921. Samuel Ullman was a German Jewish emigrant who first migrated to Natchez, Mississippi, and later to Birmingham. He became a school board member and a vocal supporter of Black education relative to Whites of his day.

32. Ibid.

33. James D. Anderson, *Education of Blacks in the South*; Bond, *Negro Education in Alabama*; Cecelski, *Along Freedom's Road*; Fairclough, *Teaching Equality*; Fairclough, *Class of their Own*; Walker, *Their Highest Potential*; and Walker, *Hello Professor*.

34. James D. Anderson, *Education of Blacks in the South*; Bullock, *History of Negro Education*; Bond, "Influence of Personalities, I"; Bond, "Influence of Personalities, II"; Gardner, "Educational Contributions of Booker T. Washington," 506–507; Jerome A. Gray, Reed, and Walton, *History of ASTA*, 39–42; McCormick, "Julius Rosenwald Fund"; National Trust for Historic Preservation, *National Rosenwald Schools Conference*; and Watkins, *White Architects of Black Education*. Washington also received support from prominent White individuals including Andrew Carnegie, John D. Rockefeller, Robert Ogden, H. H. Rogers, Collis P. Huntington, and William Baldwin.

35. James D. Anderson, *Education of Blacks in the South*; Bullock, *History of Negro Education*; Bond, "Influence of Personalities, I"; Bond, "Influence

of Personalities, II"; Jerome A. Gray, Reed, and Walton, *History of ASTA;* and Watkins, *White Architects of Black Education.*

36. Ibid; Dennis, "Schooling along the Color Line." Michael Dennis argued that progressive Southern Whites contributed more to Black education during the post–Civil War era than some historians have portrayed.

37. James D. Anderson, *Education of Blacks in the South*, 72, 83, 84, 86, 245; Bullock, *History of Negro Education*; Bond, "Influence of Personalities, I"; Bond, "Influence of Personalities, II"; Jerome A. Gray, Reed, and Walton, *History of ASTA*, 41–42; and Watkins, *White Architects of Black Education*, 161, 169, 172–74, 175, 177. The establishment of normal schools will be discussed in more detail later in this chapter.

38. Ibid.

39. Ascoli, *Julius Rosenwald*; Hoffschwelle, *Rosenwald Schools of American South*; Deutsch, *You Need a Schoolhouse*; National Trust for Historic Preservation, *National Rosenwald Schools Conference*; Encyclopedia of Alabama, "Rosenwald Schools in Alabama"; and Philanthropy Roundtable, "Julius Rosenwald." The discussion on Rosenwald that follows is guided primarily by these sources.

40. Ibid.

41. James D. Anderson, *Education of Blacks in the South*, 153; Deutsch, *You Need a Schoolhouse*, 216–17; Fultz, "Jeanes Supervisors," 96; Jerome A. Gray, Reed, and Walton, *History of ASTA*, 51–53; Watkins, *White Architects of Black Education*, 19, 91, 110,133, 149. The Jeanes Fund, known formerly as the Negro Rural School Foundation, and its relationship with early Black teacher training will be discussed in more detail later in this chapter.

42. Hoffschwelle, *Rosenwald Schools of American South*, 215.

43. Embree and Waxman, *Investment in People*, 50; and Hoffschwelle, *Rosenwald Schools of American South*, 283.

44. Hoffschwelle, *Rosenwald Schools of American South*, 283.

45. Fisk University, Rosenwald Database; and Miles College Centennial History Committee, *Miles College*, 26.

46. Harlan, *Booker T. Washington: Making of Black Leader*; Harlan, *Booker T. Washington*; Washington, *Up from Slavery;* and Feldman, *Sense of Place*, 189–90. Several of Birmingham's prominent Black businessmen and civic leaders were well connected with Washington, namely William Pettiford, Thomas Walker, Ulysses Mason, Thomas Windham, and Edward Brown. Washington's self-help message resonated with many Black middle-class residents. Birmingham's Black businessmen and civic club members showed their admiration for Washington by naming their organizations after him for example, millionaire A. G. Gaston's Booker T. Washington Insurance Company and a Colored women's club's Booker T. Washington Auxiliary of the Red Cross.

47. The classic philosophical tension between Washington and Du Bois has been addressed in a number of texts, including: James D. Anderson, *Education of Blacks in the South*; Du Bois, *Souls of Black Folk*; Harlan, *Booker T. Washington: Making of Black Leader*; Harlan, *Booker T. Washington*; David Levering Lewis, *W.*

E. B. Du Bois; August Meier, *Negro Thought in America*; Jacqueline M. Moore, *Booker T. Washington*; Sherer, *Subordination or Liberation?*, 44–64; Thelma D. Perry, *History of American Teachers Association*, 37–41, 69–86; Booker T. Washington, *Up from Slavery*; Watkins, *White Architects of Black Education*; and Watkins, "Blacks and the Curriculum." Thelma D. Perry's history of the ATA, which was the first and foremost national Black teachers association in the United States, is discussed in more detail in chapter 2. This text extends the Washington-Du Bois debate to include Washington's tensions with the Afro-American League, a late-nineteenth-century nonpartisan political rights organization made up mostly of Northerners. Sherer noted that Washington's industrial education philosophy was not adopted whole scale in Alabama's Black schools as many incorporated a blended curriculum of industrial, classical, and Black cultural heritage content.

48. Ibid.

49. Sherer, *Subordination or Liberation?*, 64.

50. Bond, *Negro Education in Alabama*, 145.

51. Ibid.

52. Bond, *Negro Education in Alabama*, 147.

53. Birmingham Public Library, *Dr. Arthur Harold Parker*; Feldman, *Sense of Place*, 119, 121–34; Parker, *Dream that Came True*; and Parker United Alumni Association, *Parker High School*. The discussion that follows is guided primarily by these texts.

54. Siebert, *Underground Railroad: From Slavery*; and Still, *Underground Railroad: Authentic Narratives*. The Underground Railroad refers to a clandestinely executed system of cooperation among an antislavery coalition made up of both Whites and Blacks to aid enslaved Blacks in reaching freedom in Northern American states and Canada.

55. Vlach, *Back of the Big House*.

56. Parker, *Dream that Came True*, 5–6.

57. Childers, "Where Pupils Study Books and Brooms."

58. Dizier, "Parker High Long Way from Single Room."

59. Ibid.

60. Birmingham Public Library, *Dr. Arthur Harold Parker*; Parker, *Dream that Came True*, 2, 36–39, 48–49; and Phillips, "History of Public Schools," 114–18.

61. Fairclough, *Class of Their Own*, 267—72; and Parker, *Dream that Came True*, 6.

62. Parker, *Dream that Came True*, 6.

63. Ibid.

64. Hayes, *Dr. Carol W. Hayes*; and Parker, *Dream that Came True*, 2.

65. Feldman, *Sense of Place*, 126.

66. Tarry, *Third Door*, 22.

67. Ibid., 25.

68. Gertrude Crum Sanders, interview by Mausiki S. Scales, Birmingham (Ala.), June 21, 1994, interview #193 (btvct02119), Behind the Veil: Documenting

African-American Life in the Jim Crow South Digital Collection, John Hope Franklin Research Center, Duke University Libraries, Durham, NC, 26.

69. Ibid., 27.

70. Ibid; and Cheryl J. Sanders, *Saints in Exile.*

71. Gertrude Crum Sanders, interview, 27.

72. Ibid., 29. Colorism, which refers to discrimination or prejudice based on skin tone, is a theme that comes up in the teacher narratives discussed in this book as well as other books related to Black teachers during the *Brown* era. For more in-depth readings see Gatewood, *Aristocrats of Color*, Berry, *Black-on-Black Discrimination*, Burch, *Skin Color and Criminal Justice*, and Hochschild and Weaver, "Skin Color Paradox." Gatewood's book, in particular, addresses how factors such as colorism, a traceable genealogy of White heritage, early emancipation status, and literacy shaped the Black social class structure in the late-nineteenth-century U.S. South.

73. E. Franklin Frazier, *Black Bourgeoisie*; and Gatewood, *Aristocrats of Color.*

74. Childers, "Where Pupils Study Books and Brooms."

75. Ibid.

76. Jerome A. Gray, Reed, and Walton, *History of ASTA*. ASTA's history will be discussed in more detail in chapter 2.

77. Birmingham Public Library, *Dr. Arthur Harold Parker.*

78. Juanita Waiters Clarke, interview by Paul Ortiz, Birmingham (Ala.), June 29, 1994, interview #159 (btvct02021), Behind the Veil: Documenting African-American Life in the Jim Crow South Digital Collection, John Hope Franklin Research Center, Duke University Libraries, Durham, NC, 17.

79. Tarry, *Third Door*, 25.

80. Fairclough, *Teaching Equality,* 15.

81. Fairclough, *Teaching Equality,* 55; Parker, *Dream that Came True*, 38–39; and Phillips, "History of Public Schools," 111–13.

82. Fairclough, *Class of their Own*, 268–72.

83. Parker, *Dream that Came True*, 59–62.

84. Ibid., 57.

85. Ibid.

86. Walker, "Architects of Black Schooling," 65; and Loder, "Dilemmas Confronting Urban Principals." Walker's collaborator and Georgia Teachers Association leader and principal Ulysses Byas explained that Black principals during his time often had to "leapfrog," or "placate their bosses," in order to get the resources they needed for their schools. I have written previously that African American principals working in contemporary urban schools encounter similar and unique dilemmas in brokering resources for their schools.

87. Ruth B. Lamonte, "Origins of an Urban Public School," 6–7, 9; Feldman, *Sense of Place*, 115, 117, 118, 120, 122, 125, 133, 136, 191; Fairclough, *Class of their Own*, 273–74; and Fairclough, *Teaching Equality*, 17.

88. Parker, *Dream that Came True*, 66–67.

89. Ibid., 67.

90. Ibid., 79.

91. Ibid.

92. *Birmingham Age-Herald*, "Dr. A. H. Parker."

93. *Birmingham News*, "Dr. A. H. Parker: Servant and Leader."

94. Ibid.

95. Birmingham Public Library, *Dr. Arthur Harold Parker*; *Birmingham News*, "Dr. A. H. Parker and 'A Dream' "; and Parker United Alumni Association, *Parker High School*.

96. Neverdon-Morton, *Afro-American Women of the South*; Perkins, "Impact of 'Cult of True Womanhood' "; and Wesley, *History of National Association of Colored Women's Clubs*.

97. Feldman, *Sense of Place*, 164–87. Birmingham sibling-teachers, Clara Moses Wilson and Sibyl Moses, were Colored Women's Club members and suffragists. Clara Moses Wilson's oral history is archived at UAB Digital Collections, www.mhsl.uab.edu/dc/.

98. Richard Bailey, *They Too Call Alabama Home*; Edgemon, *Carrie Tuggle and Tuggle Normal*; Feldman, *Sense of Place*, 171, 172–77; and Yelverton, *They also Served*. The discussion that follows is based primarily on these texts.

99. Feldman, *Sense of Place*, 172.

100. Washington, *Up from Slavery*. According to a biography published in the Black-owned *Birmingham World*, Tuggle was of mixed heritage. Her father is described as a full-blooded Indian chief, who was one of the few remaining survivors of the Mohawk tribe.

101. Ball, *Hugo L. Black*.

102. *Birmingham World*, "Education Carrie Tuggle 1859–1924."

103. Edgemon, *Carrie Tuggle and Tuggle Normal*, 7–9.

104. Ibid., 17; and Feldman, *Sense of Place*, 174.

105. Brittain, "Some Reflections on Negro Suffrage," 128; and Feldman, *Sense of Place*, 178, 192.

106. Phillips, *History of Public Schools in Birmingham*, 107–18.

107. Noble, "Education of the Negro," 405–16.

108. James D. Anderson, *Education of Blacks in the South*, 111; Fultz, "Teacher Training and African American Education"; and Walker, "African American Teaching in the South."

109. Jacqueline M. Moore, *Booker T. Washington, W. E. B. Du Bois;* Gardner, "Educational Contributions of Booker T. Washington," 507–10; Booker T. Washington, *Up from Slavery*, 153; and Watkins, *White Architects of Black Education*, 60.

110. Jerome A. Gray, Reed, and Walton, *History of ASTA*, 41.

111. Ibid.

112. Jerome A. Gray, Reed, and Walton, *History of ASTA*, 51–54; and James D. Anderson, 156, 158.

113. Jerome A. Gray, Reed, and Walton, *History of ASTA*, 51–54.

114. Alabama State University, *History of ASU,* http://www.lib.alasu.edu/archives/research/history/asu.html.

115. Ibid.

116. Ibid.

117. Miles College Centennial History Committee, *Miles College*. The discussion that follows is based primarily on information from this rare secondary source documenting Miles College's history and published during its centennial celebration in 2005.

118. Ibid., 15.

119. Miles College's role in the Birmingham civil rights movement is discussed in chapter 3. ASU's civil rights history is beyond the scope of this book, but more information may be found at the ASU Archives and Special Collections Department.

120. *Birmingham Post*, "Founder of Orphan Home."

121. The phrase "credit to your race" was used paternalistically by Whites as well as some Blacks during this era to describe noteworthy accomplishments that distinguished Blacks from the prejudiced attributions to their race.

122. Edgemon, *Carrie Tuggle and Tuggle Normal*, 14–15; and Sherer, *Subordination or Liberation?*, 3, 5, 128–30. Sherer also addressed Black school arsons in Alabama during the Reconstruction and beyond.

123. Parker, *Dream that Came True*, 32.

124. Walker, "Annual Brown Lecture"; Walker, *Hello Professor*; Walker, "African American Teaching in the South"; Fairclough, *Class of their Own*, 307–53; Fultz, "Caught between a Rock and a Hard Place"; Karpinski, *Visible Company of Professionals*; Jerome A. Gray, Reed, and Walton, *History of ASTA*; and Thelma D. Perry, *History of ATA*.

CHAPTER 2. ORGANIZING FOR EDUCATIONAL EQUITY

1. Parker, *Dream that Came True*, 18; Childers, "Where Pupils Study Books and Brooms"; Jerome A. Gray, Reed, and Walton, *History of ASTA*, 43, 60–61; and Logan, *Negro in American Life*. According to the *History of ASTA*, A. H. Parker served as president of ASTA between 1900 and 1902, although the *Birmingham News Age-Herald* published a 1905 date for his presidential inauguration speech.

2. Exodus 5:7, King James Version: "Ye shall no more give the people straw to make brick, as heretofore: let them go and gather straw for themselves."

3. Walker, "Tolerated Tokenism"; Walker, "African American Teaching in the South"; Walker, "Annual Brown Lecture"; Karpinski, "*Visible Company of Professionals*"; Fairclough, *Class of their Own*; Fultz, "Caught between a Rock"; and Thelma D. Perry, *History of ATA*.

4. Ibid.

5. Thelma D. Perry, *History of ATA*, 79.

6. Ibid.

7. Fultz, "Caught between a Rock," 68.

8. Ibid., 69.

9. Ibid., 67.

10. Thelma D. Perry, *History of ATA*, 45; and Jerome A. Gray, Reed, and Walton, *History of ASTA*, 62, 78-80. This chapter's discussion of NCTA/NATCS/ATA and ASTA is based primarily on these two books. Both books were published by the National Education Association (NEA) as a part of its merger agreement to document the histories of former Black teachers associations, which were subsumed under larger historically White teacher associations. One of the co-authors of the *History of ASTA*, Joe Reed, was a longtime leader of ASTA, who was responsible for spearheading its merger with the state arm of NEA, that is, the Alabama Education Association (AEA), in partnership with AEA president Paul Hubbert. For many years under their co-leadership, the AEA was a formidable force in Alabama education and politics. However, its power began to wane after their retirement, coupled with the resurgence of the Republican Party's dominance in the Alabama legislature in 2010. The Alabama State University Archives and Special Collections Department houses the original drafts and associated documents published in *The History of ASTA*, which I perused in great detail before locating the book on a separate floor of the library.

11. Jerome A. Gray, Reed, and Walton, *History of ASTA*, 28–30; and Sherer, *Subordination or Liberation?*, 19. There is some conflicting information between these two accounts of ASTA's origins. Jerome A. Gray et al. document one hundred inaugural participants whereas Sherer noted only sixty "teachers of black schools." Sherer's numeration evidently did not include the White participants.

12. Jerome A. Gray, Reed, and Walton, *History of ASTA*, 30–32.

13. Sherer, *Subordination or Liberation?*, 17–22.

14. Ibid., 19.

15. Ibid.

16. Jerome A. Gray, Reed, and Walton, *History of ASTA*, 125.

17. Jerome A. Gray, Reed, and Walton, *History of ASTA*, 27–29; Thelma D. Perry, *History of ATA*, 15; and Sherer, *Subordination of Liberation?*, 19, 23–31. Sherer noted that Paterson's motivation for pursuing teaching and leadership in Black schools as a White immigrant can only be speculated. Several aspects of his life trajectory are consistent with his penchant for Black education. Paterson was staunchly opposed to the terrorism of the Ku Klux Klan. He also taught Black workmen on a ditching crew at one of his earlier jobs in America. During his stint in Hale County, Alabama, he became acquainted with a plantation owner who enlisted him to start a plantation school to keep recently freed Blacks under his stead.

18. Jerome A. Gray, Reed, and Walton, *History of ASTA*, 30; and Thelma D. Perry, *History of ATA*, 37–41, 69–86. Jerome A. Gray et al. described Washington as ASTA's "energizer" although they credit William B. Paterson as the lead organizer.

19. Thelma D. Perry, *History of ATA,* 37–41, 69–86. Also, several chapters in Sherer's *Subordination or Liberation?* address philosophical differences between

Washington and some Black and White educational leaders and schools in Alabama that espoused a liberal or classical education.

20. Ibid.

21. Jerome A. Gray, Reed, and Walton, *History of ASTA*, 30.

22. Sherer, *Subordination or Liberation?*, 20–21.

23. Ibid., 20.

24. Thelma D. Perry, *History of ATA*, 39.

25. Ibid.

26. Ibid.

27. Sherer, *Subordination or Liberation?*, 20–21.

28. Ibid., 21.

29. Jerome A. Gray, Reed, and Walton, *History of ASTA*; Karpinski, "Visible Company of Professionals," 172, 175; Thelma D. Perry, *History of American Teachers Association*, 15–20; and Fultz, "Caught between a Rock and a Hard Place," 69, 71, 73, 75.

30. Jerome A. Gray, Reed, and Walton, *History of ASTA;* and Thelma D. Perry, *History of ATA*.

31. Thelma Perry, *History of ATA*, 79; Karpinski, *"Visible Company of Professionals,"* 15–27; Walker, "Tolerated Tokenism"; and Walker, "Annual *Brown* Lecture."

32. The organization continues today as the Association for the Study of African American Life and History (ASALH).

33. Jerome A. Gray, Reed, and Walton, *History of ASTA*, 91.

34. Ibid., 114.

35. Ibid., 116.

36. Ibid., 114.

37. Jerome A. Gray et al., *History of ASTA*, 126.

38. James Tyra Harris, *Alabama Reaction to Brown*, 79; and Jerome A. Gray, Reed, and Walton, *History of ASTA*, 156–57.

39. Jerome A. Gray, Reed, and Walton, *History of ASTA*, 113.

40. Ibid., 43, 60–61.

41. Rousmaniere, *Principal's Office*.

42. Jefferson County BOE, "History of Jefferson County Board," 110.

43. "JCNTA Constitution."

44. Jefferson County BOE, "History of Jefferson County Board," 110.

45. Fairclough, 309–10, 311, 344, 345, 347; Kirk, "NAACP Campaign for Teacher's Salary; Tushnet, *NAACP Legal Strategy*, 18–19, 37, 42; and Walker, "Annual Brown Lecture."

46. Kirk, "NAACP Campaign for Teacher's Salary," 529.

47. Fairclough, *Class of their Own*, 310.

48. Kirk, "NAACP Campaign for Teachers' Salary," 533–34.

49. Ibid., 534.

50. Carl V. Harris, "Stability and Change in Discrimination," 376–77.

51. Kirk, "NAACP Campaign for Teacher's Salary," 529–31; James Rawn Jr., *Root and Branch*, 66, 73, 86, 95, 101–102, 146–49; McNeil, *Groundwork*, 114–17, 135; and Tushnet, *NAACP Legal Strategy*, 20, 26–28; 45, 56, 65. The NAACP commissioned attorney Nathan Margold to strategize a legal campaign against segregation. The report called for an all-out attack on *Plessy*'s principle of separateness, which meant litigating cases that mandated separate facilities and resources for plaintiffs in hopes of fiscally wearing down the local- and state-governed school districts.

52. James T. Patterson, *Brown v. Board of Education*, 1–20.

53. Ashmore, *Negro and Schools*, 153.

54. Ibid.

55. Ibid.

56. Ibid., 157.

57. Ashmore, *Negro and Schools*, 158.

58. Ibid., 158.

59. Margo, "Teacher Salaries in Black and White," 53.

60. Ibid.

61. Ashmore, *Negro and Schools*, 159.

62. Ibid.

63. Bullock, *History of Negro Education*, 216.

64. Fultz, "African American Teachers in the South."

65. Clemon and Fair, "Making Bricks without Straw," 1138–39; Fairclough, 309–10, 311, 344, 345, 347; Karpinski, 24–25; and Kirk, "NAACP Campaign for Teachers' Salary."

66. Bailey, *They Too Call Alabama Home*, 141; *Birmingham Age-Herald*, "School Board Suit Dismissal Denied"; Clemon and Fair, "Making Bricks without Straw," 1138–39; Fairclough, *Class of their Own*, 307–53; Jerome A. Gray, Reed, and Walton, *History of ASTA*, 129–31; Karpinski, "Visible Company of Professionals," 22–27; Helen Shores Lee and Barbara S. Shores, *Gentle Giant of Dynamite Hill*, 98–102; Shircliffe, *Desegregating Teachers*, 39–44; and Tushnet, *NAACP Legal Strategy*, 92.

67. Autrey, "Can These Bones Live?"

68. Autrey, "Can these Bones Live?," 4; and Brittain, "Some Reflections on Negro Suffrage," 127–28.

69. Autrey, "Can These Bones Live?," 4.

70. Birmingham teacher Indiana Little, who was discussed in chapter 1, was a leader in this suffrage protest.

71. Autrey, "Can these Bones Live?," 4.

72. James T. Patterson, *Brown v. Board of Education*, 2. Sibyl Moses was one among several teachers and Colored Women's Club members who joined the Birmingham NAACP chapter according to her great niece, who is her namesake and a Library of Congress archivist. Moses's membership is noted in the NAACP's *Crisis*, 43, no. 5 (May 1935): 153.

73. *Birmingham Historical Society Newsletter*; and Helen Shores Lee and Barbara S. Shores, *Gentle Giant of Dynamite Hill.*

74. Ibid. Arthur D. Shores handled several high-profile civil rights cases, representing Vivian Malone and Autherine Lucy in desegregation cases against the University of Alabama as well as Fred Shuttlesworth and Martin Luther King Jr.

75. Clemon and Fair, "Making Bricks without Straw," 1132.

76. Jerome A. Gray, Reed, and Walton, *History of ASTA*, 94.

77. Clemon and Fair, "Making Bricks without Straw," 1138–39; Christopher B. Davis, *Emory O. Jackson*, 79–94; Kirk, "NAACP Campaign for Teachers' Salary"; and Helen Shores Lee and Barbara S. Shores, *Gentle Giant of Dynamite Hill*, 98–102.

78. Bullock, *History of Negro Education*, 217.

79. Jerome A. Gray, Reed, and Walton, *History of ASTA*, 91–113.

80. The Committee for the Equalization of Teacher's Salaries and School Facilities of ASTA to Fellow Teachers, 6 December 1938, Arthur D. Shores Collection, Box 3, Negro Teacher Salaries, Sit-ins, and Demonstrations, Birmingham Civil Rights Institute. The penciled notation scribed on this typed document, which reads, "The Ed. Com. and the Citizens Com.," suggests that that The Committee for the Equalization of Teacher's Salaries and School Facilities was either a subset of the Education Commission and the Citizens Commission or a previous iteration of the two commissions.

81. Jerome, A. Gray, Reed, and Walton, *History of ASTA*, 114.

82. Jerome A. Gray, Reed, and Walton, *History of ASTA*, 114; Kirk, "NAACP Campaign for Teachers' Salary," 534.

83. Jerome A. Gray, Reed, and Walton, *History of ASTA*, 113.

84. Ibid.

85. The Committee for the Equalization of Teacher's Salaries and School Facilities of ASTA to Fellow Teachers, 6 December 1938, Arthur D. Shores Collection, Box 3, Negro Teacher Salaries, Sit-ins, and Demonstrations, Birmingham Civil Rights Institute.

86. Ibid.; and Jerome A. Gray, Reed, and Walton, *History of ASTA*, 129–30.

87. Jerome A. Gray, Reed, and Walton, *History of ASTA*, 130.

88. Christopher B. Davis, "Emory O. Jackson," 83–93; and Jerome A. Gray, Reed, and Walton, *History of ASTA*, 130.

89. Christopher B. Davis, "Emory O. Jackson," 81.

90. Jefferson County BBOE, "History of the Jefferson County BOE," 98–99.

91. Ibid., 99.

92. Ibid., 99–100.

93. Ibid., 100.

94. Ibid.

95. Ibid.

96. Ibid., 101.

97. Jerome A. Gray, Reed, and Walton, *History of ASTA*, 129.

98. Jefferson County BBOE, "History of the Jefferson County BOE," 95, 100.

99. Ibid., 100.

100. Ibid.

101. Ibid., 100–101.

102. Laura Caldwell Anderson, *Civil Rights in Birmingham*, 35; Clemon and Fair, "Making Bricks without Straw," 1138–39; Christopher B. Davis, "Emory O. Jackson," 83–93; Jerome A. Gray, Reed, and Walton, *History of ASTA*, 131; Jefferson County BOE, "History of the Jefferson County BOE," 100–102; Karpinski, *"Visible Company of Professionals,"* 25, 123; Helen Shores Lee and Barbara S. Shores, *Gentle Giant of Dynamite Hill*, 102; Rutledge, "Emory O. Jackson, Warrior," 72–91; and Tushnet, *NAACP Legal Strategy*, 92.

103. Clemon and Fair, "Making Bricks without Straw," 1138–39; Helen Shores Lee and Barbara S. Shores, *Gentle Giant of Dynamite Hill*.

104. Ruby J. Gainer, President of JCNTA to Jefferson County Board of Education, 28 January 1947, Arthur D. Shores Collection, Box 3, Negro Teacher Salaries, Sit-ins, and Demonstrations, Birmingham Civil Rights Institute.

105. Jerome A. Gray, Reed, and Walton, *History of ASTA*, 130–31; and Jefferson County BOE, "Elementary and Secondary Public Education," 102.

106. Gainer v. School Board of Jeff. Co., AL et al, No. 5339, 1955 U. S. Dist. LEXIS 2613 (No. Dist. Nov. 4, 1955).

107. Christopher B. Davis, "Emory O. Jackson," 91; Helen Shores Lee and Barbara S. Shores, *Gentle Giant of Dynamite Hill*, 100; and Rutledge, "Emory O. Jackson, Warrior," 82.

108. J. E. Bryan to Ruby J. Gainer, 6 May 1947, Arthur D. Shores Collection, Box 3, Negro Teacher Salaries, Sit-ins, and Demonstrations, Birmingham Civil Rights Institute.

109. Jerome A. Gray, Reed, and Walton, *History of ASTA*, 130–31.

110. McDonald Hughes, ASTA President to E. W. Taggart, ASTA Education Commission Chairman, 25 September 1947, Arthur D. Shores Collection, Box 3, Negro Teacher Salaries, Sit-ins, and Demonstrations, Birmingham Civil Rights Institute; and E. W. Taggart, ASTA Education Commission Chairman to McDonald Hughes, ASTA President, 2 October 1947, Arthur D. Shores Collection, Box 3, Negro Teacher Salaries, Sit-ins, and Demonstrations, Birmingham Civil Rights Institute.

111. Christopher B. Davis, "Emory O. Jackson," 92.

112. Ibid.

113. Gainer v. School Board of Jeff. Co., AL et al, No. 5339, 1955 U. S. Dist. LEXIS 2613 (No. Dist. Nov. 4, 1955; and Helen Shores Lee and Barbara S. Shores, *Gentle Giant of Dynamite Hill*, 101–02.

114. Bailey, *They Too Call Alabama Home*, 141; and Karpinski, *"Visible Company of Professionals,"* 161.

115. Bailey, *They Too Call Alabama*, 141; Christopher B. Davis, "Emory O. Jackson," 92–93; Karpinski, *"Visible Company of Professionals,"* 161; Helen

Shores Lee and Barbara S. Shores, *Gentle Giant of Dynamite Hill*, 101; and *Jet*, "Ala. State Univ. Memorial Honors Ruby J. Gainer," 16. Ruby Jackson Gainer has received more recognition and honor in Pensacola, Florida, than she has in Birmingham. A school was named after her, and the Pensacola mayor proclaimed Sunday, March 9, 1969, as Ruby J. Gainer Day to honor her accomplishments. She received some recognition in Alabama as well. A June 7, 1969, article in the *The Afro-American* newspaper acknowledged that she was awarded an honorary doctorate from the formerly named Birmingham Baptist College of Religion. In addition, *Jet* magazine acknowledged a tablet memorialized in her honor at Alabama State University in 1976.

116. Rutledge, "Emory O. Jackson, Warrior," 11–12. Anne Rutledge is a former student and longtime friend of Emory O. Jackson, who has donated a collection of her correspondence with Jackson, along with other materials, to the BPL Manuscript and Archives Department. Her unpublished biography of Jackson's life is housed at the BCRI. Ms. Rutledge is also a writer and currently resides in Huntsville, Alabama.

117. Eskew, *But for Birmingham*, 196; Christopher B. Davis, "Emory O. Jackson"; and Rutledge, "Emory O. Jackson, Warrior." Christopher B. Davis described Emory O. Jackson as a "traditionalist" compared to Martin Luther King Jr. and other Birmingham civil rights foot soldiers because he chose legal strategy over direct confrontation. In a similar vein, Eskew described him as "[a]n old liberal from the popular front days of the 1940s, [who] had failed to make the transition to the civil rights movement of the 1960s, although he remained an ardent supporter of the ideology of integration." Yet, according to his former student and longtime friend, Anne Rutledge, his early career as a teacher indicates that he sometimes engaged in protest and encouraged his students to take activist stances.

118. Rutledge, "Emory O. Jackson, Warrior."

119. Ibid., 79.

120. Laura Caldwell Anderson, *Civil Rights in Birmingham*, 31–33; *Birmingham Times*, "Black History Spotlight: Dr. Emory O. Jackson"; Bryant, "Birmingham Salutes Emory O. Jackson"; Christopher B. Davis, 'Emory O. Jackson"; and Rutledge, "Emory O. Jackson, Warrior." Emory O. Jackson has received a little more recognition in Birmingham than his sister, Ruby Jackson Gainer, mainly due to a one-man campaign wielded by their youngest sibling, Lovell Jackson, whose efforts resulted in a historical marker being established at Jackson's former *Birmingham World* press office. Lovell Jackson died in March 2014 at the age of ninety-two.

121. Thelma D. Perry noted that Black presses throughout the country joined ranks with Black teachers associations in the fight for educational equity. *History of the ATA*, 87–88.

122. Christopher B. Davis, "Emory O. Jackson," 61.

123. Jerome A. Gray, Reed, and Walton, *History of ASTA*, 94, 114.

124. Rutledge, "Emory O. Jackson, Warrior," 79.

125. *The Afro-American*, "School Principal's Husband Accused," 7; Christopher B. Davis, "Emory O. Jackson," 91–92; Jerome A. Gray, Reed, and Walton, *History of ASTA*, 151–52; and Rutledge, "Emory O. Jackson, Warrior," 13.

126. Rutledge, "Emory O. Jackson, Warrior," 13.

127. Ibid.

128. Rutledge, "Emory O. Jackson, Warrior," 87.

129. Christopher B. Davis, "Emory O. Jackson," 82.

130. Jerome A. Gray, Reed, and Walton, *History of ASTA*, 133–36, 145–46.

131. Autrey, "Can These Bones Live?," 4; and James T. Patterson, *Brown v. Board of Education*, 2.

132. Colton, *Southern League*.

133. Michael Gardner, *Harry Truman and Civil Rights*.

134. Jerome A. Gray, Reed, and Walton, *History of ASTA*, 145.

135. Ibid., 147.

CHAPTER 3. SUPPORTING THE MOVEMENT INSIDE AND OUTSIDE OF THE SCHOOLHOUSE

1. Fallin, *African American Church in Birmingham,* 141–62.

2. Edwards, "From *Brown* to Bakke"; Hardy, "Study of Urban School Desegregation"; James Tyra Harris, "Alabama Reaction to *Brown*"; and Bobby M. Wilson, *Race and Place in Birmingham*, 79–80, 152, 154–55.

3. Birmingham BOE, "Meeting Proceedings," 1954, July 16.

4. Hardy, "Study of Urban School Desegregation," 127–31.

5. Ibid., 128.

6. Clemon and Fair, "Making Bricks without Straw," 114.

7. Ibid.

8. Clemon and Fair, "Making Bricks without Straw," 114; Helen Shores Lee and Barbara S. Shores, *Gentle Giant*, 161–68; and James T. Patterson, *Brown v. Board of Education*, 105, 207–208. According to Lee and Shores, Autherine Lucy's experience took a tremendous emotional toll on her, and she eventually left the state of Alabama. Thurgood Marshall sent her an encouraging letter forecasting her prominent place in history.

9. Spencer, "Reverend Fred Shuttlesworth"; and Shuttlesworth, "Remembering the Movement," 75–78.

10. Eskew, *But for Birmingham*, 140–41; Dolgin, Fryday, and Helfand, *Barber of Birmingham*; Huntley and McKerley, *Foot Soldiers for Democracy*, 92, 42–44; McWhorter, *Carry Me Home*, 127–29; Spencer, "Reverend Fred Shuttlesworth"; Shuttlesworth, "Remembering the Movement," 75–78; and Camille M. Wilson, "Starting the Bandwagon." Camille M. Wilson's recent article on African American mothers' struggles to voluntarily desegregate schools in Greensboro, North Carolina, is one among a few accounts that spotlight the contributions of ordinary families to the civil rights movement.

11. *Crisis,* "Alabama Restraining Order," 361–62.

12. Fallin, *African American Church in Birmingham*, 157–58.

13. Shuttlesworth et al. v. Birmingham Board of Education, 8914 (N. D. Al. 1958), Birmingham City Schools Miscellaneous Records, File #2033, Department of Archives and Manuscripts, Birmingham, Ala. Public Library.

14. Ibid.

15. Birmingham BOE, "Meeting Proceedings," September 6, 1957; Birmingham BOE, "Meeting Proceedings," September 20, 1957; Birmingham BOE, "Meeting Proceedings," December 20, 1957; Birmingham BOE, "Meeting Proceedings," January 3, 1957; Birmingham BOE, "Meeting Proceedings," June 6, 1958; Eskew, *But for Birmingham*, 140–41; Garrow, *Birmingham, Alabama 1956–1963*, 32–42; Huntley and McKerley, *Footsoldiers for Democracy*, 92; Leech, "Rev. Shuttlesworth, Family Relives Moment"; McWhorter, *Carry Me Home*, 127–29; and Shuttlesworth, "Remembering the Movement," 75–78.

16. "Shuttlesworth et al. Petition," Birmingham City Schools Miscellaneous Records, File #2033, Department of Archives and Manuscripts, Birmingham, Ala. Public Library.

17. Ibid.

18. Birmingham BOE, "Meeting Proceedings," September 1954 through April 1963.

19. Jerome A. Gray, Reed, and Walton, *History of ASTA*, 148–49.

20. Lillie Fincher, interview by Willoughby Anderson, October 29, 2004, interview # U-0038, Program # 4007, transcript, Southern Oral History Program Collection, University of North Carolina, Chapel Hill, 7.

21. Ibid.

22. Willie Mae L. Crews, interview by Kimberly Hill, June 16, 2005, interview # U-0020, Program # 4007, transcript, Southern Oral History Program Collection, University of North Carolina, Chapel Hill, 12.

23. Shuttlesworth et al. v. Birmingham BOE.

24. Ibid; and Hardy, "Study of Urban School Desegregation," 132–38.

25. Dwight Armstrong et al. v. Board of Education of City of Birmingham, 220 F Supp. 217 (N. D. Al. 1963).

26. W. L. Williams quoted in Faulk, "Fifty Years Ago a Federal Appeals," ¶ 4. W. L. Williams died on September 29, 2013, but was able to contribute to the fiftieth commemoration of the Birmingham civil rights movement. In addition to working on BPS school integration, he represented Shuttlesworth and King during the movement. He also helped to desegregate all public places in Birmingham. Williams was one of the first two Black residents to run for the Birmingham City Council.

27. Dolgin, Fryday, and Helfand, *Barber of Birmingham.*

28. Huntley and McKerley, *Foot Soldiers for Democracy*, 40.

29. Eskew, *But for Birmingham*, 318–19; Huntley and McKerley, *Foot Soldiers for Democracy*, 42–44; Jeremy Gray, "Birmingham School Board Officially Close"; Jeremy Gray, "State Troopers Turned Black Students Away"; and Wright, *1963*, 70.

30. Ibid.

31. Jeremy Gray, "State Troopers Turned Black Students Away," ¶ 4.

32. Ibid.

33. Wright, *1963*, 70.

34. Ibid.

35. Lydia Alexander, Charles Calhoun, Robert Corley, Louis Dale, and Peggy Harrison, community panel interview by Tondra L. Loder-Jackson, May 3, 2013, transcript, UAB Mervyn H. Sterne Library, Birmingham, AL; and Jeremy Gray, "State Troopers Turned Black Students Away." A picture of a White male standing on top of the Woodlawn High School signpost waving a large Confederate flag is featured in Jeremy Gray's *Birmingham News* article.

36. Huntley and McKerley, *Foot Soldiers for Democracy*, 103, 118; and Tara Y. White, "Black Women in Civil Rights," 103–106.

37. Tara Y. White, "Black Women in Civil Rights," 105; and Alabama Black Women Blogspot, "Fearless and Very Outspoken."

38. McKerley, *Foot Soldiers for Democracy*, 103, 118.

39. Alabama Black Women Blogspot, "Fearless and Very Outspoken"; and Tara Y. White, "Black Women in Civil Rights," 103.

40. I have yet to track down information about the Birmingham Negro Teachers Association, although I discussed the JeffCo Negro Teachers Association in chapter 2 in relation to the Ruby Jackson Gainer teacher salary equalization case. As noted previously, the Birmingham Public Schools were once under the aegis of the JeffCo Public Schools. But the two school districts have been independent since the late nineteenth century.

41. Jerome A. Gray, Reed, and Walton, *History of ASTA*, 185–86.

42. Tara Y. White, "Black Women in Civil Rights," 106.

43. Fincher, interview, 30.

44. Ibid.

45. Tara Y. White, "Black Women in Civil Rights," 106.

46. Ibid.

47. Lola Haynes Hendricks, interview by Tywanna Whorley, Birmingham (Ala.), June 22, 1994, interview #174 (btvct02013), Behind the Veil: Documenting African-American Life in the Jim Crow South Digital Collection, John Hope Franklin Research Center, Duke University Libraries, Durham, NC, 20–21.

48. Jesse Champion Sr. interview by Horace Huntley, November 1, 1995, transcript, Oral History Project, Birmingham Civil Rights Institute, Birmingham, AL, 11.

49. Ibid.

50. Ibid.

51. Birmingham Board of Education, "Meeting Proceedings," 1963, July 30.

52. Champion, interview, 12.

53. In addition to Champion, there were several high-profile teacher firings documented by the ASTA. For example, Jimmy Kidd was fired for voter's registration activities and Allie Lee Causey was fired for her published views on

integration featured in a 1956 issue of *Life* magazine. Jerome A. Gray, Reed, and Walton, *History of ASTA*, 151.

54. Christensen, "Ms. Lillie M. H. Fincher," 137.

55. Fincher, interview, 2. Gertrude Crum Sanders's oral history from the Duke University Behind the Veil Collection was discussed in chapter 2 in relation to her days as a student at Industrial High School under A. H. Parker's leadership.

56. Nelson, *Freedom Summer.*

57. Christensen, "Ms. Lillie M. H. Fincher," 137.

58. As a Social Studies curriculum director for the BPS, Fincher received nine copyrights for a Black History series and also launched innovative series district-wide on women's history and the Holocaust. Lillie M. H. Fincher's obituary, dated June 18, 2009.

59. Carolyn Cunningham, interview by Horace Huntley, March 6, 1996, transcript, Oral History Project, Birmingham Civil Rights Institute, Birmingham, AL, 8.

60. Ibid.; and Birmingham Historical Society, "Cataloguing School Closures," 5.

61. Ruth Barefield-Pendleton, interview by Horace Huntley, March 9, 1995, transcript, Oral History Project, Birmingham Civil Rights Institute, Birmingham, AL; and Barefield-Pendleton, *Minutes: Central Committee.*

62. Barefield-Pendleton, interview, 21.

63. Lydia Alexander et al., interview.

64. Aldon D. Morris, *Origins of Civil Rights*, 253–54, 266; Eskew, *But for Birmingham*, 254, 261–266; McWhorter, *Carry Me Home*, 359–61, 363–64, 390; and Wright, *1963*, 42–43.

65. Ibid.

66. Ibid.

67. Ibid.

68. Eskew, *But for Birmingham*, 261–66; Robert Hudson and Houston, *Children's March*; Huntley and McKerley, *Foot Soldiers for Democracy*, 107, 137–38; and Wright, *1963*, 42–43. According to the archives director at the Birmingham, Ala., Public Library, many more children were likely arrested but not documented in juvenile court records.

69. Eskew, *But for Birmingham*, 265; and Wright, *1963*, 98.

70. Eskew, *But for Birmingham*, 259–97; and Wright, *1963*, 41–48.

71. Eskew, *But for Birmingham*, 308.

72. Eskew, *But for Birmingham*, 265–68, 296–97; Robert Hudson and Houston, *Children's March*; Huntley and McKerley, *Foot Soldiers for Democracy*, 118–19, 145–49, 193–95, 208–11; McWhorter, *Carry Me Home*, 365–87; and Wright, *1963*, 41–55, 98.

73. Jeremy Gray, "BBOE Issued Order Expelling"; Eskew, *But for Birmingham*, 308; and Wright, *1963*, 55.

74. Barefield-Pendleton, *Minutes: Central Committee,* 43. I have referenced Ruth Barefield-Pendleton's recent publication of her copious minutes of the

Central Committee of the Joint ACMHR and SCLC. I also perused the original expanded minutes filed in the Ruth Barefield-Pendleton Collection at the BCRI Archives. In recent years, some of Birmingham's civil rights foot soldiers have been publishing their own accounts, no doubt, in response to concerns about having their stories and contributions revised, co-opted, or even misappropriated.

75. Linda Cal Woods v. Theo R. Wright, 20875, U.S. App. OPENJURIST 334 F .2D 369. (5th Cir. July 20, 1964).

76. Eskew, *But for Birmingham*, 275, 308.

77. Mary Moore, interview by Sarah Thuesen, August 17, 2006, interview # U-0193, program # 4007, transcript, Southern Oral History Program Collection, University of North Carolina, Chapel Hill. Moore has served as an Alabama legislator representing Birmingham for several years.

78. Huntley and McKerley, *Foot Soldiers for Democracy*, 128.

79. Ibid., 147.

80. Ibid., 117. Odessa Woolfolk is a longtime Birmingham civic and community leader, who helped found the Birmingham Civil Rights Institute and currently serves as its board chair emerita.

81. Ibid.

82. Ibid., 134.

83. Ibid., 120.

84. Cleopatra Goree, interview by Horace Huntley, April 29, 1998, transcript, Oral History Project, Birmingham Civil Rights Institute, Birmingham, AL, 15.

85. Ibid., 21.

86. Ibid.

87. Huntley and McKerley, *Foot Soldiers for Democracy*, 97.

88. Ibid., 80.

89. Christensen, "Ms. Lillie M. H. Fincher"; and Fincher, interview.

90. Jerome A. Gray, Reed, and Walton, *History of ASTA*, 202.

91. African American Studies scholar Martha Biondi has published an extensive analysis of Black student activism at both HBCUs and predominantly White institutions during and after the civil rights movement, titled *The Black Revolution on Campus*.

92. Eskew, *But for Birmingham*, 148–50; McPherson and Turner, *Drum Major for God*; McWhorter, *Carry Me Home*, 151–57, 245–46; Miles College Centennial History Committee, *Miles College*; Osborne, "Boycott in Birmingham"; and Thomas and Nunnelley, "The Real L. H. Pitts."

93. "The Eleventh Commandment: Thou Shalt Stay out of Downtown Birmingham!," Boycott flier, BCRI Archives Department.

94. Chambers, "Miles College Plans Events"; Chambers, "Miles College Role in Civil Rights"; and Dukes, *Stand!* The daughter of a Miles College student activist, Donna Dukes, premiered her documentary film on the college's role in the movement at a special event I attended that was held on its campus on July 27, 2013. Her father, Frank Dukes, and other activists were featured in the

program and honored as a part of the fiftieth commemoration of the Birmingham civil rights movement.

95. Chambers, "Miles College Role in Civil Rights," ¶ 8.

96. Dukes, *Stand!*; McPherson and Turner, *Drum Major for God*, 45; and McWhorter, *Carry Me Home*, 397.

97. Huntley and McKerley, *Foot Soldiers for Democracy*, 84–87; *Newsweek*, "Boycott in Birmingham, ALA"; Osborne, "Boycott in Birmingham," 397–401; Thomas and Nunnelley, "The Real L. H. Pitts," 24; and *Time*, "The South," 24.

98. Miles College Student Body, "Join the Fight" Selective Buying Campaign Flier, Miles Learning Center Archives.

99. Miles, Daniel Payne, and Booker T. Washington Colleges, "Join the Glorious Struggle" Selective Buying Campaign Flier, Miles Learning Center Archives.

100. Capossela, *John U. Monro*, 85–88; Eskew, *But for Birmingham*, 198–205; and McWhorter, *Carry Me Home*, 255–56.

101. Chambers, "Miles College Role in Civil Rights," ¶ 15; Dukes, *Stand!*; McWhorter, *Carry Me Home*, 265–266; and McPherson and Turner, *Drum Major for God*, 36.

102. Dukes, *Stand!*

103. Capossela, *John U. Monro*, 87.

104. Clemon quoted in Chambers, "Miles College Role in Civil Rights," ¶ 7; Fairclough, "Being in Field of Education"; and Fairclough, *Teaching Equality*, 21–41; Fairclough, *Class of their Own*, 383; and Gilpin and Gasman, *Charles S. Johnson*.

105. Capossela, *John U. Monro*, 84; and Miles College Centennial Committee, *Miles College*, 70.

106. McWhorter, *Carry Me Home*, 245; and Capossela, *John U. Monro*, 84.

107. Thomas and Nunnelley, "The Real Lucius Pitts," 24.

108. Jerome A. Gray, Reed, and Walton, *History of ASTA*, 169–70.

109. Ibid., 170.

110. Barefield-Pendleton, *Minutes: The Central Committee*, 72; Chambers, "Miles College Role in Civil Rights"; Miles College Centennial Committee, *Miles College*, 69–73; Osborne, "Boycott in Birmingham"; and Thomas and Nunnelley, "The Real Lucius Pitts."

111. Chambers, "Miles College Role in Civil Rights," ¶ 20. Former Miles College President William A. Bell is pictured with the Miles College Teacher Training Program Class of 1938 in chapter 2.

112. Joe Dickson quoted in Chambers, "Miles College Role in Civil Rights," ¶ 21.

113. Miles College Centennial History Committee, *Miles College*, 33.

114. Ibid; and McWhorter, *Carry Me Home*, 151.

115. Huntley and McKerley, *Foot Soldiers for Democracy*, 85; and McPherson and Turner, *Drum Major for God*, 35–37.

116. Huntley and McKerley, *Foot Soldiers for Democracy*, 64, 71.

117. Thomas and Nunnelley, "The Real Lucius Pitts," 24.

118. Ibid.

119. Eskew, *But for Birmingham,* 197, 239–40; McWhorter, *Carry Me Home*, 245–46, 255–56, 413; and Thomas and Nunnelley, "The Real Lucius Pitts."

120. Ibid.

121. Thomas and Nunnelley, "The Real Lucius Pitts," 20.

122. Ibid.

123. Ibid.

124. Ibid., 27.

125. Pitts quoted in Thelma D. Perry, *History of ATA*, 329.

126. Thomas and Nunnelley, "The Real Lucius Pitts," 24.

127. Hardy, "Study of Urban School Desegregation," 117.

128. Birmingham BOE, Meeting Proceedings, 1938 through 1963.

129. Hardy, "Study of Urban School Desegregation," 121–22.

130. Lydia Alexander et al., interview; Hayes, *Carol W. Hayes*; and Jerome A. Gray, Reed, and Walton, *History of ASTA*, 120. Louis Dale described BPS segregation during a panel at UAB commemorating the fiftieth anniversary of Birmingham's watershed civil rights year, 1963. Carol W. Hayes was a longtime BPS educator, who moved up the ranks of the system in the 1930s and 1940s. He retired as the "Superintendent of Negro Schools," who was responsible for oversight of all-Black schools. Hayes also served as president of ASTA between 1935 and 1937. As discussed earlier in this chapter, James Armstrong indicated that Hayes tried to dissuade him and his family from integrating schools in the 1950s and 1906s, but later relented from his position. Hayes's autobiographical reflections reveal his belief that Black students should possess strong Christian values, work ethic, and literacy skills. He also advocated that Black teachers spend time researching and celebrating Negro History throughout BPS. Voters' registration was another one of his initiatives. A BPS high school was named after him before his retirement in the 1960s, and the middle school that recently replaced this high school continues to bear his name.

131. Edwards, "From Brown to Bakke"; Hardy, "Study of Urban School Desegregation"; and James Tyra Harris, "Alabama Reaction to *Brown.*"

132. Ibid.

133. Letter from Kermit A. Johnson to JeffCo parents, May 1, 1967. Document may be retrieved from Public Broadcasting System's Teachers' Domain at www.pbslearningmedia.org/resource/iml04.soc.ush.civil.jefdeseg/desegregation-mandate-jefferson-county-al/.

134. Ibid.

135. Hardy, "Study of Urban School Desegregation," 127–38.

136. "Questions to be Asked of Parent," Birmingham City Schools Miscellaneous Records, File #2033, Department of Archives and Manuscripts, Birmingham, Ala. Public Library.

137. Fincher, interview, 9–10.

138. Fincher, interview, 11–12; and Shircliffe, *Desegregating Teachers*, 133–38.

139. Office of Superintendent Survey Tabulation, Birmingham City Schools Miscellaneous Records, File #2033, Department of Archives and Manuscripts, Birmingham, Ala. Public Library.

140. "BPS Desegregation," Nov. 28, 1967, BCS Misc. Records File #2033, Dept. of Archives and Manuscripts, Birmingham, Ala. Public Library.

141. A Report to the Court for the School Year 1968–69," BCS Misc. Records File #2033, Dept. of Archives and Manuscripts, Birmingham, Ala. Public Library.

142. Margaret Z. Beard, interview by Tondra L. Loder-Jackson, July 24, 2014, Urban Education Pioneers Project, UAB Center for Urban Education, Birmingham, AL; and United States and Stout et al. v. Jefferson County Bd. of Educ., 23345, 23331, 23335, 23274, 23365, 23173, 23192, U.S. App. OPENJURIST 372 F.2d 836, 837 (5th Cir. Dec. 29, 1966).

143. Beard, interview. Ms. Beard felt very strongly about her former colleague's remarks. She went on to explain that in her household there were relatives who were "Whiter than White" and others, like her father, who were dark-skinned. Yet skin color was never discussed in her family, and was certainly not used to discriminate against family members.

144. Ibid.

145. Ibid.

146. Ibid.

147. Lydia Alexander et al., interview. Lydia Alexander shared her perspectives about crossover teacher quality during her days as a JeffCo teacher in the 1960s.

148. Crews, interview, 23.

149. Ibid.

150. "1968–1969 Opposite Race Assignments for High Schools," Birmingham City Schools Miscellaneous Records #2033, Department of Archives and Manuscripts, Birmingham, Ala. Public Library.

151. Edwards, "From Brown to Bakke"; Hardy, "Study of Urban School Desegregation"; and Bobby M. Wilson, *Race and Place in Birmingham*, 154–55.

152. Jerome A. Gray, Reed, and Walton, *History of ASTA*, 216–24.

153. Ibid., 211.

154. "Birmingham Public Schools—Desegregation," Birmingham City Schools Miscellaneous Records #2033, Department of Archives and Manuscripts, Birmingham, Ala. Public Library.

155. "Birmingham Public Schools, October Enrollment," Item # 17, Birmingham City Schools Miscellaneous Records #2033, Department of Archives and Manuscripts, Birmingham, Ala. Public Library.

156. Jeremy Gray, "Birmingham School Board Officially Close"; and Bobby M. Wilson, *Race and Place in Birmingham*, 154–55.

157. Jerome A. Gray, Reed, and Walton, *History of ASTA*, 227–30; and Vanessa Siddle Walker, "Second-class Integration," 269–84.

158. Orfield, "Tenth Annual *Brown* Lecture," 276; and Frankenberg, Chungmei Lee, and Orfield, "Multiracial Society with Segregated Schools," 5–6.

159. Frankenberg, "Splintering School Districts."

160. Bobby M. Wilson, *Race and Place in Birmingham*, 155.

161. Coffin, "Black School Administrator"; Dingus, "Doing the Best We Could"; Foster, "Politics of Race"; Foster, "Self-portraits of Black Teachers"; Foster, *Black Teachers on Teaching*; Fultz, "Displacement of Black Educators"; Mildred J. Hudson and Holmes, "Missing Teachers, Impaired Communities"; Vivian G. Morris and Curtis L. Morris, *Creating Caring and Nurturing Educational Environments*; Shircliffe, *Desegregating Teachers*; Tillman, "(Un)intended Consequences?"; Tillman, "African American Principals"; Vanessa Siddle Walker, "Tolerated Tokenism, or Injustice"; and Vanessa Siddle Walker, "Second-class Integration."

162. Wesson, "Equity Issues for Women and Minorities," 152.

163. Thelma D. Perry, *History of ATA*, 299–300.

164. Fultz, "Caught between a Rock"; Jerome A. Gray, Reed, and Walton, *History of ASTA*, 235–78; Karpinski, " 'A Visible Company of Professionals"; Thelma D. Perry, *History of ATA*, 327–43; Vanessa Siddle Walker, *Hello Professor*; and Vanessa Siddle Walker, "Tolerated Tokenism, or Injustice."

165. Fultz, "Displacement of Black Educators," 44.

166. Shuttlesworth et al. v. Birmingham Board of Education, 8914 (N. D. Al. 1958), Birmingham City Schools Miscellaneous Records, File #2033, Department of Archives and Manuscripts, Birmingham, Ala. Public Library. The White state superintendent warned Shuttlesworth not to push integration, not so much out of concern for the plight of the Black plaintiffs but to protect the status quo. However, some African American scholars have prophesied or echoed his sentiment from the vantage point of African Americans' collective interest. For more insights, see W. E. B. Du Bois's classic article, "Does the Negro Need Separate Schools?," Derrick Bell's *And We Are Not Saved* (chapter 4, "Neither Separate Schools nor Mixed Schools"), and Gloria Ladson-Billings, 2004 AERA annual *Brown* lecture, "Landing on the Wrong Note."

167. Birmingham BOE, "Meeting Proceedings," #506 84-121, April 1963 through April 1983. The Birmingham BOE has consistently held a Black majority since the early 1980s, and it eventually transitioned from being an appointed to an elected board in 2001. According to some accounts, this transition was spurred by the longtime resentment of a contingent of African American civil rights leaders, teachers union members, and community activists that felt betrayed by appointed board members, namely Louis Dale, who either pushed for or tacitly supported the removal of the first African American BPS superintendent, Walter Harris. I recently published an article in the *Peabody Journal of Education*, 90:30, 336–354, that addresses the post-desegregation era of inter- and intraracial tensions in Birmingham's educational leadership.

168. Birmingham BOE, "Meeting Proceedings," #506 84-121 May 1983 through April 1990.

CHAPTER 4. RELATIVE ACTIVISM

1. Elder and Pellerin, "Linking History and Human Lives"; and Elder and Giele, *Craft of Life Course.*

2. Strauss and Howe, *Generations*; and Wellner, "Forgotten Baby Boom."

3. Ibid.

4. Eskew, *But for Birmingham*, 53. Many Southern cities experienced racial violence during this period, but bombings—which were estimated at fifty between 1947 and 1965—came to characterize the violence in Birmingham, which led to its infamous moniker, "Bombingham."

5. Spike Lee, *4 Little Girls*; and McKinstry, *While the World Watched.*

6. Hurt, *African American Life in Rural South;* and Trotter, *Great Migration in Historical Perspective.*

7. Winemiller,"Black Belt Region in Alabama," ¶ 2.

8. For a detailed analysis of how slavery in the United States extended well beyond the Civil War, particularly through convict leasing and sharecropping, see Douglas Blackmon's *Slavery by Another Name.*

9. Brooks, "Legal and Policy Issues"; Clark, *Schoolhouse Door*, 9; and www.encyclopediaofalabama.org/article/h-1480. The landmark *Knight v. State of Alabama* federal court case, which spanned thirty years between 1981 and 2003, and continues to be litigated today, concluded that many of the state's policies fostered segregation in Alabama's higher education system and stipulated that they be remedied.

10. Dan T. Carter, *Politics of Rage.*

11. Alridge, "From Civil Rights to Hip Hop," 238.

12. Patricia Hill Collins, *Black Feminist Thought*, 204.

13. Amott and Matthei, *Race, Gender, and Work*, 172–79.

14. Jerome A. Gray, Reed, and Walton, *History of ASTA*, 204.

15. Ibid.

16. Ibid.

17. Patricia Hill Collins, *Black Feminist Thought*, 201–25.

18. Ibid., 202.

19. The theme of colorism came up in some of the oral histories of Black teachers featured in Barbara Shircliffe's research in Florida and Mississippi (*Desegregating Teachers*) and Horace Huntley and John McKerley's Birmingham civil rights oral histories (*Foot Soldiers for Democracy*).

20. Alridge, "From Civil Rights to Hip Hop," 238.

21. Mays, "Moral Aspects of Segregation," 362.

22. "Isaac's" counterfactual reflection on how Martin Luther King would react to African American youth today brings to mind a provocative episode of the edgy cable television animation *The Boondocks*, created by hip-hop generation social critic and cartoonist Aaron McGruder. "Return of the King," which won a 2006 Peabody Award (http://www.peabodyawards.com/award-profile/the-boondocks-the-return-of-the-king), portrays King coming out of a thirty-two-year

coma only to find that America is far from realizing his dream for social justice and racial equity. The post-hip-hop generation protagonist, Huey, must guide him through a series of troubling scenarios, many of which indict Black intraracial cultural regression. The episode begins with two quotes that convey the painfully striking divergence between King and what some observers would describe as the "gangsta rap" contingent of the hip-hop generation. The quote attributed to King states: "I want young men and young women who are not alive today to know and see that these new privileges and opportunities did not come without somebody suffering and sacrificing for them." It is followed by a counterstatement signifying the nihilistic angst of an "anonymous" voice of the twenty-first century: "Whatever, nigga." However, Huey finds himself more sympathetic to King's sentiments than the quote attributed to his generation, pleading with King to reignite a new social movement for a new generation.

23. Loder-Jackson, "Bridging the Tradition of Activism," 162.

CHAPTER 5. INTERGENERATIONAL BRIDGE BUILDING

1. *The Cosby Show* was a watershed television show created and produced by William "Bill" Cosby in 1984. Bill Cosby was arguably the most high-profile and influential African American entertainer in mainstream popular American culture spanning across several decades between the 1960s and the 1990s. *The Cosby Show* was the first situation comedy featuring a solidly middle-class dual career professional family, the Huxtables, on a major American television network (NBC), and continues to run in syndication on several cable network stations.

2. Frankenberg, "Splintering School Districts."

3. Amy Stuart Wells, *Both Sides Now*.

4. Dyson, "Bouncing Back," 37.

5. In a chapter 4 endnote, I commented on how the dismay of a male civil rights movement educator, who lamented that Martin Luther King would be crestfallen if he returned to witness the state of affairs for African Americans in the twenty-first century, reminded me of the Peabody Award–winning "Return of the King" episode of Aaron McGruder's scathingly satirical animation, *The Boondocks*. This theme has resurfaced in the narrative of this post–civil rights generation educator.

6. McAdams, "The Redemptive Self," 81.

7. Brady and Hapenny, "Giving Back."

8. Baker, *Betrayal*.

9. Ibid.

10. Ibid.

11. Alridge, "African American Education."

12. Loder-Jackson, "Hope and Despair," 279.

13. Ibid.

14. Patricia Hill Collins, *Another Kind of Public Education*.

15. Mountain Brook is a historically upper-middle-class, predominantly White suburb of Birmingham. Hoover is a predominantly White middle-class suburb that has become increasingly racially, ethnically, and economically diverse over the past decade. Both municipalities' school districts tout high standardized test scores and college attainment, although there is a notable achievement gap and resource disparity between Hoover City schools that serve predominantly White middle-class homeowners versus racially and ethnically diverse lower middle-income, working-class, and low-income apartment residents. The Hoover City School district is currently in the midst of controversies related to how its former superintendent and school board were proposing to address budgetary constraints (i.e., through proposals to cut bus transportation altogether or to initiate bus fees that would disproportionately affect low-income, working-class, and even lower-middle-income residents across race and ethnicity) and achievement gap problems (i.e., through proposals to rezone the student population in a manner that would presumably redistribute diverse socioeconomic statuses across higher- and lower-achieving schools). See http://blog.al.com/spotnews/2013/09/hoover_bus_cuts_minority_stude.html and http://www.al.com/news/birmingham/index.ssf/2014/09/trace_crossings_elementary_sch.html.

16. No Child Left Behind (NCLB) is perhaps one of the most controversial federal education reform policies ever. Former president George W. Bush's highly touted reform was enacted by a bipartisan Congress to raise student achievement through emphasizing standards-based education and high-stakes testing as a means of making schools more accountable for the performance of students labeled as subgroups, that is, racial and ethnic minorities, free and reduced lunch participants, English Language Learners, and students with special needs and exceptionalities. NCLB critics charge that the law has dumbed down the curriculum, relegated so-called subgroups to second-class status, helped to supplant public education through its private choice provisions, and myopically defined academic achievement by a test score. See Hess and Petrilli, *No Child Left Behind*; and Deborah Meier, Kohn, Darling-Hammond, Sizer, Wood et al., *Many Children Left Behind.*

17. Higginbotham, "African-American Women's History," 272.

18. Loder-Jackson, "Hope and Despair."

19. Russell Simmons and Sean John Combs, who is also known by the stage names P. Diddy and Puff Daddy, are considered to be pioneering hip-hop moguls. Simmons, who was born in 1957, co-founded the hip-hop label Def Jam Records, and also founded the hip-hop clothing line Phat Farm. Combs, who is twelve years Simmons's junior, is a rapper who founded the hip-hop music label, Bad Boy Records, which produced major hip-hop icons such as Christopher Wallace, also known as the Notorious B.I.G., who was gunned down in Las Vegas in 1997.

20. The "J's" refers to NBA Chicago Bulls sports legend Michael Jordan's brand of athletic shoes. "Grills" refer to tooth adornments, for example, expensive gold or platinum caps with insignia. "Winifred" also refers to the "Jags,"

seemingly as a synonym to the "J's" although in the urban vernacular it refers to "Jaguar" cars or a person who is socially inept (see http://www.urbandictionary.com/define.php?term=Jag).

21. Bill Cosby and Alvin Poussaint co-authored the controversial book *Come on People: On the Path from Victims to Victors* in 2007. *New York Times* opinion editor Bob Herbert wrote an op-ed piece about the book on October 16, 2007, titled, "Tough, Sad and Smart," This is the closest reference I could find to match the commentary of this particular educator.

22. U.S. Census Bureau, "State and County Quick Facts"; Lanahan and Weyburn, "Ed's Report Card"; Hansen, "Birmingham Changes as Blacks Move"; Hansen and Leech, "City's Black Students Leaving"; and William Julius Wilson, *Truly Disadvantaged*. Birmingham's population is 73.4 percent African American and notably poor, with the latest statistics citing 26.4 percent of residents living below the federal poverty line. The city's poverty rate greatly exceeds both the state (17.1 percent) and national average (13 percent).

23. Dyson, *Between God and Gangsta Rap*; Dyson, *Know What I Mean?*; Leola Johnson, "Silencing Gangsta Rap"; Kitwana, *Hip Hop Generation*; and Lipsitz, "Hip Hop Hearings."

24. Kitwana, *Hip Hop Generation.*

25. Payne, "More Than a Symbol of Freedom."

26. Ibid., 25.

27. Patricia Hill Collins, *Black Feminist Thought*, 204.

CHAPTER 6. RESURGENT ACTIVISM?

1. Patricia Hill Collins, *Black Feminist Thought*, 204.
2. Ibid.
3. V. P. Franklin, "They Rose or Fell Together," 48.
4. Patricia Hill Collins, *Another Public Education*, 50.
5. Ibid., 51.
6. Ibid.
7. Ibid., 89.
8. Ibid.
9. Ibid; and Payne and Strickland, *Teach Freedom.*
10. Alridge, "From Civil Rights to Hip Hop"; and Dagbovie, "Strategies for Teaching African American History."
11. Taines, "What the Real World."
12. Taines, "Intervening in Alienation."
13. Ginwright, *Black Youth Rising.*
14. Hamilton, "Activists for the New Millennium."
15. Loder-Jackson, "Role of Educators in Civil Rights."
16. Generett, "Intergenerational Discussions as Curriculum."

17. Bowser, "Young Activists March"; and Underwood, "Free BCRI Youth Symposium."

18. Garrison, "Students Take to the Streets."

19. Reed, "Birmingham-area Teens Talk Politics."

20. Newsone, "Remembering Black Youth Cut Down."

21. Joseph, "How Ferguson Has Exposed."

22. Ibid.

23. Ibid.

24. Loder-Jackson, "Bridging the Tradition of Activism"; and Loder-Jackson, "Hope and Despair."

25. Cozart, "Becoming Whole"; Irvine, *In Search of Wholeness*; Ladson-Billings, *Beyond the Big House*; Ladson-Billings, *Dreamkeepers*; Milner, "Preparing Teachers for African American Students"; Norwood, "Teaching as an Emancipatory Endeavor"; and Roberts and Irvine, "African American Teachers' Caring."

26. Alridge, "From Civil Rights to Hip Hop"; Generett, "Intergenerational Discussions as Curriculum"; and Payne, "More Than a Symbol."

27. Boyd, *New H.N.I.C.*; and Bynoe, *Stand and Deliver.*

28. Ginwright, *Black Youth Rising*; and Hamilton, "Activists for the New Millennium."

29. Sawchuk, "Teacher Beat."

30. Sawchuk, "As Membership Plummets"; Sawchuck, "Feeling the Heat"; Tucker, "Blocking the Schoolhouse Door"; and Perrillo, *Uncivil Rights*. Perrillo's book chronicles the conflicting educational interests and tensions between White-led teachers unions and Black Harlemites and civil rights organizations in New York City in the 1940s and 1950s.

31. Leech, "Alabama Education Department Seizes Control."

32. Leech, "A New Era"; and Leech, "Birmingham Board of Education."

33. Loder, "Dilemmas Confronting Urban Principals."

34. Leech, 2012, "About 250 Rally in Support"; and Stock, "Birmingham Parents Quiz City School."

35. Leech, "200 Birmingham School Employees."

36. Rolen, "Yes We Can! Birmingham."

37. Loder-Jackson, Voltz, and Froning, "New Horizons for Urban Teacher."

38. Robinson, *Disintegration.*

39. Generett, "Intergenerational Discussions as a Curriculum."

40. Diann Cameron Kelly, "In Preparation for Adulthood."

41. Moses, *Radical Equations*; Theresa Perry, *Quality Education as Constitutional Right*; and Wenger, *Rising African American Leaders.*

42. Bell, *And We Are Not Saved*; Du Bois, *Souls of Black Folks*; Du Bois, "Does the Negro Need Separate Schools?"; and Ladson-Billings, "Landing on the Wrong Note."

43. Marva Collins and Tamarkin, *Marva Collins Way*; Tough, *Whatever It Takes*; and Steve Perry, *Push Has Come to Shove*. Marva Collins (Westside Preparatory, 1978–2008, Chicago, IL), Geoffrey Canada (Harlem Children's Zone, New

York City), and Steve Perry (Capital High Preparatory Magnet School, Hartford, CT) have been recognized in the past or recent years for their high-profile and entrepreneurial efforts to create schools with consistent track records of success for low-income children and adolescents of color, especially African Americans.

APPENDIX. NOTES ON METHODOLOGY

1. Loder, "Bridging the Tradition of Activism"; Loder-Jackson, "Role of Educators in Civil Rights"; and Lydia Alexander et al., "Urban Education Pioneers."

2. ALSDE, *Alabama's Education Report Card 2011–2012*, https://web.alsde.edu/Home/Reports/SDEAnnualReports.aspx; Frankenberg, "Splintering School Districts"; Lanahan and Weyburn, "Ed's Report Card"; Hansen, "Birmingham Changes as Blacks Move"; and Hansen and Leech, "City's Black Students Leaving."

3. Lanahan and Weyburn, "Ed's Report Card."

4. Ibid.

5. U.S. Census Bureau, State and County Quick Facts, quickfacts.census.gov/qfd/states/01/01073.html.

6. ALSDE, *Alabama's Education Report Card 2011–2012.*

7. ALSDE, *State Board of Education School Report Card, 2006–2007*, https://web.alsde.edu/Home/Reports/SDEAnnualReports.aspx; *Jefferson County*, 4.

8. Strauss and Howe, *Generations*; and Wellner, "Forgotten Baby Boom."

9. Kitwana, *Hip Hop Generation*; and Strauss and Howe, *Generations.*

10. Cohen, Manion, and Morrison, *Research Methods in Education*; and Foster, *Black Teachers on Teaching.*

11. Huberman and Miles, "Data Management and Analysis"; and Reissman, *Narrative Analysis.*

12. McCulloch, *Documentary Research in Education*, 129.

13. Elder and Giele, *Craft of Life Course*; and Giele and Elder, *Methods of Life Course.*

14. Elder and Pellerin, "Linking History and Human Lives."

15. Cain, "Age Status and Generational Phenomenon."

16. Mannheim, "Problem of Generations," 306.

17. Giele and Elder, *Methods of Life Course*; and Ryder, "Cohort as a Concept."

18. George, "Conceptualizing and Measuring Trajectories"; and Doherty, Laub, and Sampson, "Group-based Trajectories in Life Course," 187.

19. Mannheim, "Problem of Generations," 303.

20. Elder and Giele, *Craft of Life Course*; Giele and Elder, *Methods of Life Course*; Riley, "Aging and Cohort Succession"; and Ryder, "Cohort as a Concept."

21. Mannheim, "Problem of Generations," 297.

22. Griffin, "Generations and Collective Memory."

23. Mannheim, "Problem of Generations, 298–99.

24. Ibid., 300.

25. Ibid., 304, 309.
26. Ritchie, *Doing an Oral History.*
27. Clausen, "Life Reviews and Life Stories," 192.
28. Ibid.
29. Ibid., 196.
30. Ibid., 196–97.
31. Griffin, "Generations and Collective Memory."
32. Fredrick C. Harris, "It Takes a Tragedy."
33. Ibid.
34. Griffin, "Generations and Collective Memory."
35. Giele and Elder, *Methods of Life Course*; and Personal Narratives Group, *Interpreting Women's Lives.*
36. Ginsburg, *Contested Lives*; Newman, "Symbolic Dialects and Generations"; and Personal Narratives Group, *Interpreting Women's Lives.*
37. Giele, "Life Stories to Understand Diversity."
38. Linde, "Explanatory Systems in Oral Life Stories."
39. Ibid., 352.
40. Corti, *Archival Research*; Michael R. Hill, *Archival Strategies and Techniques*; and McCulloch, *Documentary Research in Education.*
41. Ibid.
42. Ibid.
43. Michael R. Hill, *Archival Research and Strategies*, 17.
44. Aldon D. Morris, *Origins of Civil Rights Movement*; and Romano and Raiford, *Civil Rights Movement in American Memory.*
45. Barefield-Pendleton, *Minutes: Central Committee 1963*; and McPherson and Turner, *Drum Major for God.*
46. Council for Social Foundations of Education Standards, www.uic.edu/educ/csfe/standard.htm.
47. Rossman-Reich, "School Improvement Plan"; www.yeswecanbirmingham.org; and Loder-Jackson, Voltz, and Froning, "New Horizons for Urban Teacher Preparation."
48. Titley and Chasey, "Across Differences of Age"; and Reynolds, "On Relations Between Black."

BIBLIOGRAPHY

Aamidor, Abraham. "Rosenwald Schools in Alabama." In *Encyclopedia of Alabama*. Alabama Humanities Foundation, Birmingham. Article published May 5, 2009. Last updated July 2, 2013. www.encyclopediaofalabama.org/face/Article.jsp?id=h-2126.

Afro-American. "School Principal's Husband Accused of Assault in Ala." June 14, 1947. www.news.google.com/newspapers/.

———. "Dr. Ruby J. Gainer—School of Religion Honors Dr. Gainer." June 7, 1969. www.news.google.com/newspapers/.

Akrofi, C. A., G. L. Botchey, and B. K. Takyi. *An English Akan Ewe Dictionary*. Accra: Waterville, 1996.

Alabama Black Women Blogspot. "Historical Alabama African-American Women—Fearless and Very Outspoken: Mrs. Lucinda Brown Robey, Civil Rights Activist" (blog), April 25, 2011. alabamablackwomen.blogspot.com/.

"Alabama Restraining Order." *Crisis* 63, no. 6 (June-July 1956): 361–62.

Alexander, Michelle. *The New Jim Crow: Mass Incarceration in the Age of Colorblindness*. New York: New Press, 2010.

Alridge, Derrick P. "From Civil Rights to Hip Hop: Toward a Nexus of Ideas." Special Issue, *Journal of African American History* 90, no. 3 (2005): 226–52.

———. *The Educational Thought of W. E. B. Du Bois: An Intellectual History*. New York: Teachers College Press, 2008.

———. "African American Education and the Black Intellectual Tradition," by *The Sage Handbook of African American Education*, edited by Linda C. Tillman, 23–34. Thousand Oaks, CA: Sage, 2009.

———, James B. Stewart, and V. P. Franklin. *Message in the Music: Hip Hop, History, and Pedagogy*. Washington, DC: Association for the Study of African American Life and History, 2011.

Amott, Teresa, and Julie Matthaei. *Race, Gender, and Work: A Multi-cultural Economic History of Women in the United States*. Boston: South End Press, 1996.

Anderson, James D. *The Education of Blacks in the South, 1860–1935*. Chapel Hill: University of North Carolina Press, 1988.

Anderson, Jon. 2004. "Board to Redraw Elementary Zones. Superintendent Jack Farr Retires, Cites Battle against Cancerous Brain Tumor." *Birmingham News*, April 8, 2004. www.lexisnexis.com.

Anderson, Laura Caldwell. *Images of America: Civil Rights in Birmingham*. Charleston, SC: Arcadia, 2013.

Asante Jr., M. K. *It's Bigger than Hip Hop: The Rise of the Post-Hip-Hop Generation*. New York: St. Martins, 2008.

Ascoli, Peter. *Julius Rosenwald: The Man who Built Sears, Roebuck and Advanced the Cause of Black Education in the American South*. Bloomington: Indiana University Press, 2006.

Ashmore, Harry S. *The Negro and the Schools*. Chapel Hill: University of North Carolina Press, 1954.

Autrey, Dorothy. "'Can these Bones Live?' The National Association for the Advancement of Colored People in Alabama, 1918–1930." *Journal of Negro History* 82, no. 1 (1997): 1–12.

Bailey, Cynthia. "Teaching as Activism and Excuse: A Reconsideration of the Theory-Practice Dichotomy." *Feminist Teacher* 13, no. 2 (2001): 125–33.

Bailey, Richard. *They Too Call Alabama Home: African American Profiles 1800–1999*. Montgomery, AL: Pyramid, 1999.

Baker, Houston A. *Betrayal: How Black Intellectuals Have Abandoned the Ideals of the Civil Rights Era*. New York: Columbia University Press, 2008.

Baldwin, James. "A Talk to Teachers" In *The Price of the Ticket*, edited by James Baldwin, 325–32. New York: St. Martins, 1985. First published in *The Saturday Review*, December 21, 1963.

Ball, Howard. *Hugo L. Black: Cold Steel Warrior*. Oxford: Oxford University Press, 1996.

Barefield-Pendleton, Ruth. *Minutes: The Central Committee, Alabama Christian Movement for Human Rights and Southern Christian Leadership Conference, 1963*. Birmingham Historical Society, 2013.

Barnett, Bernice McNair. "Invisible Southern Black Women Leaders in the Civil Rights Movement: The Triple Constraints of Gender, Race, and Class." *Gender and Society* 7, no. 2 (1993): 162–82.

Beauboeuf-Lafontant, Tamara. "A Movement Against and Beyond Boundaries: 'Politically Relevant Teaching' Among African American Teachers." *Teachers College Record* 100, no. 4 (1999): 702–23.

———. "A Womanist Experience of Caring: Understanding the Pedagogy of Exemplary Black Women Teachers." *Urban Review* 34, no. 1 (2002): 71–86.

———. "Womanist Lessons for Reinventing Teaching." *Journal of Teacher Education* 56, no. 5 (2005): 436–45.

Bell, Derrick. *And We Are Not Saved: The Elusive Quest for Racial Justice*. New York: Basic Books, 1987.

Berry, Bertice. *Black-on-Black Discrimination: The Phenomenon of Colorism among African Americans*. Kent, OH: Kent State University, 1988.

Bieze, Michael Scott, and Marybeth Gasman. *Booker T. Washington Rediscovered*. Baltimore: Johns Hopkins University Press, 2012.

Biondi, Martha. *The Black Revolution on Campus*. Berkeley: University of California Press, 2012.

Birmingham Age-Herald. "Dr. A. H. Parker." August, 19, 1939. Available at Birmingham (Ala.) Public Library, Digital Collections. encore.bham.lib.al.us/iii/encore/record/C__Rx1004174.

———. "School Board Suit Dismissal Denied." February 24, 1945. Available at Birmingham Civil Rights Institute Archives department, Arthur D. Shores Papers, Box 3, Negro Teacher Salaries, Sit-ins and Demonstrations.

Birmingham Historical Society. "Cataloguing School Closures," February 2–5, 2008. www.bhistorical.org/pdf/BHS_Newsletter_0208.pdf.

Birmingham News. "Dr. A. H. Parker and 'A Dream that Came True.'" May 6, 1939. Available at Birmingham (Ala.) Public Library, Digital Collections. encore.bham.lib.al.us/iii/encore/record/C__Rx1004181.

———. "Dr. A. H. Parker: Servant and Leader." August 18, 1939. Available at Birmingham (Ala.) Public Library, Digital Collections. encore.bham.lib.al.us/iii/encore/record/C__Rx1004194.

———. "Looking Back . . . First Public School, 1874." September 21, 1958. Available at Birmingham (Ala.) Public Library, Digital Collections. encore.bham.lib.al.us/iii/encore/record/C__Rx1003061.

Birmingham Post. "Founder of Orphan Home—Memory of Carrie Tuggle to be Honored with Plaque." February 6, 1954. bplonline.cdmhost.com/cdm/singleitem/collection/p4017coll2/id/1545/rec/14.

Birmingham Public Library. *Dr. Arthur Harold Parker: The Life and Legacy of a Pioneering African American Educator*. 2010. Available at Birmingham (Ala.) Public Library, Digital Collections. www.bplonline.org/resources/exhibits/ParkerA.H/gallery/parker/index.html.

Birmingham Times. "Black History Spotlight: Dr. Emory O. Jackson." February 24, 2011. Accessed February 11, 2012. www.birminghamtimesonline.com/.

Birmingham World. "Education Carrie Tuggle 1859–1924." n. d. Available at Birmingham (Ala.) Public Library, Digital Collections. encore.bham.lib.al.us/iii/encore/record/C__Rx1004768.

Blackmon, Douglas A. *Slavery by Another Name: The Re-enslavement of Black Americans from the Civil War to World War II*. New York: Anchor Books, 2008.

Bond, Horace Mann. "Negro Education: A Debate in the Alabama Constitutional Convention of 1901." *Journal of Negro Education* 1, no. 1 (1932): 49–59.

———. "The Influence of Personalities on the Public Education of Negroes in Alabama, I." *Journal of Negro Education* 6, no. 1 (1937): 17–29.

———. "The Influence of Personalities on the Public Education of Negroes in Alabama, II." *The Journal of Negro Education* 6, no. 2 (1937): 172–87.

———. *Negro Education in Alabama: A Study in Cotton and Steel.* Tuscaloosa: University of Alabama Press, 1994.

Bonvillian, Crystal. "State Earns 'A' for Schools Teaching Civil Rights History." *Birmingham News*, September 29, 2011.

Bositis, David A. *Diverging Generations: The Transformation of African American Policy Views*. Washington, DC: Joint Center for Political and Economic Studies, 2001.

Bowser, Edward. "Young Activists March in Historic Footsteps: Civil-Rights Movement Continues to Teach the Price of Freedom." *Birmingham News*, April 24, 2013.

Boyd, Todd. *The New H.N.I.C.: The Death of Civil Rights and the Reign of Hip Hop*. New York: New York University Press, 2003.

Bracey Jr., John H., and August Meier. *Papers of the NAACP, Part 20: White Resistance and Reprisals, 1956–1965*. Frederick, MD: University Publications of America, 1996. www.lexisnexis.com

Brady, Loretta C., and Amanda Hapenny "Giving Back and Growing in Service: Investigating Spirituality, Religiosity, and Generativity in Young Adults." *Journal of Adult Development* 17, no. 3 (2010): 162–67.

Branch, Taylor. *Pillar of Fire: America in the King Years 1963–1965*. New York: Simon and Schuster, 1998.

Brittain, Joseph M. "Some Reflections on Negro Suffrage and Politics in Alabama—Past and Present." Special issue, *Journal of Negro History 47*, no. 2 (1962): 127–38.

Brooks, F. Erik. "Legal and Policy Issues: Removing the Residue of Past Segregation in Higher Education." Special issue, *Journal of Negro Education* 73, no. 3 (2004): 350–64.

Bryant, Joseph D. "Birmingham Salutes Emory O. Jackson, Early Editor, Reformer with New Marker." *Al.com/Birmingham News*, October 16, 2012. blog.al.com/spotnews/.

Bullock, Henry A. *A History of Negro Education in the South, from 1619 to the Present*. Cambridge: Harvard University Press, 1967.

Burch, Traci. *Skin Color and the Criminal Justice System: Beyond Black-White Disparities in Sentencing*. Cambridge: Harvard University Press, 2005.

Butchart, Ronald E. *Schooling the Freed People: Teaching, Learning, and the Struggle for Black Freedom, 1861–1876*. Chapel Hill: University of North Carolina Press, 2010.

Bynoe, Yvonne. "Connected but Distinct: Hip-Hop Culture versus Hip-Hop Activism." *The Network Journal*, April 2004. www.tnj.com/archives/.

———. *Stand and Deliver: Political Activism, Leadership, and Hip Hop Culture*. Brooklyn: Soft Skull, 2004.

Cain, Leonard D. "Age Status and Generational Phenomena: The New Old People in Contemporary America." *Gerontologist*, 7 (1967): 83–92.

Callejo-Perez, David M. *Southern Hospitality: Identity, Schools, and the Civil Rights Movement in Mississippi 1964–1972*. New York: Peter Lang, 2001.

Capossela, Toni-Lee. *John U. Monro: Uncommon Educator*. Baton Rouge: Louisiana State University Press, 2012.

Carsen, Clayborn. *In Struggle: SNCC and the Black Awakening of the 1960s*. Cambridge: Harvard University Press, 1981.

Carter, Dan T. *The Politics of Rage: George Wallace, the Origins of the New Conservatism, and the Transformation of American Politics*. Baton Rouge: Louisiana State University Press, 2000.

Carter, Patricia A. *"Everybody's Paid but the Teacher" The Teaching Profession and the Women's Movement*. New York: Teachers College Press, 2002.

Cecelski, David S. 1994. *Along Freedom Road*. Chapel Hill: University of North Carolina Press, 1994.

Chabot, Sean. "Framing, Transnational Diffusion, and African American Intellectuals in the Land of Gandhi." *International Review of Social History* 149, no. S12 (2004): 19–40.

Chambers, Jesse. "Miles College Plans Events to Celebrate its Role in the Civil Rights Movement." *Birmingham News*, April 5, 2013. www.blog.al.com.

———. "Miles College Role in Civil Rights Movement Has Created a Permanent Legacy." *Birmingham News*, July 7, 2013. www.blog.al.com.

Charron, Katherine. M. *Freedom's Teacher: The Life of Septima Clark*. Chapel Hill: University of North Carolina Press, 2009.

Childers, James. S. "Where Pupils Study Books and Brooms." *Birmingham News Age-Herald*, May 28, 1933. Available at Birmingham Public Library, Digital Collections. encore.bham.lib.al.us/iii/encore/record/C__Rx1004217.

Christensen, Lois M. "Ms. Lillie M. H. Fincher: A Luminary African-American Educator in the Pre- and Post-integration in the South." *Social Science Research and Practice* 4 (2009): 131–39. www.socstrp.org/issues/PDF/4.2.13.pdf.

———, Tondra L. Loder, Virginia Volker, and Lillie M. H. Fincher. "The Historical Legacy of the Civil Rights Movement." Paper presented at the annual meeting of the American Educational Research Association, San Francisco, CA, April 2006.

Clark, E. Culpepper. *The Schoolhouse Door: Segregation's Last Stand at The University of Alabama*. New York: Oxford University Press, 1995.

Clausen, John A. "Life Reviews and Life Stories." In *Methods of Life Course Research: Qualitative and Quantitative Approaches*, edited by Janet Z. Giele and Glen H. Elder Jr., 189–212. Thousand Oaks, CA: Sage, 1998.

Clemon, U. W., and Bryan K. Fair. "Making Bricks without Straw: The NAACP Legal Defense Fund and the Development of Civil Rights Law in Alabama 1940–1980." *Alabama Law Review* 52 (2001): 1121–52.

Cohen, Louise, Lawrence Manion, and Keith Morrison. *Research Methods in Education*. 5th edition. London: Routledge Farmer, 2000.

Coffin, G. C. "The Black School Administrator and How He's Being Pushed to Extinction." *American School Board Journal* 159, no. 11 (1972): 33–36.

Cole, Antrenise. "50 Years Later: Racial Divide Shown in School Enrollment Figures." *Birmingham Business Journal*, July 18, 2013. www.bizjournals.com/birmingham/.

Collier-Thomas, Bettye, and V. P. Franklin. *Sisters in the Struggle: African American Women in the Civil Rights-Black Power Movement*. New York: New York University Press, 2001.

Collins, Marva, and Civia Tamarkin. *Marva Collins' Way*. New York: Penguin Putnam, 1990.

Collins, Patricia Hill. *Black Feminist Thought: Knowledge, Consciousness, and the Politics of Empowerment*. 2nd edition. New York: Routledge, 2000.

———. *From Black Power to Hip Hop: Racism, Nationalism, and Feminism*. Philadelphia: Temple University Press, 2006.

———. *Another Kind of Public Education: Race, Schools, the Media, and Democratic Possibilities*. Boston: Beacon, 2009.

Colton, Larry. *Southern League: A True Story of Baseball, Civil Rights, and the Deep South's Most Compelling Pennant Race*. New York: Grand Central Publishing, 2013.

Corti, Louise. "Archival Research." In *Sage Encyclopedia of Social Science Research Methods*, edited by Michael S. Lewis-Beck, Alan Bryman, and Tim Futing Liao, 20–21. Thousand Oaks, CA: Sage, 2004.

Cose, Ellis. *The End of Anger: A New Generation's Take on Race and Rage*. New York: Harper Collins, 2011.

Cozart, Sheryl Conrad. "Becoming Whole: A Letter to a Young, Miseducated Black Teacher." *Urban Review* 42 (2010): 22–38.

Crawford, Vicki L., Jacqueline Anne Rouse, and Barbara Woods. *Women in the Civil Rights Movement: Trailblazers and Torchbearers 1941–1965*. Bloomington: Indiana University Press, 1993.

Crocco, Margaret S., Petra Munro, and Kathleen Weiler. *Pedagogies of Resistance: Women Educator Activists, 1880–1960*. New York: Teachers College Press, 1999.

Crosnoe, Robert, Monica K. Johnson, and Glen H. Elder Jr. "Intergenerational Bonding in School: The Behavioral and Contextual Correlates of Student-Teacher Relationships." *Sociology of Education* 77, no. 1 (2004): 60–81.

Dagbovie, Petro. G. "Strategies for Teaching African American History: Musings from the Past, Ruminations for the Future." *Journal of Negro Education* 75 (2006): 635–48.

Dailey, Jane, Glenda Elizabeth Gilmore, and Bryant Simon. *Jumpin' Jim Crow: Southern Politics from Civil War to Civil Rights*. Princeton: Princeton University Press, 2000.

Davis, Allison, B. Burleigh Gardner, and Mary Gardner. *Deep South: A Social Anthropological Study of Caste and Class*. Columbia: University of South Carolina Press, 2009.

Davis, Angela Y. *Women, Race and Class*. New York: Vintage Books, 1981.

Davis, Christopher B. "Emory O. Jackson: A Traditionalist in the Early Civil Rights Fight in Birmingham, Alabama." MA thesis, University of Alabama at Birmingham, 2006.

De Moraes, Lisa. "Kanye West's Torrent of Criticism, Live on NBC." *Washington Post*, September 3, 2005. www.washingtonpost.com.

Dennis, Michael, J. "Schooling along the Color Line: Progressives and the Education of Blacks in the New South." *Journal of Negro Education* 67, no. 2 (1998): 142–56.

de Schweinitz, Rebecca. *If We Could Change the World. Young People and America's Struggle for Racial Equality*. Chapel Hill: University of North Carolina Press, 2009.

Deutsch, Stephanie. *You Need a Schoolhouse: Booker T. Washington, Julius Rosenwald, and the Building of Schools for the Segregated South*. Evanston: Northwestern University Press, 2011.

Dillon, Ernie H. *A Brief History of Birmingham Public Schools, 1883–1972*. Available at Birmingham (Ala.) Public Library Southern History Collection.

Dingus, Jeannine E. "Doing the Best We Could: African American Teachers' Counterstory on School Desegregation." *Urban Review* 38 (2006): 211–33.

Dittmer, John. *Local People: The Struggle for Civil Rights in Mississippi*. Urbana: University of Illinois Press, 1994.

Dixson, Adrienne D. " 'Let's Do This!' Black Women Teachers' Politics and Pedagogy." *Urban Education* 38 (2003): 217–35.

———, and Jeannine E. Dingus. "In Search of Our Mothers' Gardens: Black Women Teachers and Professional Socialization." *Teachers College Record* 110 (2008): 805–37.

Dizier, Byron, S. "Parker High Long Way from Single Room." *Birmingham News*, May 24, 1985. encore.bham.lib.al.us/iii/encore/record/C__Rx1004204.

Doherty, Elaine, John H. Laub, and Robert J. Sampson. "Group-based Trajectories in Life Course Criminology." In *The Craft of Life Course Research*, edited by Glen H. Elder Jr. and Janet Z. Giele, 187–210. New York: Guilford, 2009.

Dolgin, Gail, Robin Fryday, and Judith Helfand. *The Barber of Birmingham: Foot Soldier of the Civil Rights Movement*, 2011. Documentary film. United States: Chicken and Egg Pictures, Interfaze Educational Productions, and Purposeful Productions.

Dougherty, Jack. " 'That's When We Were Marching for Jobs': Black Teachers and the Early Civil Rights Movement in Milwaukee." *History of Education Quarterly* 38, no. 2 (1998): 121–41.

Du Bois, W. E. B. "Does the Negro Need Separate Schools?" *Journal of Negro Education* 4 (1935): 328–35.

———. *The Souls of Black Folk*. New York: Fawcett Publications, 1961. First published 1953 by Blue Heron Press.

Dukes, Donna. *Stand!* 2013. Documentary film. Birmingham, AL: Donna Dukes Production.

Dyson, Michael Eric. *Between God and Gangsta Rap: Bearing Witness to Black Culture*. New York: Oxford University Press, 1996.

———. *Know What I Mean? Reflections on Hip Hop*. New York: Basic Civitas, 2007.

Edgemon, Catherine. "Carrie Tuggle and the Tuggle Normal and Industrial Institute." College thesis. Birmingham, AL. Available at Birmingham Public Library Rare Books Collection, 1995.

Edwards, JohnMark Allen. "From *Brown* to *Bakke*: Race, Change and the Birmingham City Schools 1963–1983." Master's thesis, University of Alabama at Birmingham, 2011.

Elder, Glen H., and Janet Z. Giele. *The Craft of Life Course Research*. New York: Guilford, 2009.

Elder, Glen H., and Lisa A. Pellerin. "Linking History and Human Lives." In *Methods of Life Course Research: Qualitative and Quantitative Approaches*, edited by Janet Z. Giele and Glen H. Elder Jr., 264–94. Thousand Oaks, CA: Sage, 1998.

Embree, Edwin R., and Julia Waxman. *Investment in People: The Story of the Julius Rosenwald Fund*. New York: Harper and Brothers, 1949.

Epps, Edgar G. "Race and School Desegregation: Contemporary Legal and Educational Issues." In *Messages for Educational Leadership: The Constance E. Clayton Lectures 1998–2007*, edited by Diana T. Slaughter-Defoe, 26–49. New York: Peter Lang, 2012.

Eskew, Glenn T. 1997. *But for Birmingham: The Local and National Movements in the Civil Rights Struggle*. Chapel Hill: The University of North Carolina Press.

Fairclough, Adam. *To Redeem the Soul of America: The Southern Christian Leadership Conference and Martin Luther King, Jr.* Athens: University of Georgia Press, 1987.

———. " 'Being in the Field of Education and also Being a Negro . . . Seems . . . Tragic': Black Teachers in the Jim Crow South." *Journal of American History* 87, no. 1 (2000): 65–91.

———. *Teaching Equality: Black Schools in the Age of Jim Crow*. Athens: University of Georgia Press, 2001.

———. "The Cost of *Brown*: Black Teachers and School Integration." *Journal of American History* 91, no. 1 (2004): 43–55.

———. *A Class of Their Own: Black Teachers in the Segregated South*. Cambridge: Harvard University Press, 2007.

Fallin Jr., Wilson. 1997. *The African American Church in Birmingham Alabama, 1815–1963: A Shelter in the Storm*. New York: Garland.

Faulk, Kent. "Lola Hendricks, Key Behind the Scene Worker in Civil Rights Group, Dies." *Birmingham News*, May 23, 2013. www.blog.al.com/spotnews/2013/05/lola_hendricks_key_behind_the.html.

———. "Fifty Years Ago a Federal Appeals Court Ordered Desegregation of Birmingham Schools." *Birmingham News*, July 12, 2013. www.blog.al.com/spotnews/2013/07/fifty_years_ago_a_federal_appe.html.

Feldman, Lynne B. 1999. *A Sense of Place: Birmingham's Black Middle-Class Community, 1890–1930*. Tuscaloosa: University of Alabama Press.

Fields-Smith, Cheryl. "African American Parents Before and after *Brown*." *Journal of Curriculum and Supervision* 20, no. 2 (2005): 129–35.

Fleming, Nora. "Magnets Reimagined as School Option." *Education Week*, May 1, 2012. www.edweek.org.

Flynt, Wayne. *Dixie's Forgotten People, New Edition: The South's Poor Whites*. Bloomington: Indiana University Press, 2004.

Foster, Michele. "The Politics of Race: Through the Eyes of African-American Teachers." *Journal of Education* 172 (1990):123–41.

———. "Self-portraits of Black Teachers: Narratives of Individual and Collective Struggle Against Racism." In *Naming Silenced Lives: Personal Narratives and Processes of Educational Change*, edited by Daniel McLaughlin and William G. Tierney, 155–76. New York: Routledge, 1993.

———. *Black Teachers on Teaching*. New York: Norton, 1997.

Frankenberg, Erica. "Splintering School Districts: Understanding the Link between Segregation and Fragmentation." *Law and Social Inquiry* 34, no. 4 (2009): 869–909.

———, Lee Chungmei, and Gary Orfield. "A Multiracial Society with Segregated Schools: Are We Losing the Dream?" (report). Cambridge: Civil Rights Project at Harvard University, 2003.

Franklin, V. P. " 'They Rose or Fell Together': African American Educators and Community Leadership, 1795–1954." In *The Sage Handbook of African American Education*, edited by Linda C. Tillman, 35–51. Thousand Oaks, CA: Sage, 2009. First published in *Journal of Education* (1990.172: 39–64).

Frazier, E. Franklin. *Black Bourgeoisie*. New York: Free Press, 1957.

Freire, Paulo. *Pedagogy of the Oppressed*. 30th anniversary edition. New York: Continuum, 2005.

Fultz, Michael. "African American Teachers in the South, 1890–1940: Powerlessness and the Ironies of Expectations of Protest." *History of Education Quarterly* 35 (1995): 401–22.

———. "Teacher Training and African American Education in the South, 1900–1940." *Journal of Negro Education* 64, no. 2 (1995): 196–210.

———. Review of *The Jeanes Supervisors: Striving to Educate*, DVD, by Vernon F. Clarke and James C. Isaac. Atlanta: BNG Media. *Journal of Negro Education* 65, no. 1 (1996): 95–96.

———. "The Displacement of Black Educators Post-Brown: An Overview and Analysis." *History of Education Quarterly* 44 (2004): 11–45.

———. "Caught between a Rock and a Hard Place: The Dissolution of Black State Teachers Associations, 1954–1970." In *Sage Handbook of African American Education*, edited by Linda C. Tillman, 67–82. Thousand Oaks, CA: Sage, 2009.

Gaddis, John L. *The Landscape of History: How Historians Map the Past*. New York: Oxford University Press, 2002.

Gardner, Booker, T. "The Educational Contributions of Booker T. Washington." *Journal of Negro Education* 44, no. 4 (1975): 502–18.

Gardner, Michael R. *Harry Truman and Civil Rights: Moral Courage and Political Risks*. Carbondale: Southern Illinois University Press, 2002.

Garrison, Greg. "Students Take to the Streets to Remember Children who Marched for Civil Rights in 1963." May 2, 2013. *AL.com/Birmingham News*. blog.al.com/spotnews//.

Garrow, David J. *Birmingham, Alabama 1956–1963: The Black Struggle for Civil Rights*. Brooklyn: Carlson, 1989.

Gasman, Marybeth. "Perceptions of Black College Presidents: Sorting through Stereotypes and Reality to Gain a Complex Picture." *American Education Research Journal* 48, no. 4 (2011): 836–70.

Gatewood, Willard B. *The Aristocrats of Color: The Black Elite, 1880–1920*. Bloomington: Indiana University Press, 1990.

Generett, Gretchen G. "Intergenerational Discussions as a Curriculum Strategy: Modeling Audacious Hope in Action." Special issue, *Urban Review* 37 (2005): 267–77.

George, Linda K. "Conceptualizing and Measuring Trajectories." In *The Craft of Life Course Research*, edited by Glen H. Elder Jr. and Janet Z. Giele, 163–86. New York: Guilford, 2009.

Giddings, Paula J. *When and Where I Enter: The Impact of Black Women in America*. New York: HarperCollins, 1984.

Giele, Janet Z. "Life Stories to Understand Diversity—Variations by Class, Race, and Gender." In *The Craft of Life Course Research*, edited by Glen H. Elder Jr. and Janet Z. Giele, 236–57. New York: Guildford, 2009.

———, and Glen H. Elder Jr., eds. *Methods of Life Course Research: Qualitative and Quantitative Approaches*. Thousand Oaks, CA: Sage, 1998.

Gilkes, Cheryl T. "'Liberated to Work Like Dogs!' Labeling Black Women and their Work." In *The Experience and Meaning of Work in Women's Lives*, edited by Hildreth Y. Grossman and Nia Lane Chester, 165–68. Hillsdale, NJ: Lawrence Erlbaum Associates, 1990.

Gilmore, Glenda E. *Gender and Jim Crow: Women and the Politics of White Supremacy in North Carolina, 1896–1920*. Chapel Hill: University of North Carolina Press, 1996.

Gilpin, Patrick J., and Marybeth Gasman. *Charles S. Johnson: Leadership Beyond the Veil in the Age of Jim Crow*. Albany: State University of New York Press, 2003.

Ginsburg, Faye D. *Contested Lives: The Abortion Debate in an American Community*. Berkeley: University of California Press, 1989.

Ginwright, Shawn. *Black in School: Afrocentric Reform, Urban Youth, and the Promise of Hip-Hop Culture*. New York: Teachers College Press, 2004.

———. *Black Youth Rising: Activism and Radical Healing in Urban America*. New York: Teachers College Press, 2009.

Gray, Jeremy. "Civil Rights Institute Honors Lowery." *Birmingham News*, November 13, 2009. www.al.com/birmingham.

"Birmingham-area Poverty Rises 1.5 Percent, U.S. Census Bureau Says." *Birmingham News*, September 24, 2011. www.al.com/birmingham.

______. "Birmingham Board of Education Issued Order Expelling or Suspending 1,081 Student Protestors." *Birmingham News*, May 20, 2013, www.al.com/birmingham.

———. "Birmingham School Board Officially Close Integrated Schools." *Birmingham News*, September 5, 2013. blog.al.com/birmingham-news-stories.

———. "State Troopers Turned Black Students Away from Birmingham Schools." *Birmingham News*, September 9, 1963. blog.al.com/birmingham-news-stories.

Gray, Jerome, Joe L. Reed, and Norman W. Walton. *History of the Alabama State Teachers Association*. Washington, DC: National Education Association, 1987. Available at Alabama State University Levi Watkins Learning Center Archives and Special Collections.

Green, Keisha L., and Marcella Runell. "Hip Hop and Education: An Exploratory Dialogue." Paper presented at the annual conference of the National Association for Multicultural Education, Phoenix, Arizona, November 2006.

Greene, Christina. *Our Separate Ways: Women and the Black Freedom Struggle in Durham, North Carolina*. Chapel Hill: University of North Carolina Press, 2005.

Griffin, Larry J. " 'Generations and Collective Memory' Revisited: Race, Region, and Memory of Civil Rights." *American Sociological Review* 69 (2004): 544–57.

———, and Kenneth A. Bollen. "What Do These Memories Do? Civil Rights Remembrance and Racial Attitudes." *American Sociological Review* 74, no. 4 (2009): 594–614.

Hagestad, Gunhild O. "Introduction: Thoughts about the Life Course." In *The Meaning of Age: Selected Papers by Bernice L. Neugarten*, edited by Dail A. Neugarten, 81–87. Chicago: University of Chicago Press, 1996.

Hall, Jacquelyn Dowd. "The Long Civil Rights Movement and the Political Uses of the Past." *Journal of American History* 91, no. 4 (2005): 1233–63.

Hamilton, Kendra. "Activists for the New Millennium." *Black Issues in Higher Education* 20 (April, 24, 2003): 16–21.

Hansen, Jeff. "Birmingham Changes as Blacks Move to the Suburbs." *Birmingham News*, March 27, 2011. www.al.com/birmingham.

———, and Marie Leech. "City's Black Students Leaving for the Suburbs." *Birmingham News*, August 6, 2006. www.al.com/birmingham.

Hardy, Ernest A. "A Study of Urban School Desegregation with Implications for the City School System of Birmingham, Alabama." PhD diss., University of Alabama, 1977.

Harlan, Louis R. *Booker T. Washington: The Making of a Black Leader, 1856–1901*. 2 vols. New York: Oxford University Press, 1972.

———. *Booker T. Washington*. New York: Oxford University Press, 1983.

Harley, Sharon. "Beyond the Classroom: The Organizational Lives of Black Female Educators in the District of Columbia, 1890–1930." *Journal of Negro Education* 51 (1982): 254–65.

———. "For the Good of Family and Race: Gender, Work, and Domestic Roles in a Black Community, 1880–1930." *Signs* 15, no. 2 (1990): 336–49.

Harris, Carl V. "Stability and Change in Discrimination against Black Public Schools: Birmingham, Alabama, 1871–1931." *Journal of Southern History* 51, no. 3 (1985): 375–416.

Harris, Fredrick. C. "It Takes a Tragedy to Arouse Them: Collective Memory and Collective Action during the Civil Rights Movement." *Social Movement Studies* 5, no. 1 (2006): 19–43.

Harris, James Tyra. "Alabama Reaction to the Brown Decision, 1954–1956: A Case Study in Early Massive Resistance." PhD diss., Middle Tennessee State University, 1978.

Harris-Perry, Melissa. *Sister Citizen: Shame, Stereotypes, and Black Women in America*. New Haven: Yale University Press, 2011.

Hayes, Carol W. *Think-Work-Serve: A Profile of Carol William Hayes*. Birmingham, AL: Author, 1966.

———. "Dr. Carol W. Hayes: The Man and the Legend" (school program booklet). Birmingham, AL: Carol W. Hayes High School, 1980.

Henig, Jeffrey R., Richard C. Hula, Marion Orr, and Desiree S. Pedescleaux. T*he Color of School Reform: Race, Politics, and the Challenge of Urban Education*. Princeton: Princeton University Press, 1999.

Hess, Fredrick M., and Michael J. Petrilli. *No Child Left Behind*. New York: Peter Lang, 2009.

Higginbotham, Elizabeth Brooks. "African-American Women's History and the Metalanguage of Race." *Signs* 17, no. 2 (1992): 251–74.

Hill, Marc Lamont. *Beats, Rhymes, and Classroom Life: Hip-Hop Pedagogy and the Politics of Identity*. New York: Teachers College Press, 2009.

Hill, Michael R. *Archival Strategies and Techniques*. Thousand Oaks, CA: Sage, 1993.

Hine, Darlene Clark. *Hine Sight: Black Women and the Re-construction of American History*. Bloomington: Indiana University Press, 1996.

———, ed. *Black Women in America*. 2nd edition. New York: Oxford University Press, 2005.

Hochschild, Jennifer L., and Velsa M. Weaver. "The Skin Color Paradox and the American Racial Order." *Social Forces* 86, no. 2 (2007): 643–70.

Hoffschwelle, Mary S. *The Rosenwald Schools of the American South*. Gainesville: University Press of Florida, 2006.

hooks, bell. *Ain't I a Woman: Black Women and Feminism*. Boston: South End Press, 1981.

———. *Teaching to Transgress: Education as the Practice of Freedom*. New York: Routledge, 1994.

Huberman, Michael A., and Matthew B. Miles. "Data Management and Analysis Methods." In *Handbook of Qualitative Research*, edited by Norman K. Denzin and Yvonne S. Lincoln, 428–44. Thousand Oaks, CA: Sage, 1994.

Hudson, Mildred J., and Barbara. J. Holmes. "Missing Teachers, Impaired Communities: The Unanticipated Consequences of *Brown vs. Board of Education* on the African American Teaching Force at the Precollegiate Level." *Journal of Negro Education* 63 (1994): 388–93.

Huntley, Horace H., and John W. McKerley, eds. *Footsoldiers for Democracy: The Men, Women, and Children of the Birmingham Civil Rights Movement*. Birmingham, AL: Birmingham Civil Rights Institute, 2009.

Hurt, R. Douglas, ed. *African American Life in the Rural South, 1900–1950*. Columbia: University of Missouri Press, 2003.

Irvine, Jacqueline Jordan. *In Search of Wholeness: African American Teachers and Their Culturally Specific Classroom Practices*. New York: Palgrave, 2002.

James, Joy. *Transcending the Talented Tenth: Black Leaders and American Intellectuals*. New York: Routledge, 1997.

James Jr., Rawn. *Root and Branch: Charles Hamilton Houston, Thurgood Marshall, and the Struggle to End Segregation*. New York: Bloomsbury, 2010.

Jarrett, Robin L., and Linda M. Burton. "Dynamic Dimensions of Family Structure in Low-Income African American Families: Emergent Themes in Qualitative Research." *Journal of Comparative Family Studies* 30 (1999): 177–87.

Jean-Marie, Gaetane, Channell James, and Shirley Bynum. "Black Women Activists, Leaders, and Educators: Transforming Urban Educational Practice." In Vol. 1 of *The Praeger Handbook of Urban Education*, edited by Joe L. Kincheloe, kecia hayes, Karel Rose, and Philip M. Anderson, 59–70. Westport, CT: Greenwood, 2006.

Jefferson County Board of Education. Vol. 1 of "Elementary and Secondary Public Education in Jefferson County, Alabama: History of the Jefferson County Board of Education, 1819–1868" (report). Homewood, Alabama: Jefferson County Board of Education, 1976.

Jefferson County Board of Education, Vickie M. Chandler, and Pamela S. King. Vol. 2 of "Elementary and Secondary Public Education in Jefferson County, Alabama: History of the Jefferson County Board of Education, 1868–1975" (report). Homewood, Alabama: Jefferson County Board of Education, 1978.

Johnson, Jeff. "Young, Black and in Decline in the Obama Age?" *The Root*, June 10, 2008. www.theroot.com/id/46761/output/print.

Johnson, Karen A. "On Classical versus Vocational Education: The Educational Ideas of Anna Julia Cooper and Nannie Helen Burroughs." In *Education as Freedom: African American Educational Thought and Activism*, edited by Noel S. Anderson and Haroon Kharem, 47–68. Lanham, MD: Lexington Books, 2009.

———. "Cooper, Anna Julia Haywood (1860–1964)." In Vol. 1 of *Encyclopedia of African American Education*, edited by Kofi Lomotey, 184–86. Thousand Oaks, CA: Sage, 2010.

———. "Septima Poinsette Clark's Literacy Teaching Approaches for Linguistic Acquisition and Literacy Development for Gullah-Speaking Children." In

African American Women Educators: A Critical Examination of their Pedagogies, Educational Ideas, and Activism from the Nineteenth to the Mid-Twentieth Century, edited by Karen A. Johnson, Abdul Pitre, and Kenneth L. Johnson, 73–105. Lanham, MD: Rowman and Littlefield, 2014.

———, Abdul Pitre, and Kenneth L. Johnson, eds. *African American Women Educators: A Critical Examination of their Pedagogies, Educational Ideas, and Activism from the Nineteenth to the Mid-Twentieth Century*. Lanham, MD: Rowman and Littlefield, 2014.

Johnson, Leola. "Silencing Gangsta Rap: Class and Race Agendas in the Campaign against Hardcore Rap Lyrics." *Temple Political and Civil Rights Law Review* 3, no. 19 (October 1993).

Joseph, Peniel E. "How Ferguson Has Exposed a Civil Rights Generational Divide." *The Root*. www.theroot.com.

———, ed. *The Black Power Movement: Rethinking the Civil Rights-Black Power Era*. New York: Routledge/Taylor and Francis, 2006.

Karpinski, Carol. F. *"A Visible Company of Professionals": African Americans and the National Education Association during the Civil Rights Movement*. New York: Peter Lang, 2008.

Kelley, Robin D. G. *Into the Fire: African Americans since 1970*. New York: Oxford University Press, 1996.

Kelly, Diann Cameron. "In Preparation for Adulthood: Exploring Civic Participation and Social Trust among Young Minorities." *Youth and Society* 40, no. 4 (2009): 526–40.

Kelly, Hilton. "What Jim Crow's Teachers Could Do: Educational Capital and Teachers' Work in Under-resourced Schools." *Urban Review* 42 (2010): 329–50.

———. *Race, Remembering, and Jim Crow's Teachers*. New York: Routledge, 2010.

———. " 'Just Something Gone, but Nothing Missing': Booker T. Washington, Nannie Helen Burroughs, and the Social Significance of Black Teachers Theorizing across Two Centuries." Special issue, *Educational Studies: Journal of the American Educational Studies Association* 48, no. 3 (2012): 215–19.

King, Joyce E. "A Declaration of Intellectual Independence for Human Freedom." In *Black Education: A Transformative Research and Action Agenda for the New Century*, edited by Joyce E. King, 19–44. Washington, DC, and Mahwah, NJ: American Educational Research Association and Lawrence Erlbaum Associates, 2005.

———, ed. *Black Education: A Transformative Research and Action Agenda for the New Century*. Washington, DC, and Mahwah, NJ: American Educational Research Association and Lawrence Erlbaum Associates, 2005.

King, Sabrina Hope. "The Limited Presence of African-American Teachers." *Review of Educational Research* 63, no. 2 (1993): 115–49.

Kirk, John A. "The NAACP Campaign for Teachers' Salary Equalization: African American Women Educators and the Early Civil Rights Struggle." *Journal of African American History* 94, no. 4 (2009): 529–52.

Kitwana, Bakari. *The Hip Hop Generation: Young Blacks and the Crisis in African American Culture*. New York: Basic Civitas Books, 2002.

Klarman, Michael J. *Brown v. Board of Education and the Civil Rights Movement*. New York: Oxford University Press, 2007.

Knight, David. "Why Schools Must Talk about Trayvon Martin." *Education Week*, September 23, 2013. www.edweek.org/ew/articles/2013/09/25/05knight.h33.html?qs=trayvon+martin.

Ladson-Billings, Gloria. "2004 DeWitt-Wallace Reader's Digest Distinguished Lecture: Landing on the Wrong Note: The Price We Paid for *Brown*." *Educational Researcher* 33, no. 7 (2004): 3–13.

———. *Beyond the Big House: African American Educators on Teacher Education*. New York: Teachers College Press, 2005.

———. *Dreamkeepers: Successful Teachers of African American Children*. 2nd edition. San Francisco: Jossey-Bass/John Wiley and Sons, 2009.

Lamonte, Edward S. *Politics and Welfare in Birmingham, 1900–1975*. Tuscaloosa: University of Alabama Press, 1995.

Lamonte, Ruth B. "The Origins of an Urban School System: Birmingham, 1873–1900." *Journal of the Birmingham Historical Society* 5, no. 2 (1977): 5–17.

Lanahan, D., and J. Weyburn. *Ed's Report Card*, PhD capstone project, Vanderbilt University and Birmingham Education Foundation, Spring 2013. Available at Vanderbilt Peabody School of Education website. discoverarchive.vanderbilt.edu/handle/1803/5201.

Lee, Carol D. "The State of Knowledge about the Education of African Americans." In *Black Education: A Transformative Research and Action Agenda for the New Century*, edited by Joyce E. King, 45–71. Matwah, NJ, and Washington, DC: Lawrence Erlbaum Associates and American Educational Research Association, 2005.

———, and Diana Slaughter-Defoe. "Historical and Sociocultural Influences on African American Education." In *Handbook of Research on Multicultural Education*, edited by James A. Banks and Cherry A. McGee Banks, 348–71. New York: Macmillan, 1995.

Lee, Helen Shores, and Barbara S. Shores. In collaboration with Denise George. *The Gentle Giant of Dynamite Hill: The Untold Story of Arthur Shores and his Family's Fight for Civil Rights*. Grand Rapids: Zondervan, 2012.

Lee, Spike. *Four Little Girls*, 1997. Documentary film. New York: 40 Acres and a Mule Productions and Home Box Office.

Leech, Marie. "200 Birmingham School Employees Demoted or Laid off after Alabama Superintendent Implements Cost-cutting Plan." *Birmingham News*, July 24, 2010. blog.al.com/spotnews/2012/07/200_birmingham_school_employee.html.

———. "Efforts Afoot to Abolish Birmingham Board of Education." *Birmingham News*, August 21, 2010. www.al.com/birmingham.

———. "Rev. Shuttlesworth, Family Relives a Moment in History with Return to Birmingham School Where They were Beaten." *Birmingham News*, September 17, 2010. www.al.com/birmingham.

———. "About 250 Rally in Support of Birmingham School Superintendent Craig Witherspoon." *Birmingham News*, April 6, 2012. blog.al.com/spotnews/2012/04/about_250_rally_in_support_of.html.

———. "Alabama Education Department Seizes Control of Birmingham School Board." *Birmingham News*, April 13, 2012. www.al.com/birmingham.

———. "Alabama Department of Education Officially Takes over Birmingham City Schools." *Birmingham News*, June 27, 2012. www.al.com/birmingham.

———. "Accrediting Agency Tells Birmingham School Board there is 'Little to No Evidence of Improvement,' Gives Board Dec. 1 Deadline for Plan." *Birmingham News*, November 1, 2012. blog.al.com/spotnews/2012/11/accrediting_agency_tells_birmi.html.

———. "A New Era: Birmingham Board of Education Members Sworn In." *Al.com/Birmingham News*, October 22, 2013. blog.al.com/spotnews/2013/10/a_new_era_birmingham_board_of.html.

———. "Birmingham Board of Education: Woodfin Named President, Collins Vice President." *Al.com/Birmingham News*, October 23, 2013. blog.al.com/spotnews/2013/10/birmingham_board_of_education_48.html.

Levinson, Cynthia. *We've Got a Job: The 1963 Birmingham Children's March*. Atlanta: Peachtree Publishers, 2012.

Lewis, Andrew B. *The Shadows of Youth: The Remarkable Journey of the Civil Rights Generation*. New York: Hill and Wang, 2009.

Lewis, David Levering. *W. E. B. Du Bois: Biography of a Race 1868–1919*. New York: Henry Holt and Company, 1993.

Linde, Charlotte. "Explanatory Systems in Oral Life Stories." In *Cultural Models in Language and Thought*, edited by Dorothy Holland and Naomi Quinn, 343–66. Cambridge: Cambridge University Press, 1987.

Lipsitz, George. "The Hip Hop Hearings: Censorship, Social Memory, and Intergenerational Tensions among African Americans." In *Generations of Youth: Youth Cultures and History in Twentieth Century America*, edited by Joe Austin and Michael Willard, 395–411. New York: New York University, 1998.

Loder, Tondra. "Bridging the Tradition of Activism and Professionalism within the Context of Contemporary Urban Education: Perspectives from Birmingham Educators Born Pre- and Post–Civil Rights Movement," #200500140. Small Research Grant funded by Lyle M. Spencer Foundation, Chicago.

———. "African-American Women Principals' Reflections on Social Change, Community Othermothering, and Chicago Public School Reform." *Urban Education* 40 (2005): 298–320.

———. "On Deferred Dreams, Callings, and Revolving Doors of Opportunity: African-American Women's Reflections on Becoming Principals." Special issue, *Urban Review* 37 (2005): 243–65.

———. "Dilemmas Confronting Urban Principals in the Post–Civil Rights Era." In Vol. 1 of *The Praeger Handbook of Urban Education: An Encyclopedia*, edited by Joe L. Kincheloe, Kecia Hayes, Karel Rose, and Philip M Anderson, 70–77. Westport, CT: Greenwood, 2006.

Loder-Jackson, Tondra L. The Role of Educators in the Civil Rights Movement. Community symposium convened at the annual Archival Department Series of the Birmingham Civil Rights Institute, Birmingham, AL, September 2007.

———. "The Confluence of Race, Gender, and Generation in the Lives of African-American Women Principals." In *The Sage Handbook of African American Education*, edited by Linda C. Tillman, 223–36. Thousand Oaks, CA: Sage, 2009.

———. "Mary McCleod Bethune." In Vol. 1 of *Encyclopedia of African American Education*, edited by Kofi Lomotey, 71–74. Thousand Oaks, CA: Sage, 2010.

———. "Bridging the Legacy of Activism across Generations: Life Stories of African American Educators in Post–Civil Rights Birmingham." *Urban Review* 43, no. 2 (2011): 151–74.

———. "Hope and Despair: Southern Black Women Educators across Pre- and Post–Civil Rights Cohorts Theorize about Their Activism." Special issue, *Educational Studies: Journal of the American Educational Studies Association* 48, no. 3 (2012): 266–95.

———. "The Generational Challenge for African American Educators in the Post–Civil Rights Era." In *Messages for Educational Leadership: The Constance E. Clayton Lectures, 1998–2007*, edited by Judy Alston (series ed.) and Diana T. Slaughter-Defoe (vol. ed.), 214–22. New York: Peter Lang, 2012.

———, Deborah L. Voltz, and Michael Froning. "New Horizons for Urban Teacher Preparation and Parent Engagement in the Post–Civil Rights South." In *A Nation of Students at Risk: Advancing Equity and Achievement in America's Diversifying Schools*, edited by Camille Wilson and Sonya Douglas Horsford, 186–99. New York: Routledge, 2014.

Logan, Rayford W. *The Negro in American Life and Thought: The Nadir, 1877–1901*. New York: Dial, 1954.

Lomotey, Kofi, ed. *Encyclopedia of African American Education*, 2 vols. Thousand Oaks, CA: Sage, 2010.

Mannheim, Karl. "The Problem of Generations." In *Essays on the Sociology of Knowledge*, edited by Paul Kecskemeti, 276–322. London: Routledge and Kegan Paul, 1952. First published as "Das Problem der Generationen" in 1928.

Margo, Robert A. "'Teacher Salaries in Black and White': Pay Discrimination in the Southern Classroom." In *Race and Schooling in the South, 1880–1950: An Economic History*, edited by Robert A. Margo, 52–67. Chicago: University of Chicago Press, 1990.

Marshall, Catherine, and Amy L. Anderson, eds. *Activist Educators: Breaking Past Limits*. New York: Routledge, 2009.

Massey, Douglas S., and Nancy A. Denton. *American Apartheid: Segregation and the Making of the Underclass*. Boston: President and Fellows of Harvard College, 1993.

Mays, Benjamin E. "The Moral Aspects of Segregation Decisions." *Journal of Educational Sociology* 29 (1956): 361–66.

McAdams, Dan P. "The Redemptive Self: Generativity and the Stories Americans Live By." *Research in Human Development* 3, no. 2/3 (2006): 81–100.

McCluskey, Audrey Thomas. *Forgotten Sisterhood: Pioneering Black Women Educators and Activists in the Jim Crow South.* Lanham, MD: Rowman and Littlefield, 2014.

McCormick, J. Scott. "The Julius Rosenwald Fund." *Journal of Negro Education* 3, no. 4 (1934): 605–26.

McCulloch, Gary. *Documentary Research in Education, History and the Social Sciences.* New York: Routledge Falmer, 2002.

McGruder, Aaron, Reginald Hudlin, and Rodney Barnes. "Return of the King." *The Boondocks.* Cable television series. Directed by Kalvin Lee. Aired January 15, 2006. Culver City, CA: Adelaide Productions, Rebel Base, and Sony Productions.

McGuire, Danielle L. *At the Dark End of the Street: Black Women, Rape, and Resistance—A New History of the Civil Rights Movement from Rosa Parks to the Rise of Black Power.* New York: Vintage Books, 2010.

McKinstry, Carolyn Maull. *While the World Watched: A Birmingham Bombing Survivor Comes of Age during the Civil Rights Movement.* Carol Stream, IL: Tyndale House, 2011.

McNeil, Genna Rae. *Groundwork: Charles Hamilton Houston and the Struggle for Civil Rights.* Philadelphia: The University of Pennsylvania Press, 1984.

McPherson Sr., Jonathan. *A Drum Major for God and a Perfume Sprinkler to Man: The Life and Theology of Unsung Civil Rights Hero Reverend Dr. Jonathan McPherson, Sr.* In collaboration with Nathan Hale Turner Jr. Jonesboro, AR: Grant House, 2013.

McWhorter, Diane. *Carry Me Home: Birmingham, Alabama, The Climactic Battle of the Civil Rights Revolution.* New York: Touchstone, 2001.

Meier, August. *Negro Thought in America, 1880–1915.* Ann Arbor: University of Michigan and Ann Arbor Paperbacks, 1963.

Meier, Deborah, Alfie Kohn, Linda Darling-Hammond, Theodore Sizer, R., George Wood, and others. *Many Children Left Behind: How the No Child Left Behind Act Is Damaging our Children and our Schools.* Boston: Beacon, 2004.

Mighty Times: The Children's March. Directed by Robert Hudson and Bobby Houston. Montgomery, AL: Southern Poverty Law Center and Home Box Office, 2004.

Miles College Centennial History Committee. *Miles College: The First One Hundred Years.* Charleston, SC: Arcadia, 2005.

Milner, H. Richard. "Preparing Teachers of African American Students in Urban Schools." In *The Sage Handbook of African American Education*, edited by Linda C. Tillman, 123–39. Thousand Oaks, CA: Sage, 2009.

Moore, Jacqueline M. *Booker T. Washington, W. E. B. Du Bois, and the Struggle for Racial Uplift*. Wilmington, DE: Scholarly Resources, 2003.

Morris, Aldon D. 1984. *The Origins of the Civil Rights Movement: Black Communities Organizing for Change*. New York: The Free Press.

———. "A Retrospective on the Civil Rights Movement: Political and Intellectual Landmarks." *Annual Review of Sociology* 25 (1999): 517–39.

Morris, Jerome E. *Troubling the Waters: Fulfilling the Promise of Quality Public Schooling for Black Children*. New York: Teachers College Press, 2009.

Morris, Vivian G., and Curtis L. Morris. *Creating Caring and Nurturing Educational Environments for African American Children*. Westport, CT: Bergin and Garvey, 2000.

Moses, Robert P. *Radical Equations: Civil Rights from Mississippi to the Algebra Project*. Boston: Beacon, 2001.

Moyers, Bill. "Interview with Melissa Harris-Lacewell." *Bill Moyers Journal*. Television news broadcast. Aired on May 11, 2007. New York: Public Broadcasting Service. www.pbs.org/moyers/journal/05182007/profile.html.

Murray, Shailagh. "Black Leaders Divided over Endorsement: Clinton and Obama Present a Tricky Choice." *Concord Monitor*, December 2, 2007. www.concordmonitor.com/article/black-leaders-divided-over-endorsement.

National Center for Education Statistics. "Fast Facts: Teacher Trends." 2014. nces.ed.gov/fastfacts/.

National Trust for Historic Preservation. *National Rosenwald Schools Conference: 100 Years of Pride, Progress, and Preservation*. Conference held at Tuskegee University. Tuskegee, AL, July 2012.

Nelson, Stanley. *Freedom Summer*. Documentary film. United States: Fireflight Films for *American Experience*, Public Broadcasting System, 2014.

Neverdon-Morton, Cynthia. "Self-Help Programs as Educative Activities of Black Women in the South, 1895–1925: Focus on Four Key Areas." *Journal of Negro Education* 51 (1982): 207–21.

———. *Afro-American Women of the South and the Advancement of the Race, 1895–1925*. Knoxville: University of Tennessee Press, 1989.

Newby, Idus A. *Black Carolinians: A History of Blacks in South Carolina from 1865 to 1968*. Columbia: University of South Carolina Press, 1973.

Newman, Katherine S. "Symbolic Dialects and Generations of Women: Variation in the Meaning of Post-Divorce Downward Mobility." *American Ethnologist* 13 (1986): 230–52.

Newsone. "Remembering Black Youth Cut Down by Violence," February 21, 2014. newsone.com/playlist/from-emmett-till-to-trayvon-martin-black-youth-killed-over-the-years/item/2909257/.

Newsweek. "Boycott in Birmingham, ALA . . . Time to Sit Down and Talk," May 14, 1962.

Norwood, Pamela M. "Teaching as an Emancipatory Endeavor: Can 'Racial Uplift' be Taught?" *Negro Educational Review* 49 (1998): 119–27.

Orfield, Gary. "Tenth Annual *Brown* Lecture in Education Research—A New Civil Rights Agenda for American Education." *Educational Researcher* 43, no. 6 (2014): 273–92.

Osborne, George R. "Boycott in Birmingham." *The Nation* (May 5, 1962): 397–401.

Parker, Arthur Harold. *A Dream that Came True: Autobiography of Arthur Harold Parker*. Birmingham, AL: Printing Department of Industrial High School, 1932–1933 Academic Year.

Patterson, James T. *Brown v. Board of Education: A Civil Rights Milestone and its Troubled Legacy*. New York. Oxford University Press, 2001.

Patterson, Nick. *Birmingham Foot Soldiers: Voices from the Civil Rights Movement*. Charleston, SC: The History Press, 2014.

Pattillo, Mary. *Black Picket Fences: Privilege and Peril among the Black Middle Class*. 2nd edition. Chicago: University of Chicago Press, 2013.

Payne, Charles M. *I've Got the Light of Freedom: The Organizing Tradition and the Mississippi Freedom Struggle*. Berkeley: University of California Press, 1995.

———. "More Than a Symbol of Freedom: Education for Liberation and Democracy." *Phi Delta Kappan* 85 (2003): 22–28.

———, and Carol Sills Strickland, eds. *Teach Freedom: Education for Liberation in the African-American Tradition*. New York: Teachers College Press, 2008.

Perkins, Linda M. "The Impact of the 'Cult of True Womanhood' on the Education of Black Women." *Journal of Social Issues* 39 (1983): 17–28.

———. 1989. "The History of Blacks in Teaching." In *American Teachers: Histories of a Profession at Work*, edited by Donald Warren, 344–69. New York: MacMillan.

Perlstein, Daniel. "Minds Stayed on Freedom: Politics and Pedagogy in the African-American Freedom Struggle." *American Educational Research Journal* 39, no. 2 (2002): 249–77.

Perrillo, Joann. *Uncivil Rights: Teachers, Unions, and Race in the Battle for School Equity*. Chicago: University of Chicago Press, 2012.

Perry, Steve. *Push Has Come to Shove: Giving our Kids the Education They Deserve—Even If It Means Picking a Fight*. New York: Broadway, 2012.

Perry, Thelma D. *History of the American Teachers Association*. Washington, DC: National Education Association, 1975.

Perry, Theresa, Robert P. Moses, Joan T. Wynne, Ernesto Cortes Jr., and Lisa Delpit. *Quality Education as a Constitutional Right: Creating a Grassroots Movement to Transform Public Schools*. Boston: Beacon, 2010.

———, Claude Steele, and Asa Hilliard. *Young, Gifted, and Black: Promoting High Achievement among African American Students*. Boston: Beacon, 2003.

Personal Narratives Group. *Interpreting Women's Lives: Feminist Theory and Personal Narratives*. Bloomington: Indiana University Press, 1989.

Petchauer, Emery. "Framing and Reviewing Hip-hop Educational Research." *Review of Educational Research* 79 (2009): 946–78.

Phi Delta Kappa International. "Curriculum Audit of the Birmingham City Schools" (report). Bloomington, IN: International Curriculum Management Audit Center, Phi Delta Kappa, 2011.

Philanthropy Roundtable. "Julius Rosenwald." n. d. Accessed on July 25, 2014. www.philanthropyroundtable.org/almanac/hall_of_fame/julius_rosenwald.

Phillips, Marshall Fred. "A History of the Public Schools in Birmingham, Alabama." Master's thesis. Tuscaloosa: University of Alabama, 1939.

Pratt-Harris, Natasha C. "Pedagogy and Trayvon Martin" (blog). *Journal of Blacks in Higher Education.* July 21, 2013. www.jbhe.com/2013/07/pedagogy-and-trayvon-martin/.

Preston-Grimes, Patrice. "Fulfilling the Promise: African American Educators Teach for Democracy in Jim Crow's South." *Teacher Education Quarterly* 37 (2010): 35–52.

Rabinowitz, Howard N. "Half a Loaf: The Shift from White to Black Teachers in the Negro Schools of the Urban South, 1865–1890." *Journal of Southern History* 40, no. 4 (1974): 565–94.

Ramsey, Sonya. "Caring Is Activism: Black Southern Womanist Teachers Theorizing and the Careers of Kathleen Crosby and Bertha Maxwell-Roddey, 1946–1986." *Educational Studies: Journal of the American Educational Studies Association* 48 (2012): 244–65.

Ransby, Barbara. *Ella Baker and the Black Freedom Movement.* Chapel Hill: University of North Carolina Press, 2003.

———. *Eslanda: The Large and Unconventional Life of Mrs. Paul Robeson.* New Haven: Yale University Press, 2013.

Rawn, James Jr. *Root and Branch: Charles Hamilton Houston, Thurgood Marshall, and the Struggle to End Segregation.* New York: Bloomsbury.

Ray, Tiffany. "Desegregation Order Ended at Vestavia." *Birmingham News*, December 14, 2007. www.al.com.

Reardon, Sean F. and Kendra Bischoff. "Income Inequality and Income Segregation." *American Journal of Sociology* 116, no. 4 (2011): 1092–1153.

Reed, Jon. "Birmingham-area Teens Talk Politics, Future and Community Involvement at 'Next Movement' Forum." *AL.com/Birmingham News.* August 13, 2013. blog.al.com/spotnews/.

Reynolds, Tracey. "On Relations between Black Female Researchers and Participants." In *Qualitative Research in Action*, edited by Tim May, 300–309. London: Sage, 2002.

Riley, Matilda W. "Aging and Cohort Succession: Interpretations and Misinterpretations." *Public Opinion Quarterly* 37 (1973): 35–49.

Ritchie, Donald A. *Doing Oral History: A Practical Guide.* New York: Oxford University Press, 2003.

Roach, Ronald. "The Scholar-Activists of *Brown*." *Black Issues in Higher Education* 21, no. 7 (May 20, 2004): 26–31.

Roberts, Mari Ann, and Jacqueline Jordan Irvine. "African American Teachers' Caring Behaviors: The Difference Makes a Difference." In The *Sage*

Handbook of African American Education, edited by Linda C. Tillman, 141–52. Thousand Oaks, CA: Sage, 2009.

Robinson, Eugene. *Disintegration: The Splintering of Black America*. New York: Anchor Books, 2010.

Rolen, Karen. "Yes We Can! Birmingham Polishing up New Vision for City Schools." *Birmingham News*, February 10, 2008. blog.al.com/bn/2008/02/yes_we_can_birmingham_polishin.html.

Romano, Renee C. and Leigh Raiford. *The Civil Rights Movement in American Memory*. Athens: University of Georgia Press, 2006.

Rose, Tricia. "'Fear of a Black Planet': Rap Music and Black Cultural Politics in the 1990s." *Journal of Negro Education* 60, no. 3 (1991): 276–90.

Rossman-Reich, Philip. "School-improvement Plan in Works." *Birmingham News*, August 13, 2008. www.al.com/birmingham.

Roth, Wendy D., and Jal D. Mehta. "The Rashomon Effect: Combining Positivist and Interpretivist Approaches in the Analysis of Contested Events." *Sociological Methods and Research* 31, no. 2 (2002): 131–73.

Rousmaniere, Kate. *The Principal's Office: A Social History of the American School Principal*. Albany: State University of New York Press, 2013.

Rustin, Bayard. "From Protest to Politics: The Future of the Civil Rights Movement." *Commentary* 39 (1965): 25–31.

Rutledge, Anne G. "Emory O. Jackson, Warrior" Unpublished manuscript. Available at Birmingham Civil Rights Institute Archives Department. Lovell Jackson Papers, Emory O. Jackson Collection (Box 1 of 1). Birmingham, AL.

Ryder, Norman B. 1965. "The Cohort as a Concept in the Study of Social Change." *American Sociological Review* 30: 843–61.

Sanders, Cheryl J. *Saints in Exile: The Holiness-Pentecostal Experience in African American Religion and Culture*. Oxford: Oxford University Press, 1996.

Sartain, Lee. *Invisible Activists: Women of the Louisiana NAACP and the Struggle for Civil Rights, 1915–1945*. Baton Rouge: Louisiana State University Press, 2007.

Sawchuck, Stephen. "As Membership Plummets, NEA Retools Mission. *Education Week* 31, no. 36, July 13, 2012. www.edweek.org.

———. "Feeling the Heat, AFT's Reform Resolve Wavers." *Education Week* 31, no. 36, August 6, 2012. www.edweek.org.

———. "Teacher Beat: Surveys Probe Generational Attitudes of Teaching Force" (blog). *Education Week*, October 22, 2012. www.edweek.org.

Schwartz, Barry, and Howard Schuman. "History, Commemoration, and Belief: Abraham Lincoln in American Memory, 1945–2001." *American Sociological Review* 70 (2005): 183–203.

Schweninger, Loren. "The American Missionary Association and Northern Philanthropy in Reconstruction Alabama." *Alabama Historical Quarterly*, 33 (1970): 129–56.

Sealey-Ruiz, Yolanda, and Perry Greene. "Embracing Urban Youth Culture in the Context of Education." *Urban Review* 43 (2010): 339–57.

Shaw, Stephanie. *What a Woman Ought to Be and to Do: Black Professional Women Workers during the Jim Crow Era*. Chicago: The University of Chicago Press, 1996.

Sherer, Robert G. *Subordination or Liberation: The Development and Conflicting Theories of Black Education in Nineteenth Century Alabama*. Tuscaloosa: University of Alabama Press, 1977.

Shircliffe, Barbara J. *Desegregating Teachers: Contesting the Meaning of Equality of Educational Opportunity in the South Post Brown*. New York: Peter Lang, 2012.

Shuttlesworth, Fred. "Remembering the Movement." In *Birmingham Revolutionaries: The Reverend Fred Shuttlesworth and the Alabama Christian Movement for Human Rights*, edited by Marjorie L. White and Andrew M. McManis, 75–78, Macon, GA: Mercer University Press, 2000.

Siebert, Wilbur H. *The Underground Railroad—From Slavery to Freedom*. New York: Macmillan, 1898.

Spencer, Thomas. "The Reverend Fred Shuttlesworth 1922–2011: Minister Breathed Life into Civil Rights Story." *The Birmingham News*, October 9, 2011.

Stack, Carol. *Call to Home: African Americans Reclaim the Rural South*. New York: Basic Books, 1996.

Stephens, Challen. "Alabama Leads Nation in Desegregation Cases; Huntsville Looks to Shed 42-year-old Order." *Al.com/Birmingham News*, October 12, 2012. blog.al.com/breaking//print.html.

Still, William. *The Underground Railroad—Authentic Narratives and First-Hand Accounts*. Edited by Ian F. Finseth. Mineola, NY: Dover, 2007.

Stock, Erin. "Birmingham Parents Quiz City School Officials in Range of Issues in Pending School Closings." *Birmingham News*, May 12, 2008. www.al.com/birmingham.

Strauss, William, and Howe, Neil. *Generations: The History of America's Future, 1584–2069*. New York: William Morrow, 1991.

Taines, Cynthia. "'What the Real World in Schools Is Like': Urban Youth in Dialogue about Educational Inequality." *Urban Review* 43 (2010): 414–35.

———. "Intervening in Alienation: The Outcomes for Urban Youth of Participating in School Activism." *American Educational Research Journal* 49, no. 1 (2012): 53–86.

Tarry, Ellen. *The Third Door: The Autobiography of an American Negro Woman*. Tuscaloosa: University of Alabama Press, 1996. Full Text e-book.

Tavernise, Sabrina. "Outside Cleveland, Snapshots of Poverty's Surge in the Suburbs." *New York Times*, October 24, 2011. www.nytimes.com.

Thomas, Barbara, and Carol Nunnelley. "The Real L. H. Pitts: Uncle Tom or Radical?" *In Dixieland*, May 2, 1971. Available at Miles College Learning Resource Center, Birmingham, AL. Originally archived at University of Alabama at Birmingham Archives, Series 3.3.1, Folder 6.20. Also available in *Birmingham News*, May 2, 1971.

Tillman, Linda C. "African American Principals and the Legacy of *Brown*." *Review of Research in Education* 28 (2004): 101–146.

———. "(Un)intended Consequences? The Impact of *Brown vs. Board of Education* Decision on the Employment Status of Black Educators." *Education in Urban Society* 36 (2004): 280–303.

———, ed. *The Sage Handbook of African American Education*. Thousand Oaks, CA: Sage, 2009.

Time. "The South—How Not to Have Anything." May 4, 1962, 24.

Titley, Marian, and Becky Chasey. "Across Differences of Age: Young Women Speaking of and with Old Women." In *Representing the Other: A Feminism and Psychology Reader*, edited by Sue Wilkinson and Celia Kitzinger, 147–51. Thousand Oaks, CA: Sage, 1996.

Tough, Paul. *Whatever It Takes: Geoffrey Canada's Quest to Change Harlem and America*. New York: Houghton Mifflin, 2008.

Trotter Jr., Joe William, ed. *The Great Migration in Historical Perspective: New Dimensions of Race, Class, and Gender*. Bloomington: Indiana University Press, 1991.

Tucker, Cynthia. "As I See It: D. C. Schools Controversy Shows It's Hard to Shake Things Up." *Atlanta Journal Constitution* (blog), September 8, 2010. www.uexpress.com/asiseeit/?uc_full_date=20100908.

———. "Blocking the Schoolhouse Door." *AL.com/Birmingham News*, July, 27, 2014.

Tushnet, Mark V. *The NAACP Legal Strategy against Segregated Education, 1925–1950*. Chapel Hill: University of North Carolina Press, 2004.

Underwood, Madison. "Free BCRI Youth Symposium Teaches Lessons of the Civil Rights Movement, Kicks off Today with All-Star Local Panel." *AL.com/Birmingham News*, April 25, 2013. blog.al.com/spotnews/.

U. S. Census Bureau. *State and County Quick Facts* (electronic file), June 6, 2012. Washington DC. quickfacts.census.gov.

Vaughn, J. T. "Historical Sketches of Birmingham Public Schools." Master's thesis, 1926. Available at Birmingham (Ala.) Public Library Southern History Collection.

Vlach, John Michael. *Back of the Big House: The Architecture of Plantation Slavery*. Chapel Hill: University of North Carolina Press, 1993.

Walker, Vanessa Siddle. *Their Highest Potential: An African American School Community in the Segregated South*. Chapel Hill: University of North Carolina Press, 1996.

———. "Valued Segregated Schools for African American Children in the South,1935–1969: A Review of Common Themes and Characteristics." *Review of Educational Research* 70 (2000): 253–85.

———. "African American Teaching in the South: 1940–1960." *American Educational Research Journal* 38, no. 4 (2001): 751–79.

———. "The Architects of Black Schooling in the Segregated South: The Case of One Principal Leader." *Journal of Curriculum and Supervision* 19 (2003): 54–72.

———. "Organized Resistance and Black Educators' Quest for School Equality, 1878–1938." *Teachers College Record* 107, no. 3 (2005): 355–88.

———. *Hello Professor: A Black Principal and Professional Leadership in the Segregated South*. Chapel Hill: University of North Carolina Press, 2009.

———. "Second-Class Integration: A Historical Perspective for a Contemporary Agenda." *Harvard Educational Review* 79, no. 2 (2009): 269–84.

———. "The Annual *Brown* Lecture in Education Research: Black Educators as Educational Advocates in the Decades before *Brown v. Board of Education*." *Educational Researcher* 42, no. 4 (2013): 207–22.

———. "Tolerated Tokenism, or the Injustice in Justice: Black Teacher Associations and their Forgotten Struggle for Educational Justice, 1921–1954." *Equity and Excellence in Education* 46, no. 1 (2013): 64–80.

Ward Randolph, Adah. "'It Is Better to Light a Candle Than to Curse the Darkness': Ethel Thompson Overby and Democratic Schooling in Richmond, Virginia, 1910–1958." *Educational Studies: Journal of the American Educational Studies Association* 48, no. 3 (2012): 220–43.

Washington, Booker T. *Up from Slavery*. New York: Doubleday, Page and Co., 1907. Originally published in 1900.

Watkins, William H. *The White Architects of Black Education: Ideology and Power in America, 1865–1954*. New York: Teachers College Press, 2001.

———. "Blacks and the Curriculum: From Accommodation to Contestation and Beyond." In *Race and Education: The Role of History and Society in Educating African American Students*, edited by William H. Watkins, James H. Lewis, and Victoria Chou, 40–65. Boston: Allyn and Bacon, 2001.

Wellner, Alison S. "The Forgotten Baby Boom." *American Demographics* 23 (2001): 48–51.

Wells, Amy Stuart. *Both Sides Now: The Story of School Desegregation's Graduates*. Berkeley: University of California Press, 2009.

———, Julie Slayton, and Janelle Scott. "Defining Democracy in the Neoliberal Age: Charter School Reform and Educational Consumption." *American Educational Research Journal* 39, no. 2 (2002): 337–61.

Wenger, Michael R. *Rising African American Leaders: Challenges for a New Generation*. Washington, DC: Joint Center for Political and Economic Studies, 2006.

Wesley, Charles Harris. *The History of the National Association of Colored Women's Clubs: A Legacy of Service*. Washington, DC: National Association of Colored Women's Clubs, 1984.

Wesson, L. Hampton. "Equity Issues for Women and Minorities in Educational Administration." In *Women as School Executives: Voices and Visions*, edited by Beverly Irby and Genevieve Brown, 149–57. Austin: Texas Association of School Administrators, 1995.

White, Marjorie L., and Andrew M. McManis. *Birmingham Revolutionaries: The Reverend Fred Shuttlesworth and the Alabama Christian Movement for Human Rights*. Macon, GA: Mercer University Press, 2000.

White, Tara Y. "Black Women in the Civil Rights Movement, 1954–1963. Women of the Alabama Christian Movement for Human Rights in Birmingham, AL." Master's thesis. SUNY-Oneonta, Cooperstown Graduate Program, 2002. Available at the Birmingham (Ala.) Public Library Department of Manuscripts and Archives.

Whitmire, Kyle. "Southern Association of Colleges and Schools puts Birmingham City School System on Probation." *Al.com/Birmingham News*, July 25, 2013. www.al.com/birmingham.

Williams, Juan. *Eyes on the Prize: America's Civil Rights Years, 1954–1965*. New York: Penguin Books, 1987.

Wilson, Bobby M. *Race and Place in Birmingham: The Civil Rights and Neighborhood Movements*. Lanham, MD: Rowman and Littlefield, 2000.

Wilson, Camille M. "Starting the Bandwagon: A Historiography of African American Mothers' Leadership during Voluntary School Desegregation, 1954–1971." *Advancing Women in Leadership* 34 (2014): 38–47.

Wilson, William Julius. *The Truly Disadvantaged: The Inner City, the Underclass, and Public Policy*. Chicago: The University of Chicago Press, 1987.

Winemiller, Terance. L. "Black Belt Region in Alabama." *Encyclopedia of Alabama*, September 17, 2009. www.encyclopediaofalabama.org.

Witherspoon, Craig. *Birmingham City Schools: 2011–2012 Financial Realities, Projections and Considerations*. Power Point Prepared by the Birmingham City Schools Superintendent.

Woodson, Carter G. *The Mis-education of the Negro*. Trenton: African World Press, 1990. First published in 1933 by Carter G. Woodson.

Wright, Barnett. "W. L. Williams Jr. 1930–2013 Civil Rights Lawyer Helped Integrate Schools." *Al.com/Birmingham News*, October 2, 2013. www.al.com/birmingham/.

———. 1963: *How the Birmingham Civil Rights Movement Changed America and the World*. Birmingham, AL: Birmingham News, 2013.

Yasin, Jon A. "Hip Hop: A Source of Empowerment for African American Male College Students." In *The Sage Handbook of African American Education*, edited by Linda C. Tillman, 283–96. Thousand Oaks, CA: Sage.

Yelverton, Mildred Griffin. *They also Served: Twenty-five Remarkable Alabama Women*. Dothan, AL: Ampersand, 1993.

INDEX

Note: Page references enclosed in square brackets indicate textual references found only in the Notes section (denoted by "n").